Parker Gillmore

A Hunter's Adventures in the great West

Parker Gillmore

A Hunter's Adventures in the great West

ISBN/EAN: 9783337177447

Printed in Europe, USA, Canada, Australia, Japan

Cover: Foto ©ninafisch / pixelio.de

More available books at **www.hansebooks.com**

A HUNTER'S ADVENTURES

IN

THE GREAT WEST.

BY

PARKER GILLMORE,
("UBIQUE")
AUTHOR OF 'GUN, ROD, AND SADDLE,' ETC. ETC.

BULL MOOSE LAKE.

LONDON:
HURST AND BLACKETT, PUBLISHERS,
13, GREAT MARLBOROUGH STREET.
1871.

The Right of Translation is reserved.

CONTENTS.

CHAPTER I.

MONTANA — SOIL, CLIMATE, AND APPEARANCE OF THE COUNTRY — MINERAL WEALTH — LAST HOME OF THE RED MAN — TRAVELLERS IN A SORRY PLIGHT — THE CAMP-FIRE — WAKING DREAMS — ARDUOUS AND FATIGUING TRAVELLING — FAITHFUL COMPANIONS — SOLITUDES 1

CHAPTER II.

DISAPPEARANCE OF MY NAGS — UNWELCOME SERENADE — FIRST APPEARANCE OF BUFFALO — DESERTED ENCAMPMENT — REMARKABLE SUGAR-LOAF MOUNTAIN — A FAMILY OF BEARS — MAKING A PAIR OF TROUSERS — BIG-HORNS AND ROCKY-MOUNTAIN SHEEP — THE TURKEY BUZZARD — GOOD CAMPING-GROUND 20

CHAPTER III.

EXCELLENT FISHING — VICINITY OF FRIENDS OR FOES — AN AMBUSCADE — THE SQUAW AND HER PAPOOSE — A WIDOW'S ATTENTIONS — CHANGE OF CAMP — ABUNDANCE OF GAME — INDIAN DOGS — PROCESS OF TANNING — CANVAS-BACK DUCKS — THEIR HABITAT, AND METHODS OF CAPTURING THEM . . 38

CHAPTER IV.

SUBSTITUTES FOR BAIT — FISHING EXPERIENCE — THE BLUE-BIRD — ALABAMA — RICH AND POOR — HOOD'S SPERMOPHILUS — A WOUNDED WAPITI — THE MODEST VIOLET — SUPPLY OF AMMUNITION — UNEXPECTED PROPOSAL — DOGS AND WOLVES — FRIENDS OF LONG STANDING — LUDICROUS POSITION — HOSPITABLE TEAMSTERS 57

CONTENTS.

CHAPTER V.

WAGGONS ON THE WESTERN WILDS — SHOT AT A BUFFALO — BY THE CAMP-FIRE — THE BOSS'S STORY 75

CHAPTER VI.

COON OR SHELL-DRAKE CREEK — MUSK-RATS — THE SKUNK — RACOON HUNTING — STORY OF A SKUNK — A RECOLLECTION OF MINNESOTA — ANAS OBSCURA, BLACK DUCK — ALARM IN CAMP — PRAIRIE DOGS — FAITHFUL SENTINELS — UNWELCOME GUESTS — ANIMAL BAROMETER 105

CHAPTER VII.

AN INDIAN MOTHER — DEATH OF THE PAPOOSE — BID ADIEU TO THE TRADERS — VOLUNTEER GUIDE — HIS HISTORY — EXCITING ADVENTURE — ENCOUNTER WITH THE GREY WOLF OF THE NORTH — A TRAPPER'S COURTING — DREADFUL TRAGEDY — CONCLUSION OF THE OLD MAN'S STORY 121

CHAPTER VIII.

ECCENTRICITIES OF CATTLE — RED-HEADED WOODPECKERS — STRANGE CAPERS OF AN OLD DOE — RATTLESNAKE KILLED BY A DEER — THE BOBOLINK, OR REED-BIRD — TRAIL OF INDIANS — ATTEMPT TO BURN A BEAR OUT OF A CAVE — ROUGHED GROUSE — OBSTINATE COURAGE OF MY OLD GUIDE . . 154

CHAPTER IX.

ANTELOPES — THE GARTER-SNAKE — THE JAW AND TEETH OF SNAKES — KILDEES — SPRIG-TAIL OR PHEASANT-DUCKS — ZEAL IN THE STUDY OF NATURAL HISTORY — SPOOR OF THE BEAR — A DAINTY MARAUDER — THE VARIEGATED HARE — THE MISSOURI — ENCAMPMENT OF TRAPPERS . . 171

CHAPTER X.

LOOKING FOR GAME — ON THE TRACK OF WAPITI DEER — ENCOUNTER WITH A PUMA — AN 'OLD HOSS'S' STORY — SOULÉ AND HIS MEN — SHAMEFUL TREATMENT OF INDIANS — RATTLESNAKES — DEPARTURE FROM THE CAMP — WILD STRAWBERRIES — SHOT AT A BLACK-TAILED DEER — BEAR AND WOLVES — EXCITING ADVENTURE 192

CHAPTER XI.

BEAUTIFUL SCENERY — THE CHAIN-MOUSE — PLEASANT SHOWER-BATH — UNSUCCESSFUL ATTEMPT TO BRING DOWN A BUFFALO COW — SOLITARY REGION — ENDURING FATIGUE — BEAUTIFUL LAKE — COMMUNION WITH NATURE — WILD DUCK . . 211

CHAPTER XII.

BLACK SPRUCE — MINIATURE LAKE — THE MINK — NATURAL ARBOUR — UNSUCCESSFUL STALK AFTER A COW MOOSE — THE CANADA PORCUPINE — SNIPE — WATER-SNAKES — CURLEWS — ROASTED OWL — ENCAMPED ON THE MARGIN OF A LAKE — INGRATITUDE OF A GREY WOLF 224

CHAPTER XIII.

GOOD CAMPING-GROUND — NIGHT FISHING ON THE LAKE — TRAPPERS' STOCK-HOUSE — SALE OF MY QUADRUPEDS — IMMENSE SWAMP — THE AMERICAN RAIL — BEAUTIFUL SCENERY — MY DEBUT IN RAIL-SHOOTING — MY 'PUSHER' SOLD . . 242

CHAPTER XIV.

JOURNEY TO THE BARRENS — ROCK CREVICES — MINERAL WEALTH — UNUSUAL CONFIDENCE OF THE WILD ANIMALS — ECONOMY IN THE USE OF AMMUNITION — LAST NIGHT IN CAMP — AGAIN EN ROUTE — TIMBER — A BEE-TREE — MY COMPANION — BEE-HUNTERS — PTARMIGAN — ADVENTURE WITH A GLUTTON 256

CHAPTER XV.

THE RED-MEN — AN INDIAN 'FLITTING' — INTERVIEW WITH AN INDIAN FAMILY — HORSE-INDIANS — TIMBER-INDIANS — FISH-INDIANS — THE MUSTANG — PICTURESQUE CAMP — AMERICAN CHAR — RECKLESSNESS OF MY FELLOW-TRAVELLER — VIOLENT GALE — EMIGRATION 271

CHAPTER XVI.

PRAIRIE-FIRES — TERROR AND FLIGHT OF WILD ANIMALS — CARIBOO-TRACKS — SPONGY SOIL — UNSUCCESSFUL STALK — LARGE GREY WOLF — WILD DUCKS — SIGNS OF A CHANGE OF WEATHER — WILD GEESE — MOOSE RIVER — CONSTRUCTION OF A RAFT — VOYAGE OF DISCOVERY — BIRCH-BARK CANOES . 285

CHAPTER XVII.

DELICATE LUXURY — A HURRICANE — CONTRETEMPS TO THE CANOE — DISTURBED IN A DAY-DREAM — NARROW ESCAPE FROM A BEAR — TICKS — GREY WOLVES — MUSIC OF THE WINDS — THE CANOE IN A RAPID — HUMBUG — AN AUTHORITY ON NATURAL HISTORY 302

CHAPTER XVIII.

DANGEROUS NAVIGATION — NARROW ESCAPE — MOOSE RIVER — BEAUTIFUL CASCADE — AMERICAN RIVERS — BRILLIANTLY-COLOURED FISH — BEAVERS — TRACES OF AN ENCAMPMENT — MAN AND NATURE — EFFRONTERY OF A WHITE EAGLE — THE CANOE OVERTURNED BY A BEAR — DINNER AT THE SOUTHERN HOTEL, ST. LOUIS 320

A HUNTER'S ADVENTURES.

CHAPTER I.

MONTANA—SOIL, CLIMATE, AND APPEARANCE OF THE COUNTRY—MINERAL WEALTH—LAST HOME OF THE RED MAN—TRAVELLERS IN A SORRY PLIGHT—THE CAMP-FIRE—WAKING DREAMS—ARDUOUS AND FATIGUING TRAVELLING—FAITHFUL COMPANIONS—SOLITUDES.

ALMOST in the centre of the vast continent of North America is situated an immense extent of country called Montana, the interior of which was but little known a few years since beyond what had been gathered from information afforded by adventurous white trappers, Indian traders, and small surveying parties in search of possible rail or telegraph routes from the Atlantic to the Pacific Ocean.

Although this is now a portion of the United States, it is more than probable that, from its geographical position, the absence of navigable rivers, the roughness of its surface, and the hostility of the aborigines, it will still be many years before the advance of civilisation materially affects it; for it does not hold out to the emigrant those inducements which promise remuneration for the cultivation of the earth. Neither is the climate of a nature likely to attract settlers, for both the rigours of a Canadian winter and the heat of a tropical summer are experienced within its limits; while the fluctuations from the one extreme of temperature to the other are so sudden, that only persons possessed of the hardiest constitutions are able to bear them with impunity.

At the same time, it must not be imagined that this territory is all a barren waste; for such is not the case. Valleys, sometimes of great extent, intersect its limits; but these are so small in proportion to the rugged mountain-tracts and precipitous sierras, that they are the exceptions, not the rule.

Since the discovery of gold in California the Pacific slopes of the North American continent have undergone changes, by the building of cities, the constant influx of emigrants from East and West, and the formation of routes for traffic, that cannot probably be paralleled in the history of the earth; but, as might naturally be supposed, these transformations have been confined to those localities most favoured by nature; and great as they have been, there still remains farther to the south so much wild and untenanted land, suitable for tillage, that a quarter of a century at the very least will be required before the greater portion of it has been surveyed, formed into counties, and allotted to resident white men. And until this is so effectually done that no space is left on which the hardy squatter can at will take up his residence, build his home, and exercise the authority of lord and master over all that surrounds him, Montana will remain, comparatively speaking, deserted.

If we had to search for other reasons that might be urged against the probability of these rugged highlands soon becoming the resting-place of a portion of those seeking new homes, we might add that it is out of the line usually chosen by the exodus of people that annually, with increased numbers, rolls across from the Atlantic to the Pacific. Thus it is not even honoured by an occasional straggler, who, dropping from the immense human tide, either from faintness of heart or by incapacity for further progression, produced by bodily infirmity, is satisfied to remain where circumstances have placed him.

Still, there is an attraction in this wild territory that may falsify my prediction regarding the time that will be required to elapse before the patient steer will toil in front of the plough breaking up its virgin soil; or the voices of children playing round the homestead wake the echoes with their merry laugh; or the sierras and crags repeat the monotonous sound of the stroke of the destructive axe. The attraction is mineral wealth—iron, silver, and gold are among its productions; and should these be here found in greater abundance than in more accessible places, the craving for the possession of wealth will soon induce speculators to overflood the country with a host of miners, as a rule the most dissipated, cruel, and reckless people upon the face of the earth. That such may not occur I sincerely hope. I hope it for the sake of the Indian—for the sake of the wild game; for it will be to them the signing of their death-warrant. Indeed, I may already say that the extermination of both is fixed for an early date.

. Forty years ago, the whole extent of territory from the Mississippi to the Pacific, from the Gulf of Mexico to Hudson's Bay, belonged to the red man. All over this space their cattle, the wild game, roamed free, and the white man only dwelt within its limits as a guest, or on tolerance. And how has such hospitality been requited? In the same way as is written in every page of the history of our race —the lawful possessors have been dispossessed, their lands have been appropriated, and the children of the soil have been driven forth, to wander homeless and despoiled, to starve and die. Montana is now almost their only sanctuary remaining; and if the lessons of the past have not taught them how little faith can be reposed in treaties and promises—if their hearts fail in courage, their hands in strength, and their tongues in the deception practised by the invaders, this last resting-place will follow in the wake of those lands that have ceased to know the camp-fires of their forefathers.

The British nation, and the Americans sprung from their loins, are professors of Christianity; they repudiate, and express indignation, when foreign powers act upon the principle of 'might is right:' but let them look at home, and they will see that their treatment of the Indian is without a parallel for inhumanity—contrary as day is to night to what is inculcated by the religion in which they profess to believe.

'What's in a name?' is a question very often asked. To such a query our reply would be, that there is great value in an appropriate appellation. Thus, for example, in Montana there is both poetry and music; and he who proposed its adoption deserves to be handed down to posterity. The enunciation of it pictures to the mind the very place which it designates, by conjuring up views of steep mountains, secluded valleys, and sparkling streams. Perhaps it was the name that first attracted my attention: in fact, I believe it was; for when I learned that here a secluded life could be enjoyed in perfection—that I could reside in this remote region cut off from the selfish outer world—that it was a place where I might contemplate some of the wildest and most beautiful scenes of nature, undefiled by the brand of man's handiwork—I determined to avail myself of the first chance to visit it. The coveted opportunity at last arrived, and I now propose to give a description of my existence in a place so little known to the majority of readers; with the observations I made on its climate, zoology, and botany, during my residence in its sierras, and on my homeward journey from them.

Less than four years since, if the peruser of these

pages could have been transplanted to the northern portion of Montana, and have gazed upon the southern slope of a mountain the summit of which was lost in clouds, a *cortége*, consisting of a man, horse, and mule, might have been seen slowly, and apparently with great difficulty, making its way through snow and boulders towards the East. Over each there was an air of languor that spoke of fatigue and short commons; while the neglected, nay, dirty appearance of all, proclaimed that many days had elapsed since they had been in a settlement, or had time to devote that attention to appearances which is no less necessary to brutes than to men, to make them presentable to civilised eyes.

We three were, indeed, in a sorry plight—for your humble servant, the Author, claimed to be the chief of the triumvirate: could we have been transplanted to the fashionable precincts of Rotten Row in the state in which we then were, we should have doubtlessly caused curiosity, possibly contempt.

Although both the animals were without a load of any consequence, the descent was so steep, and the ground so rough, that they repeatedly stumbled or slid, with such force that I expected momentarily to see them continue their descent headlong into the ravines beneath, where a broken neck would have been their certain destiny.

It was near sunset, and if earlier in the day a suitable halting-place could have been found I would have camped long before; for I was fearfully tired, and my poor companions were even in a worse plight. Had I been alone, with no one to consider but myself, the sheltered side of a rock or boulder would have afforded sufficient protection to enable me to get through the night; but my faithful followers had to be considered, for a night on the exposed mountain-side would probably have cost them their lives: therefore I had no alternative but to push forward, with the hope that fortune would favour us.

But a few minutes more and the sun would dip the horizon, and in an hour all would be enveloped in utter darkness; yet far as I could see, looking to every point of the compass, nothing greeted my vision but an ocean of sterile hills. As we continued our journey, stumble followed stumble; and at length my exclamation of 'Hold up!' was unavailing. The poor mare, that I loved as well,—ay, and far better, than many I know of my own kith and kin—after making violent efforts to recover herself, gathering speed as she advanced, fell with fearful force down a drop of many feet, and disappeared from my solicitous gaze. In a few moments I was at her side. She had not risen, and, only that she did not struggle, I should have felt convinced that some of her limbs were broken: but I was spared such a trial; only a little of her hide was lost, and after a few efforts I had her again upon her pins.

'Out of evil cometh good,' is a proverb which, in this instance, proved correct, for in seeking an opening by which the animal might ascend to my old position, I found a small plateau which had an inviting appearance, was well sheltered, and fairly covered with bush, which not only promised shelter but grazing. With the intention of selecting the most suitable spot for my camp—that is where, if possible, wood and water could be obtained—I traversed possibly a couple of hundred yards, when, resting my gun upon a rock, I undid the girths that bound my saddle to the mare, removed the bit from her mouth, and giving her a slap on the rump, ordered her and her companion to go and seek their suppers, while I prepared mine. What a dreadful thing affectionate mothers think it is for their sons to have damp feet! but here I was so wet that I was positively soaked almost to the loins, and had been so for days, sleeping and travelling in that condition, and yet no harm had resulted. Soon the camp-fire threw out an invigorating blaze, my string of jerked venison sputtered in front of its embers; and as day waned into darkness, the surrounding objects within easy distance of the blaze stood out in bold relief, and this little secluded spot became imbued with all the attractions usually implied in the word 'home.' How gratefully I enjoyed my repose! Fatigue rendered it unnecessary for me to seek a position in which to be comfortable; and although clouds of steam rose from my limbs under the influence of the heat, I felt that I was not an unfit object for envy when I compared my present circumstances and position with those I had been placed in for days previously. I even relaxed my habitual watchfulness, and yielded myself more entirely to repose; for there was an air of such perfect seclusion and safety over everything, that I did not even hesitate to wander off in mind into the realms of dreamland, or into the vast fields of memory.

Like the soldier reposing after the hard-contested battle, familiar faces and sounds flitted before me. I saw in imagination a family circle around a bright coal fire, or a stile on a woodland path, and a graceful figure with golden tresses illumined by the moon's soft light; then the visionary scene changed to innumerable white tents on an extended plain, interspersed with tropical trees, the silence being broken by the shrill call of the bugle, the hoarse note of the trumpet, or the musical 'All's well.'

While I was thus communing with memories of the past, I was recalled to reality by the breaking of brush in my vicinity; but the noise was not ominous of evil, for it was produced by my foot-tired quadrupeds returning to seek the companionship of their lord and master. This confidence in my mare ever pleased me, for it was an expression of regard, plainer even than could have been made by words, that I was not looked upon by her as a tyrant, but was relied on as a protector and friend; the more gratifying as this sentiment was not the result of selfishness on her part.

Having scratched the old lady's muzzle and pulled her ears, caresses which she always acknowledged with an expression of gratitude, I returned to my blanket, and although fitful angry gusts of wind rushed madly across the mountain's sides, screaming as they struck the sharp edges of the rocks and brush, and producing many a weird note, as if old Boreas was giving vent to his wrath for such interruptions in his headlong course; I was soon dead to all consciousness of the outer world; and when I awoke next day the sun was already above the horizon, the horse and mule were gone to seek their breakfast, and my fire of the previous evening no longer existed, leaving only its tell-tale mark to remind me of the services which it had rendered me.

Previous to the date on which I commence my narrative, I was settled in a valley some distance to the southward of my present position, and my intention had been to remain there for possibly a month more; but this decision was altered from my accidentally discovering that Indians had found out my fastness, and had already prowled around it, disguising in every possible manner the evidences of their vicinity. Now, if these Red-skins had not been possessed of evil intentions towards me, knowing as they did that I was alone and comparatively defenceless, they would have come and made a friendly call; we would have had a grave smoke together, and afterwards a grand pow-wow, consisting of big words and bigger speeches; utterly incomprehensible in detail, but strongly significant when taken all together.

Thus arguing the matter over, I determined to

give up possession, and make my exodus into a new land, not halting except for necessary rest till many, many leagues were between me and my old camping-ground. In the lapse of a week I expected to accomplish this purpose, but the further I advanced the less inviting became the country, vegetation became scarcer, and snow more abundant; while, from the rugged nature of the surface of the land, travelling was monotonous, arduous, and fatiguing in the extreme.

Fortunately in this land water was always to be obtained, and though food was scarce, I had exercised so much economy as to possess a fair supply for my own use; otherwise I should have starved, for game was scarce. From day's end to day's end scarcely a wild animal was to be seen, and then so wary were the denizens of this almost untrodden desert that they constantly kept themselves beyond reach of my missiles. My poor mule and mare, however, were absolutely starving, for I verily believe, if every particle of edible vegetation had been collected from a hundred of the surrounding acres, it would not have sufficed to make them one good meal.

Having hoped from day to day that a change would occur, I continued progressing to the northward, until it was too late to think of retracing my steps, and hope deferred had already caused my heart to become sick. With the least enviable feelings I ever remember to have experienced, day by day I observed the clearly-defined ribs and prominent points of my poor quadrupeds become more conspicuous, their hides more tightly bound, their coats more staring, and their eyes more enlarged and glassy. Their loss would not have necessarily entailed upon me death, but it would have subjected me to immense inconvenience, for, although now unable to bear my weight, they still carried my small stock of worldly wealth. Moreover, I am not ashamed to confess the grief I should have felt at being deprived of two old and tried companions, for whom I possessed the strongest feelings of affection.

Each of these animals was a character in its way, and although excessively dissimilar, they exhibited for each other the strongest regard. This might have been the result of their hard fate, for misery is sometimes a bond of sympathy; and although petulance and irascibility were occasionably manifested, these displays of feeling never for a moment produced a spirit of retaliation.

When first I became their possessor they were high-spirited, proud, sleek, and fat. Though the comparison of their present state with their past was not with me a favourite occupation, yet I sometimes looked forward with pleasure to the prospect of what they might again become after months of regular rest and abundant food. But there was still another reason for my anxiety that they should be spared me; viz. that if ever I again reached the confines of civilisation, or found my way to a traders' camp, they were almost the only property I possessed convertible into the sinews that would supply me with ammunition, tobacco, and other necessaries requisite to enable me to reach a population susceptible to the influences of letters of credit and introduction. It is true I did not like the idea of selling my pets, but I was too poor to retain them, much less give them away. To mollify the gentle monitor who whispered reproaches at the heinousness of bartering the servants who had so faithfully served me, I promised inwardly that no effort should be spared to obtain for them a good and kind master. Yet I knew full well that it might be impossible for me to succeed in this, for circumstances would compel me to take the highest offer for them.

What a good thing it is that we have a conscience, for it is a most valuable addition to our far from perfect characters! Still, what scurvy tricks we occasionally play it; too frequently lulling its uneasiness to rest by prevarication and false promises, actually lying to ourselves—a proof of our proneness to practise deception.

But I will return to the morning after the day on which the reader and myself first met. The sun was a couple of hours high before I was ready for the road. The weather had improved, and there was sufficient genial warmth to invest my frame with a little more than usual elasticity, and raise my spirits above their wonted elevation.

Taking hold of the mare's lariat-rope, I proceeded to investigate the vicinity in which I had passed the night. The further I progressed the more inviting became the landscape. Vegetation increased in abundance, the snow lay in smaller and less deep patches, while the footing was good and the surface smooth.

After an hour and a half's tramp, which led nearly all down a slight incline, the descent became more rapid; brush gave way to dwarf trees, occasional tufts of grass struggled through the soil for existence, and a stray track of game here and there proclaimed that we were not the only living creatures left upon the earth.

Have you ever been a long voyage, in which you have traversed some of the remote solitudes of ocean, when for weeks the straining eye has not been able to detect upon the furthest limits of the horizon a solitary sail? Again and again the effort is made to discern some indications of a ship. The last thing you do before darkness envelopes your floating habitation is to gaze wistfully around; the first thing in the morning, in the rarefied atmosphere that precedes the rising sun, you resume your search for the discovery of land, or for the appearance of a vessel, till at length continued disappointment maketh the heart grow sick, and the hope which had so long sustained you gives way, and is replaced by despair. Next morning, however, at the grey dawn, when with languid step and fevered brow you gain the deck, you find the breeze of last night has died away into a calm, and the great heaving bosom of the deep at comparative rest, and the distant view curtailed by mists. At length the sun dispels the fog-bank, which evaporating into nothingness, the distance becomes revealed, and in it you behold the object of your search.

Your first feeling is gratitude that you are not alone—that there are still others in the world. Such thoughts I experienced when far south of the Cape; again I felt them when I came upon the deep, clean impressions cut in the surface of the earth by the hoofs of an antlered monarch of the wild highlands of the Far West.

Who that has wandered through America does not love the birch-tree? Of all the dwellers of the forest to me it is the most attractive, for it combines qualities as varied as numerous. In wild life it is of great utility to man, for from its bark can be made anything, from a canoe to writing-paper or a cooking utensil. Its long flaccid boughs provide a capital, almost a luxurious bed; it is well suited for torches and firewood; while no tree is more graceful in outline, or in its aspect more enlivening to the landscape. When, in turning an angle of rock, one stood before me, its appearance recalled so many pleasant memories that I almost hugged it with joy.

'*Fortuna favet fortibus.*' Can I be egotistical enough to accredit myself with bravery, for fortune has certainly turned, and is favouring me with unexpected kindness? Every mile presents new attractions, and my increased buoyancy of spirit appears to become infectious, for my animals step out more gaily and appear more happy, even mustering courage to pluck the herbage as they advance.

To-day I am satisfied with my progress. The position I have reached is eminently suited for camping, as a stream purls by in close proximity and fuel is abundant, while the shelter is all that can be desired. Although the sun had not passed the meridian more than an hour, I determined to halt, and give self and nags a long rest. As I could not, however, sleep through the intervening space between this and night, and my ponies did not require attention, for I knew when they had satisfied their appetites they would return to the smouldering camp-fire, I determined to explore the neighbourhood, and, if chance offered me an opportunity, to add to my low stock of provisions.

Wherever there is a brook or river, almost all descriptions of animal life are to be found most abundant in its vicinity; so I directed my steps in the direction from which the murmuring of rapid-running water appeared to emanate. Having reached a rivulet, I followed its course for a mile or more. The further I progressed along its margin the more it appeared to expand, and to lose its previously rapid and precipitous character. At length its neighbourhood became so swampy, that I had to make a considerable *détour* to obtain walkable ground. Suddenly I reached a spot where the stunted cedars and hemlocks that had encircled me became scarce; their places being taken by willows, which massed themselves together in such a way as to form an impenetrable labyrinth. Evidences of the vicinity of beavers were scattered around on every hand: trees that had lost portions of their bark, and limbs which had been gnawed, were here as plentiful as if a whole host of these animals had just completed a meal after a long fast. Practising every caution of which I was cognisant, I made an essay to reach the water's margin, and succeeded after much difficulty. My labour, however, was well rewarded; for at the first glance I found over a dozen beavers within view, while some were not more than thirty feet from my position. Beavers (*Castor fiber*) are so excessively wary, that it is very seldom such a sight as that which I enjoyed has been gazed upon by white men, and then only in such remote and undisturbed districts as that in which I wandered.

But I will try to describe the scene. The side of the stream near to my position was margined with a sand-bank several yards in width, while further off stretched the gliding water, dotted with numerous dome-like houses. The distant view was shut out by a dense growth of evergreens, which formed an impenetrable obstacle to vision. On the foreground were a brace of beavers, whose serious, sedate manner indicated that they were engaged in conversation upon some subject of vital importance. In the water and on the houses something like half-a-dozen of the same race were busily occupied repairing their domiciles, or floating down stream material with which to do so. Now beaver-meat is very nice, particularly when served in the shape of a stew; and the very thoughts of such succulent food caused my mouth to water, by enjoying it in anticipation. My vision of *ragoûts* and pasties, however, was dissipated by the sound of a steady, monotonous succession of splashes. Cautiously I listened, and in endeavouring to turn my eyes in the direction from whence the noise emanated, I nearly screwed my head off; for an awkward or hurried movement might have alarmed the quarry, or exposed my position to an enemy. For a few moments the sounds ceased, but were again renewed, and I felt convinced more substantial game was now within reach. My anticipations turned out to be correct, for a very large Wapiti stag (*Cervus Canadensis*) emerged from the cover into the open meadow. Although within easy gunshot, the handsome creature was quite ignorant of my presence, and unsuspectingly crossed the wet ground, cropping stray mouthfuls of browse from the willow-bushes that chanced to be in his course. The beautiful animal seemed to move with as much indolence, and with as perfect an absence of purpose, as the most thorough exquisite could evince in his dawdle down the Row on a warm day in the height of the season. So little did the beavers regard the presence of the antlered monarch, that they scarcely halted from their occupation for more than a moment to greet his intrusion with a stare of indifference.

The question now arose in my mind, which of these animals was, under existing circumstances, best suited as food to my palate, for I had now before me a choice; but as the buck was rather low in flesh, rough in coat, and unquestionably a veteran in years, I decided for beaver-flesh, and took aim at the nearest of the two cronies hobnobbing on the sand-flat, stretching him lifeless ere the echoes of the report had died away. The uninjured beaver fled; took to the water, dived, reappeared, looked around, halted, and turned about, as if intent on learning why he was not followed by his companion; while the buck stood still, evincing symptoms of nervous curiosity. 'Good!' thought I to myself. 'At length I have gained a sanctuary that (lately, at least) has not been contaminated by the presence of man.' The utter ignorance which these timid representatives of the animal kingdom evinced of the danger attending the white man's thunder was just ground for such a supposition.

CHAPTER II.

DISAPPEARANCE OF MY NAGS — UNWELCOME SERENADE — FIRST APPEARANCE OF BUFFALO — DESERTED ENCAMPMENT — REMARKABLE SUGAR-LOAF MOUNTAIN — A FAMILY OF BEARS — MAKING A PAIR OF TROUSERS — BIG-HORNS AND ROCKY-MOUNTAIN SHEEP — THE TURKEY BUZZARD — GOOD CAMPING-GROUND.

ON reaching home I found the camp-fire extinguished, and was unable to discover any traces of my nags. The former was unimportant in itself, as my flint and steel would soon produce a fresh blaze ; and to the extinction of the fire I attributed the absence of the animals.

At break of day, as there was no indication of my quadrupeds being in the vicinity, I shouldered my double-barrel, and followed for more than a mile their indistinct tracks. After a time, from the soil becoming firmer, I was compelled to give up the trail, and trust to luck. About noon I could not have been possibly less than six or seven miles from home ; still there were not the slightest signs of the truants. I observed in a hollow a considerable drift of snow, and on its surface the fresh imprint of a large bear's feet. A little alarmed lest Bruin might have a *penchant* for horse-flesh, and had indulged his taste at my cost, I endeavoured to get some clue to his retreat, and from whence he had come : but all without success. Tired and disappointed I returned homewards, angry with myself for not having hobbled the objects of my search, and cross with them for making such an ungrateful return for the confidence I reposed in them.

A wolf found me out that evening, and, doubtless with the intention of according my advent a suitable reception, honoured me with a serenade all night— a compliment which a tired traveller who seeks repose could have very well dispensed with.

Awaking next morning not particularly refreshed, for my rest had been disturbed by dreams of all kinds, my depression of spirits was in no way removed on finding that the morning was gloomy and threatening, while the wind whispered warnings of coming change in the weather. The heaviness of the low dark clouds predicted rain; and not feeling disposed to stray far, I proceeded to the stream, in the hope of procuring fish for this day's sustenance. I had an unsuccessful search for worms, a bait in which I had most confidence. From under a decayed log I obtained, however, a small lizard and a grub, which both answered my purpose admirably, for the fish were voracious, and ere many minutes I had made half-a-dozen captures. My prizes were identical with the char. of the Eastern States (*Salmo fontinalis*), both in flavour and colour. A fish dinner once in a way is all very well, but if too often indulged in is apt to surfeit; though it has one recommendation, that little skill and but a short time are necessary for its preparation.

Ascending from the stream to where my camp-fire was burning, and where reposed my *lares* and *penates*, thus constituting the spot 'home,' I had to traverse a narrow belt of brush, which was sufficiently dense to shut out a view of what was beyond. With my thoughts far away, and not the most remote idea of the surprise in store for me, I had passed through the cover, when, to my delight and astonishment, I beheld the two truants not fifty yards from me. The mare, who was standing up, whinnied a note of welcome; while the mule, who was rolling upon the ground, as soon as he became aware of my presence got on his pins, and, flapping his rabbit-like ears, inquired after my health through the medium of the language of the eyes—a dialect in which I have known young ladies in England fairly proficient, and señoras in Spain perfect adepts: but none of them, in this accomplishment, excelled my old mule.

The distended paunches of my favourites told me that they had fared well, and from their indolence I concluded that they had just finished a hearty meal. Their absence, therefore, I now rejoiced over, though at the same time I took steps to prevent its recurrence, by hobbling the old lady's fore feet when dismissed to seek her dinner.

Next morning, as soon as the animals had had time to fill their stomachs, I saddled up, and, for the first time for many days, rode. I continued to push my course to the north. Travelling was sufficiently good to enable me to make a fair journey —possibly twenty miles. About two hours before sundown we halted for the night, and, fatigued as I was, I lost no time in seeking the rest which I needed. I had got soundly into dreamland when (as I imagine from the appearance of the few stars visible, it wanted a couple of hours to midnight) I was awakened by a subdued rushing sound, the origin of which was explained by a glance in the direction from whence the wind came. I was about to witness a specimen of the mountain-storms peculiar to this region. Not possessing a tent, it was not incumbent on me to rush to the storm-rope and see that it was secure. I was far more independent. I only pulled my blanket more tightly around me, kicked the balance of the fuel upon the glowing embers, squeezed myself into the smallest possible compass, in order that the diminutive log to windward of my position should not be overtaxed in its efforts to ward off the coming deluge, and waited the issue. I was not long detained in suspense. A few large drops pattered upon the soil, and in a moment after the floodgates of heaven were opened to their full extent, and a perfect waterfall descended. The thunder was loud and terrific, and the flashes of lightning were remarkable for their brilliancy.

Reader, have you ever hunted a water-rat till the poor creature is on the verge of death, from the length of time it has remained submerged, in order to save itself from the unrelenting terriers? If you have indulged in such a chase you will know what they call in Scotland his *drookit* state. Such is the expression which will give the best idea of my appearance at daybreak on the following morning. A bright sun and a clear sky, however, prevented me from yielding to depression of spirits, and as I had not yet obtained a camping-ground suited to my fastidious taste, a further advance to the north was undertaken. Game was more abundant than usual, and the first buffalo (*Bison Americanus*) which I had seen for a month was discovered in some low ground, half meadow, half swamp. Not being partial to beef of so tough a nature as this veteran was certain to make, I left him alone in his glory.

About half-past three I came to a spot which had evidently been used as a camping-ground; though from the rotten state of the few scattered camp poles, and the ashes (ever tell-tales of the existence of fire) having vegetation protruding through them, I came to the conclusion that the place had long been deserted. It was, however, an excellently selected site, and I determined to remain there for the night.

For days there had been to the north-west of my line of march a mountain peak, I should imagine quite as lofty as the highest point of the Sierra Nevada. In shape it was like a sugar-loaf, with an excrescence projecting from one side, about one-third of the way from its summit. I did not see it marked in my map, which from its size, and the ignorance that exists in reference to this locality, was necessarily very imperfect. At some future period it doubtless will be well known, for it is remarkably steep, while its outline is peculiar. Judging as well as I could from the distance at which I was from it, my impression is that it was one mass of stone.

After turning the animals loose to feed, I ascended a bluff which overtopped my resting-place, to obtain a survey in the direction I wished to proceed. The view to the east was extensive, and the appearance of the country promising, encouraging me to hope that my intention to reach the upper waters of the Missouri, or some of its tributaries, might yet turn out successful.

While enjoying my anticipations of once more setting my feet upon the plains beneath me, I observed an animal, reduced by distance to the size of a puppy about two weeks old. When it first caught my attention it was in motion, but soon came to a halt. Surmising it to be a young bear, I made my way down to within fifty yards of where I had marked it, having carefully kept a large rock between me and the object of my stalk. On peering out from my ambush I was amazed to find that it had disappeared, but an opening in the rock close by suggested to me the idea that there was a cave somewhere, into which the youngster had retired. Not being desirous of meeting the mother of this fascinating child, I was about to return, when two cub bears came forth from their hiding-place, followed by their maternal parent. Fortunately their course was not in my direction, and as they started on their evening's foray I retraced my way to camp. My four-footed companions had arrived there before me, thus saving me the trouble of hunting them up—a precaution necessary for their safety when such a dangerous family was abroad.

The horses found so much food about here that I determined to remain for another day; my gun, too, sadly needed cleaning, and my clothes required patching—reasons which also induced me to decide on a protracted halt.

When I was a boy, a fond mother, either out of regard for my future welfare, or to keep me out of mischief, and thus save herself trouble, taught me to sew and to work kettle-holders. Although years have elapsed since then, the lesson of my youth has not been forgotten, but on several occasions has turned out useful. If some unprejudiced person were to see the patches and darning I have accomplished, he would pronounce them miracles of skill. Of course they are not so regular as the stitches of a sewing-machine, but bear the same relation to them that the drill of a regiment of militia or volunteers does to that of a battalion of the Guards. I would not give a fig for a man who is deterred from undertaking a task because there are obstacles to prevent its accomplishment. I once undertook to make a pair of trousers. With the legs, which required merely straight cutting, I succeeded admirably, though I had only a hunting-knife to do the duty of shears; but the fork, or seat of the inexpressibles, beat me. First, it was too high up, and almost split me; then it was too low down, and braced my thighs so closely together that I was like a hobbled horse. Ultimately I determined to fill up the vacancy which I had made by too free a use of 'my knife, with pieces skilfully sewn in. These, however, were so numerous that the garment became ponderous, and the weight was exactly where it was least desirable. I made another attempt to render this maiden effort in tailoring successful, but not having a goose with which to press the seams, their edges chafed me so dreadfully that, much against my will, I was obliged to wear for some time a kilt—a costume not suited for climates that produce mosquitoes. However, I have the consolation of knowing that ultimately I succeeded in obtaining a good fit,—a salve that helped to soften much the wounds of disappointment and insects' mandibles.

If the wild animals that I have met form an estimate of my consequence by the amount of destruction I have committed upon their respective races, they must regard me, in the language of the States, as 'very small punkins.' I wish more of my countrymen could say the same. Unless for sustenance, or to obtain information on subjects of natural history, I now never killed any animal; but this night my objection to useless slaughter almost cost me my life.

Before going to sleep I fastened up the old mare with more than usual care. To the mule I always granted perfect freedom, as he would not leave his companion, and, further, performed most thoroughly the duties of watch-dog. The hooting of several owls told me that rain might be expected, so I piled on more than the ordinary amount of fuel, moved off further from the fire to obtain better shelter, and, curling up like a dormouse, soon fell into a sleep, in which I had many strange dreams. How long I had been wandering in imagination far from where I lay I know not, when a snort from the mule, and the violent struggling of the mare, awoke me. Without waiting to wipe the cobwebs from my eyes, I jumped to my feet and seized my gun. For some moments I could not distinguish anything more than a few feet from me, for the night was intensely dark, and the glare from the fire enshrouded the distance in impenetrable obscurity. The fact that the mare still struggled violently, and that the mule, strange to say, had bolted, seemed ominous of trouble. As an Indian would not have alarmed the horses so much, I felt convinced that it was a bear, which, although as yet I could not see him, I had no doubt was close at hand. Prepared to act promptly if called upon to defend my faithful companions, I looked around on all sides, and at length discovered Bruin, whom I had previously been unable to see in consequence of the fire being situated between me and him. His attitude was one of uncertainty; for though he was hankering after horse-flesh, he seemed to be balancing in his mind whether the reward would be commensurate with the risk. I believe my presence was unknown to him; however, I soon introduced myself to his attention by whirling a burning limb almost between his legs. This demonstration only caused him to change his place. A second fagot I aimed more successfully, for I hit the enemy on the flank, the missile dropping almost under his nose. Such a reception was not to his taste, so he bolted, running as if pursued by a pack of furies.

While I patted my mare, and spoke to her words of confidence, the mule returned, and as all was quiet, and the animals had apparently recovered from their alarm, I again turned in.

In all probability two or three hours had elapsed, and the fresh-made fire had subsided from a blaze to a mass of glowing embers, when a second time I was awoke by the agitation of the horses, whose manner seemed to evince their dread of a not far-distant foe. Without moving I peered from under my blanket. The moon had risen, and as less light emanated from the fire, I could see more distinctly than on the former occasion. Some animal was certainly near. I sprang to my feet, gun in hand. A movement behind me attracted my attention in that direction. Not five yards off stood the bear, his upper lip curled up so as to show his tusks, giving a fierce expression to his visage, denoting the innate ferocity for which his family have a reputation. In a moment I comprehended the situation, and intuitively cocked both barrels, so that in an instant my gun could be employed. Well it was that I was thus prepared, for, with wonderful suddenness, the aggressor reared himself on his hind legs, and rushed upon me. There was no use in delaying hostilities longer, so I aimed the right barrel at his chest, and fired. With the report he staggered, but only for an instant. In a moment more I should have been within reach of his formidable claws, but I took aim with the left barrel, and lodged its contents in a vulnerable spot. The foe, rearing himself to his greatest height on his hind toes, and grasping madly in the air with his fore feet, rushed forward, as if the last impulse of his instinct was to annihilate his slayer; but he fell headlong, with his purpose unfulfilled, within a yard of the camp-fire.

Fearing the struggle was not over, I had dropped my gun and drawn my revolver, which, with a sigh of relief that its services were not wanted, I was now able to replace.

The whole affair had been so sudden and unexpected, that, even while viewing the carcass, I could not realise the exciting scene I had just gone through. Daylight did not surprise me napping or indulging in idle dreams that morning; I had obtained too much food for thought to quit the real for the ideal.

When sufficiently light I carefully examined the dead animal. Its size for a moment caused me disappointment, for in the darkness in which the struggle had taken place I had fancied that I had never before seen its equal in magnitude. The first shot was well placed, possibly a little too far forward, for a bear's heart is situated well back in the carcass. Nevertheless, after the lapse of a short time it must have proved fatal. The second shot was placed so admirably that, under the most favourable circumstance, I could not have fired with a more thoroughly destructive aim. Entering between the junction of the lower ribs the bullet had ranged upwards, bearing to the left, and splitting the heart in two. Both were snap-shots, but the range was so short that room for missing was scarcely allowed : so little credit is due to me on this occasion for skill in marksmanship.

Four hundred and fifty pounds I should suppose was quite as much as this bear weighed, but he was much out of condition. If the season had been the fall instead of early spring, twenty per cent at least might have been calculated as its probable weight. The colour of its hair was a light tawny-brown, which almost induced me for the moment to adopt the mistaken hypothesis that the cinnamon bear (*Ursus cinnamomus*) is only a variety of the grizzly bear (*Ursus ferox*).

I am aware that both mammals and fishes will

often change the colour of their coat, the better to adapt themselves to changes of temperature, or to new ranges of country and rivers they may be removed to ; but I am still unaware of either of these influences causing a change in their features, or in the general outline of their shape.

This day I continued my slow and tedious route over a very rugged country, but the diminution in elevation of the mountain ridges to the east, as well as their less bold and jagged outlines, induced me to hope that I was at length approaching the upper table-lands of North America, situated between the Prairies and the Rocky Mountains. In many of the ravines, and on one or two flat-surfaced, elevated slabs of rock, that are frequent in this neighbourhood, I observed the droppings of both big-horns and Rocky-mountain sheep. These animals occupy the same position in reference to this continent that the ibex and chamois do to Europe. They are both extremely wary, and during day select the elevated plateaux and ridges, but at night descend in search of their food to places where vegetation is less scant and more diversified.

The first turkey-buzzard (*Vultur aura*) observed for months I saw to-day, perched upon what I should suppose to be the remains of a lynx, but as the bones of the limbs and cranium were wanting, I was unable to decide with certainty on its identity. Though this bird, from its filthy habits, rank, putrid smell, and dirty, unkempt plumage, has ever been the reverse of a favourite, still to-day I welcomed its appearance with most pleasurable feelings, the mutability of my own sensations recalling the often inexplicable changeability of many of my race. Thus, the snob who would be passed by in Piccadilly as almost unworthy of a nod of recognition, if met in distant lands, particularly where travel is dangerous, would be accorded a thorough shake of the hand. 'No, he's not a bad fellow, but d—n it, I must give him the cold shoulder before I get home. What would the Honourable Tom, or my Lord —— say, if they saw me in such society?'

There was a period when I did as others, particularly youngsters, do. Time, I hope, has taught me sense. Although these birds had incurred my dislike, they are wondrously useful, for they devour quantities of putrid animal matter that otherwise would impregnate a whole neighbourhood with its noxious exhalations. In the Southern States of the Union, where they are numerous, they are protected by law, for their utility has long been known by their practical inhabitants. Few creatures are made perfect; cowardice and gluttony are their besetting faults—another cause for my dislike. A human being that possessed such characteristics I would despise.

This night I had to put up with a bad camping-ground, little fuel, no shelter, and scarcely any food for the ponies. Poor things! their lot was a hard one. Just compare it for a moment with the pampered life of an English thoroughbred. The contrast is as great as that between the existence of an *habitué* of

White's or the 'Rag,' and the lad who sweeps the crossing in front of either of these comfortable retreats from domestic tyranny. Still I hoped better days were in store for my ponies. The wielder of the broom hopes the same, but are his anticipations ever realised?

Although kept awake for several hours by some half-starved native of these wastes, who howled his lungs nearly out of his carcass, I awoke betimes, and hurrying over my simple breakfast, saddled up, and got under way. The landscape continued very uninviting, for even dwarf vegetation was scarce. Still the surface of the soil was less packed with boulders, and the mountains did not appear so elevated.

A little after the sun had crossed the meridian, I mounted for an hour's ride. After being possibly thirty minutes in the saddle, the mare, who had been previously walking so listlessly as to toe several stones, and once almost to pitch on her head, voluntarily accelerated her pace. Soon after her ears became pricked, and an unwonted animation told that some living creature was in our vicinity. From my long acquaintance with the old lady, I knew her peculiarities thoroughly. In fact, she was almost equal to a pointer in telling me to prepare for a shot.

Why she did so I never could tell, unless that she associated my killing game with the half-hour's or more rest she generally obtained, while I was removing the hide of the victim, or selecting such tit-bits as most pleased my appetite.

Nevertheless, I unslung my gun, and, cocking it, placed it across my saddle-bow. At the time we were rounding the base of an almost perpendicular cliff. In a few moments the entrance to a ravine of sixty or more yards in width was disclosed, and from its bottom, disturbed by my presence, a brace of Big-horns rushed to ascend the only practicable path that appeared upon its sides. This brought the animals closer to me. The range was not over a hundred and fifty feet. The old nag comprehended the situation and halted. The position she selected was admirable for my purpose, and I cut down the larger animal in splendid style.

Who does not feel gratified when he is conscious of having made a very clever shot? But my satisfaction was not unalloyed with sorrow, for the carcass was lean and unfit for food, and the splendid head and horns were a load too great to think of carrying with me, that they might at some future time become an ornament to my dwelling. So all had to be left a prey to ravens and vultures, or, worse still, to putrefy, and serve no other purpose than that of manure to the uncultivated soil.

At sunset, when I had been in camp more than an hour, it commenced to rain—a Scotch mist it might have been called; but whatever appellation was most applicable, it inflicted on the unsheltered a most perfect ducking. Half the night I submitted without murmur to my fate, but when constantly replenished puddles had formed under each prominent portion of my figure—puddles which from the influx and egress of fresh liquid were not permitted to get warm—I fear I uttered a malediction against mountainous countries in general and this one in particular.

It is often a great consolation to our wounded feelings to know that there are others as painfully situated as ourselves. Whether this is a Christian sentiment or not, it is certainly one by no means uncommon among Christians. On a knoll not a hundred yards off was a wolf, whose lair had been invaded by the penetrating rain. The ejected tenant made the neighbourhood echo with his discordant howlings. When day dawned he still remained at his post. Nothing would have induced me to harm him. I suppose I was actuated by the fellow-feeling that both were houseless.

Although the trumpet did not sound 'to horse' at an early hour, I was soon on foot, leading along my disreputable-looking 'Rosinante.' About noon the country commenced to improve, the hills becoming less rugged and the valleys showing some symptoms of vegetation, while here and there, even in exposed situations, a dwarf fir-tree could be discerned. Snow still was to be found, but only in patches, its position generally denoting a ravine. Several buffalo, all of which were bulls, I saw in various directions; but, having enough and to spare of bear-meat, I left them to die patriarchs.

When the sun was an hour from the horizon I

arrived at a notch between two bluffs, from which I looked into a long and wide valley; its lower margin was abundantly clothed with timber, gradually decreasing in quantity as the sides were ascended. Such a scene was too attractive to pass, so I entered through its portals, and found a good camping-ground, with a capital sheltered corner for myself, plenty of browse for the nags, and firewood galore, as Pat is supposed to say.

In searching over my traps to take stock of the quantity of ammunition I had remaining, I discovered, in an old cap pouch, a piece of plug tobacco, as black as coal, and which, from it richness, cut like a piece of cheese. This Godsend afforded me great satisfaction, increased also by its appearance, which was a proof of its strength. A neighbouring yellow willow I soon afterwards denuded of a portion of its bark, which, when dried, I mixed with the Nicotian leaf in about equal proportions—thus doubling the amount of smoking material, and spinning two pipes out into four. That night half my supply was consumed. In each puff which I inhaled I saw outlines of home, of dear friends, of valued companions; and when I fell asleep I do not believe I turned till the bright rays of the sun whispered to my eyelids that I should be up and doing homage to their Producer.

CHAPTER III.

EXCELLENT FISHING — VICINITY OF FRIENDS OR FOES — AN AMBUSCADE — THE SQUAW AND HER PAPOOSE — A WIDOW'S ATTENTIONS — CHANGE OF CAMP — ABUNDANCE OF GAME — INDIAN DOGS — PROCESS OF TANNING — CANVAS-BACK DUCKS — THEIR HABITAT, AND METHODS OF CAPTURING THEM.

IN this spot I determined to halt for four days, for with such shelter, water, and vegetation, game must be abundant. Descending after breakfast to the stream that coursed lengthways through the valley, I found indisputable evidences of the presence of beavers, as well as numerous deer and buffalo tracks.

My rough but ready fish-line was always carried in a corner of my bullet-bag. Hoping to find the water as prolific in game as the land promised to be, I cut a wand for a rod, and with some thread ravelled from a few scraps of rag I retained for gun-washing, lashed a diminutive piece of the tail of my scarlet shirt upon the hook's shank. Taking my stand where there was a rush of water, produced by a choke caused by the jamming of logs and vegetable matter, I made a cast. In a moment I had hooked a splendid fellow. For a few minutes I gave him the butt, to gain time to find a landing-place. This I succeeded in doing, and pulled my prey ashore, in spite of his most urgent remonstrances and struggles. Again and again the operation was repeated with equal success, till I began to regret that my horses would not eat fish, and thus justify me in continuing my sport.

Returning homewards I could have killed several deer, but, satisfied that I had obtained sufficient food to sustain the inward man, I desisted from useless slaughter. Not to take too much credit upon myself for what by some may be considered self-denial, my reduced stock of ammunition might have had no small amount of influence in producing such commendable conduct. As I had enjoyed a pipe in the middle of the day, there was only sufficient of my tobacco mixture left for an after-supper smoke. Was it because one of these luxuries was not enough, and the body craved for more, that I slept but indifferently, and during the night felt convinced on several occasions that I heard dogs barking? If my surmises were correct, either white men or Indians—either friends or foes—must have been in the vicinity. As my animals had not returned to camp, I felt more uneasy than I otherwise should have done from such indications of the vicinity of my own race.

Having scattered the remains of my fire and hid my saddle and blankets in the neighbouring bush, I started in search of the truants as soon as the sun was over the eastern ridges. The bottom ground I knew they would make for, as there more abundant food could be expected. An hour's unsuccessful search brought me out on a ridge from whence a tolerable view could be obtained. In the north-east, to my astonishment, hovered several turkey-buzzards. From my knowledge of these birds I felt assured that they were near a camp or dead game: the first was a probable, the other a certain indication of man's presence.

'My luck all over!' I exclaimed inwardly. Now. that I had reached an elysium I found that it had other occupants. It was, to use a not very elegant expression, a confounded sell, for the odds were all in favour of their being enemies, not friends. Always thinking it better to know the worst, I proceeded at once to do so. If the mare and mule had not been absent, it is more than probable that I should have retired without gratifying my curiosity; but, *minus* these, I could not depart, and in following out my search for them it was quite possible I should be discovered, and thus placed at a disadvantage. I therefore got to leeward of the place I wished to reconnoitre, and then advanced upon it directly up-wind. If this is neglected, and the strangers happen to possess dogs, they will be winded by them before they are within half-a-mile of the object of their search.

Now, believing that the dogs I heard last night belonged to the hunters whose handiwork had attracted these carrion-feeders, I was more than usually guarded in my advance. Each step was made with caution; no rotten limb was tramped upon, and the intervening boughs that prevented my progress were parted with the utmost care. From the abundant indications of game to be seen on every hand, I concluded that the unknown were either new arrivals or numerically few.

The caution that I was obliged to exercise prevented my approach from being rapid, so that almost an hour elapsed before I believed myself within such distance that I could obtain an observation of the immediate locality I sought. From being a little out in my reckoning I had to alter my course, and stalk further than I expected. The trees and brush, as I advanced, became less abundant, and a few yards further on it would be difficult to find shelter from observation; but fortunately, before I was in such a predicament, I was rewarded with an elucidation of the mystery. By a charred piece of ground where there had once been a fire were two Indian dogs; both of which appeared large, well-fed specimens of their race. The one was amusing himself with a shank-bone; the other, half asleep, nodded and blinked over the imaginary warmth of the extinguished fire. The surface of the soil was here clothed with grasses, and, except immediately around the remains of the fire, was not trodden down and disturbed; while at the base of a rock, not ten yards removed from where the cooking had been performed, stood a shanty, composed of cedar-boughs skilfully laid in lairs so as to overlap each other and be waterproof. The slight appearance of traffic and the smallness of the bush residence were conclusive evidence that two or three persons at most claimed this for their camp.

For more than half-an-hour I remained in ambush, but not a vestige could I see of the owners. Several times the dogs got up, stretched themselves, and took an observation of the immediate vicinity; causing me on one occasion much alarm, lest I should be discovered: the larger of the brutes actually came within thirty or forty yards of my hiding-place.

The person or persons, however, who I supposed resided at this spot, were evidently away hunting, for all around was in a state of repose. No sound broke the solitude, except the plaintive note of the peabiddy bird or the hammering of a woodpecker on a neighbouring tree. Commencing to feel uneasy at the delay, I repeated mentally the proverb about 'patience and perseverance,' and argued with myself on the necessity of being cautious. However, I was soon recalled from this intellectual amusement by both dogs springing to their feet and rushing towards my left, with anything but anger in their manner or ferocity in their bark.

Very little over pistol-range from where I was secreted they halted, and evinced every demonstration of joy. What did this mean? In altering my position, and straining my eyes to learn the cause, I betrayed my presence to the curs, who in a moment rushed at me with the impetuosity and savageness of a brace of fiends. However, I had little to fear from their attack, but a great deal to dread from the discovery their angry barking was sure to entail.

But no time was left for thought; for, looking in their direction, I perceived the head and shoulders of a figure projecting above a log. Closer examination disclosed a rifle-barrel. Here was a pretty kettle of fish! for I was taken in rear, and, therefore, was without shelter. At the same time the enemy had cover that would have warmed the heart of the most fastidious rifleman. To attempt to make a bolt in hopes of securing shelter, would very possibly induce my opponent to open fire; and certainly the curs would lose no time in trying the quality and flavour of my calves. I must have been discovered before aware of it; and if so, and the intention of the unknown had been hostile, ere this I should have received the contents of the long ominous-looking barrel, the muzzle of which frowned more than a foot over the owner's shoulder.

If obliged to make a virtue of necessity, it is always best never to appear hurried, or to take any step but with the greatest precision and formality. The adverse party is thus prepossessed in your favour—possibly overawed by your self-possession, and not unfrequently, instead of remaining master of the position, he becomes, from want of strength of mind, willing to play second-fiddle instead of wielding the *bâton* of leader. In order to impress my foe I gave my moustache a pull—a way we have in the army—straightened myself to my full height, assumed a benign but at the same time determined aspect, and marched up with measured tread towards the ambuscade, the dogs in advance, like two heralds, vociferously proclaiming my approach.

The rifle of the stranger remained directed towards me, the figure never altering its position, and the black eyes looking straight into mine. Though they were mild yet they said, 'If you harbour guile, beware!' Not being an apt linguist I hesitated how to open conversation, for the long snake-like optics bespoke plainly that the person before me was an Indian. Having been lately in China, my first salutation was '*Chin-chin!*' '*Comment vous portez-vous?*' my second: mother-English for the time being quite forgotten. It is usual to forget our native dialect when we address foreigners. At length the figure stepped from its concealment, exclaiming at the same moment, in shrill, high-pitched accents,—

'How you do?'

The speaker I looked at—could I be mistaken? no, certainly not!—was a woman.

'A what?' I hear the reader exclaim.

A woman—a squaw—I repeat, and, as squaws run, not a bad-looking one, although sufficiently aged to be beyond mark of mouth, for where teeth should have been visible there were none. Her manner was timid, but not distrustful. Broken English, interspersed with an occasional word of French, she spoke fluently. We directed our steps to the camp, when, having reached the fire, we halted. As she observed me anxiously gazing around, she read in my eye that I was searching for her husband; so, without my even asking the question, she exclaimed, 'No chief, no brave, no Injun here. I all alone, except papoose.' Then she went to the cedar wigwam, and returned with her almost naked baby, a little copper-skinned, dark-eyed, good-looking brat of about a year old, who coyly hid his face in his mother's bosom when he saw the stranger's eyes fixed upon him. The parent hugged him to her heart, maternal love and pride beaming in her countenance as she gazed upon her progeny, or listened to the few words of praise I bestowed on young hopeful's looks.

Full of confidence in my good intentions, she deposited her baby on the ground, and entered the wigwam. In a few moments she returned with a minx-skin pouch in her hand; from it was produced a plug of tobacco, which she cut up, and having—after the most approved plan on such occasions—rubbed it into shreds between the palms of her hand, filled a pipe, lighted it, and handed it to me. After a few puffs I wished to return the attention, but she declined the glowing bowl with the exclamation, 'Me no smoke;' so I, in no way loath, enjoyed the luxury to the dregs.

From this woman I learned where my quadrupeds were, and that my whereabouts had been discovered through them. Last night my mare and mule had come to her camp with her horse. Alarmed, she had endeavoured to separate them, and drive off the strangers, lest their owners, when in search of them, should discover her retreat. This she failed to do, for the three nags, unseparated, wandered off into a neighbouring meadow. Not satisfied, she extinguished her fire, searched for the horses' back-trail, found it, and with the skill so peculiarly characteristic of the North American Indian, followed it up to within a short distance of my camp. As it was then nearly dark she desisted till dawn of day, when she renewed her exertions, and easily discovered me by the smoke from my tell-tale fire. She had closely watched all my movements, followed me in my search for my horses, and in my stalk up to her camp. Perceiving nothing hostile in my manner, she perhaps saw—gentle reader, do not consider me conceited—the prospect of a future husband, for hers had been dead some months— killed, as she told me, by the falling of a limb of a neighbouring tree in one of the gales of wind of last winter; and Indian widows, as well as English ones, often think this quite long enough to mourn in solitude the loss of a dear departed.

As is very common among the Western tribes, the husband of this squaw had been a trapper. An Indian beauty would sooner link her fate with such a man than with the proudest chief of her tribe. This preference most probably results from the fact that the red man expects all manual labour, it matters not how severe, to be performed by the women.

For the benefit of my horses I removed my camp next day, and chose my new dwelling within earshot of the powerful lungs of the half-bred baby, who by-the-bye was rather a model child, and worthy of being taken as a pattern for good behaviour by many of our infants claiming to be well bred, and who are continually quoted by their aristocratic parents as models of all that is charming and loveable.

Rest and abundant food wonderfully improved my horses, for after three days' idleness they became so skittish that it was always an hour's work to secure them. On such occasions I became so worried in temper that, to prevent the recurrence of the annoyance, the would-be truants were no longer allowed to wander without hobbles.

Game of every description peculiar to these latitudes was here most abundant. Deer were to be frequently seen within gunshot of the camp-fire; bears nightly put in an appearance, and received a welcome from the two Indian dogs, noble specimens of a deservedly honoured race; while each night wolves sung out a challenge to their domesticated relations, which was returned by them in language doubtless as defiant, but less malicious in intonation. I have heard travellers say that they never could distinguish any difference between the voice of an Indian dog and that of the wolf. My experience,— and I think those readers who have had the opportunity of judging will agree with me,—is, that the wild animal's note is more shrill, protracted, and of less volume than the voice of man's companion in this part of the world.

In this out-of-the-way part of the earth the dog plays a very important part. He is the watchman *par excellence,* he is a beast of burden, a romping companion with the youngsters, and furnishes a favourite food on occasions of great ceremony. In appearance he much resembles what is erroneously denominated in England a Pomeranian dog, but is generally twenty-four inches high at the shoulder, sometimes more, and of a yellowish-tawny colour. He is possessed of excellent sight, a sharp nose, and acute hearing. As a rule, instead of being treated with confidence by their owners, these animals are fearfully abused and knocked about. If they were treated with more kindness and carefully trained, they doubtless would develop much sagacity. *N'importe,* I have not as yet been able to gain the confidence of the squaw's two companions. They brook my presence, but do not like me. Even the half-picked bones I throw them are regarded with distrustful eyes.

In some of their traits of character they display much of the wild animal. Thus, when we are at meals all that is given them is at once carried off and secreted, unless it be such a small morsel as will constitute a mouthful, when it will be swallowed with a spasmodic gulp.

My companion informs me that she is of the Crow tribe. Around I see proofs that she is an excellent trapper. She had already a large stock of peltries collected, to be disposed of at the nearest trading post when spring was sufficiently advanced for trade to open. Every day she visited her line of traps, for she was possessed of eight, and seldom returned empty-handed.

The process of tanning is very simple among the Indians, but my efforts had never been satisfactory, although I had followed as closely as possible their example. It was doubtless in consequence of my imperfect manipulation that the garments which I then wore—though, indeed, they had gone through much wear and tear—showed evidences of dissolution. My new friend voluntarily undertook to remedy these defects, and in a few days I was much more presentable.

Having proposed to purchase her supply of tobacco, the pouch and its contents were handed over to me, and all attempts to force her to accept any remuneration failed. 'We are friends, therefore I will not take your money,' was her answer, while a sad look—possibly if she had been more juvenile it would have been called a pout—said as plainly as words could express, 'I will have my own way.'

The weather had been very changeable lately, and if our elevation had been greater we must have felt it severely. Squalls succeeded squalls, accompanied by rain or hail. Those mountain-peaks within sight were all dressed in their winter covering, yet the meadow where the horses fed was almost without snow. The buffalo-grass was already cropping out through the decayed vegetation of last year, and migration was going on rapidly among aquatic fowls. For an hour this morning they continued going north in immense phalanxes, returning southward in the evening.

As I expected, soon after dark there was a considerable fall of temperature, and in the morning a thin coat of snow was visible everywhere over the low grounds.

By the river I fired into a flock of duck, which proved to be canvas-backs (*Anas vallisneria*), thus knocking on the head the supposition of some would-be authorities, that this species are not to be found west of the Atlantic sea-board; but, alas! they were poor and insipid—how different from those found on the Chesapeake River during winter!

From the reputation Epicurus has obtained there can be scarcely a doubt that he was a gastronome of great experience, yet he was unacquainted with the canvas-back duck, which in my belief deserves to be placed at the head of any enumeration of delicacies. Among educated sportsmen—and in England few others exist—this bird is well known by name. The very rich may even have had their tables graced with them, but they are only to be obtained in America. Such being the case, a description of their appearance and habits, as well as the methods adopted for their successful pursuit, may not be uninteresting. The naturalist Wilson thus describes a drake:—

'The canvas-back is two feet long and three feet in extent, and when in good order weighs three pounds. The bill is large, rising high in the head, three inches in length, and one inch and three-eighths thick at the base, of a glossy black; eye very small, irides dark red; cheeks and fore parts of the head blackish brown; rest of the head and greater part of the neck bright, glossy, reddish chestnut, ending in a broad space of black that covers the upper part of the breast and spreads round to the back; back, scapulars, and tertials white, faintly marked with an infinite number of transverse waving lines or points, as if done with a pencil; whole lower parts of the breast, also the belly, white, slightly pencilled in the same manner, scarcely perceptible on the breast, pretty thick towards the vent; wing-coverts gray, with numerous specks of blackish; legs and feet very pale ash, the latter three inches in width—a circumstance which partly accounts for its great power of swimming.'

The female is a trifle smaller than the male, and less brilliant in colour, while the characteristic markings are not in her so distinct. Still both sexes much resemble each other, and are not distinguishable by the wide difference in plumage so apparent in the majority of wild-fowl.

Essentially migratory, few birds have a wider habitat, the Arctic regions being their breeding-ground, while the estuaries of the slimy, mud-margined rivers of that portion of North America situated between the 40th degree of latitude and the verge of the tropics, are their winter retreat. Nor are they confined only to the Atlantic sea-board, but are found in equally great numbers (as I have learned from a close observer) on the Pacific margin. However, they are not scattered like the mallard (*Anas boschas*) all over this extensive region, but confine themselves to certain localities. Thus, on the great Western prairies, although on occasions I have seen a flight of these birds, I have but seldom killed them. On the harbours and bays of Northern New England the sportsman rarely brings a number of canvas-back ducks to bay, yet they must have passed over each of these extensive ranges in their journeys from their breeding-grounds to their winter quarters. Two reasons are urged to account for this eccentricity or partiality. First, that the intermediate space does not produce food suitable for their support; secondly, that their powers of flight are so great that they almost disregard space. Temperature, which operates so powerfully upon nearly all aquatic fowls, as almost invariably to force them to assemble in the greatest numbers where the line of demarcation is drawn between frost and thaw, does not in this particular case appear to assert its influence in the same way, for without resting, all, save the stragglers, pass from one region to another, jumping as it were from hyperborean latitudes to tropical climates.

One peculiarity in the canvas-back duck must

not pass unnoticed, viz. that its food so affects its flesh that it is either the greatest table delicacy or the reverse. On the Chesapeake, where they are procured in the greatest perfection, these birds, at the period of their arrival, are poor in flesh and insipid in taste. After a week or two of rest in this favourite haunt they become fat, and reach the greatest perfection in flavour. This is, doubtless, to be attributed to the abundance of the aquatic plant, *Vallisneria Americana*, which in Maryland and Virginia is found most abundant, and appears there to constitute their sole food. This plant, which much resembles celery, and grows to several feet in length, is firmly attached to the bottom, and is only procurable by diving. Many species of ducks, among which may be enumerated Red Heads (*Anas ferina*), and the American Widgeon (*Anas Americanus*), also show a marked preference for this aquatic vegetable; but as their strength and diving powers are inferior to those of the canvas-back, they constantly follow the latter, robbing them and bullying them out of the result of their labours.

The Chesapeake and its tributaries generally are visited, about the end of October or early in November, by canvas-backs. There they remain throughout the winter, but being extremely shy, they are easily frightened from their feeding-ground; more especially as the season advances, if the weather is mild. Frequently they go so far off into open water, that the visitor or sportsman might well imagine the locality deserted that yesterday abounded with them. At a distance they are easily recognised from other wild fowl, for when on the water they never appear a moment at rest, but continue incessantly diving. On the wing they pursue their flight in the form of a wedge. When wounded they dive to immense depths, and if closely pursued in this crippled state, and escape appears impossible, they will lay hold of aquatic vegetation on the bottom, the strength of their bill keeping the body attached to the weeds long after life has become extinct. That water-fowl are capable of such resolution as thus to become suicides in preference to permitting themselves to fall into the hands of their pursuers, I have often heard doubted; but this peculiarity is not only possessed by many Transatlantic ducks, but by several of our home species.

The modes pursued for their capture are numerous. It is considered most sportsmanlike to shoot them from stands at the hours of flight, as they pass to and from their feeding-grounds. Such points of land as project into the tidal portion of rivers, or lie directly in the course of these broad-bills to and fro during their flight, are much valued, and are generally strictly preserved, the owners inviting their friends from far and near to participate in the sport; and such compliments are regarded by American gentlemen in the same light as an invitation among us to shoot over a well-stocked cover or moor.

Another method by which they are taken is that of attracting them to the gunner, by employing a dog to play and gambol on the beach within their sight. Soon after the canvas-backs have arrived from their breeding-haunts this plan answers best; and such is their extraordinary stupidity, that the same flock can be again and again enticed within range. By this means very heavy bags are frequently made, but it is not by all regarded as a fair way of attaining game. In fact, the majority of shooting-clubs have issued a positive injunction against the employment of such a device on their grounds. They are also shot from a surface-boat, not inaptly called, from its appearance, a coffin, around and on which are placed a number of decoys. The quantity of birds that have been killed in a season by one man, by this means, is sometimes so enormous that, if the author were to state the numbers, the English sportsman would be apt to believe he was dealing in the marvellous. In this case, however, the labourer is worthy of his hire, for the discomfort attending so novel a means of obtaining sport is so great, that an immense return is required as an adequate compensation for the inconvenience incurred.

The danger, however, is inconsiderable; and whatever may be the impression of the *débutant* on first inspecting one of these extraordinary-looking machines, he may safely trust himself in its limited accommodation, even supposing it be blowing half a gale of wind. In fact, I have always found blustering cold weather better for this sport, for the motion imparted to the decoys by the dapple of the sea makes them much more attractive to their animated counterparts.

CHAPTER IV.

SUBSTITUTES FOR BAIT — FISHING EXPERIENCE — THE BLUE-BIRD — ALABAMA — RICH AND POOR — HOOD'S SPERMOPHILUS — A WOUNDED WAPITI — THE MODEST VIOLET — SUPPLY OF AMMUNITION — UNEXPECTED PROPOSAL — DOGS AND WOLVES — FRIENDS OF LONG STANDING — LUDICROUS POSITION — HOSPITABLE TEAMSTERS.

THIS morning, when the sun was sufficiently high in the heavens for the earth to feel its invigorating influence, I went down to the stream to try my luck among its speckled denizens. For some time I was delayed in commencing fishing by the difficulty I experienced in obtaining bait. However, after turning over innumerable stones, and displacing several decayed logs, I secured a specimen of an unknown grub. With this victim impaled upon my hook, I selected the top of a long reach of comparatively dead water, where wide-circling dark eddies proclaimed considerable depth. Among the grass and rushes that margined the water I discovered a flat rock, of many feet in diameter, only protruding a few inches above the surface. In the centre of this was a natural basin fifteen or sixteen inches in depth, in appearance not unlike an exaggerated foot-bath. In this natural tub I determined to place the anticipated results of my sport.

As split-bamboo, greenheart, or even lance-wood fishing-rods, jointed and spliced ready for use, are not to be procured here, I was satisfied to employ in their place a young tamarach-tree, about twelve or thirteen feet long. Of course this formed rather a clumsy instrument, but as no better was at hand, I was forced to be content with it. When the first cast was made scarcely had the bait disappeared when the line was tightened with a jerk, and I had a fine fish fast. With such strong tackle I could afford to be less cautious than the disciples of the gentle art usually are with such worthy game, so I put on pressure, gave the victim of his appetite the butt, and in a moment had him struggling at my feet. But in his efforts to escape my bait dropped off in the stream, and half-a-dozen of the inhabitants of the brook appearing as claimants for it, instantly bore it off. Thus I was again without this important aid. Only one resource was left me. As I did not desire to lose half-an-hour in searching for another, I determined to slice a piece off the pure white, silvery belly of my capture. Such a course was repulsive, but 'where needs drives——' —I will not complete the sentence. My hook was again in the circling eddies, and by degrees the glittering bait became more and more indistinct as it sunk deeper and deeper into the water, at length entirely disappearing. After a pause, a sudden, spasmodic jerk was felt at the line for a moment, and then all was still; but this inertion was of short duration, for almost instantly afterwards my pole—I will not say rod—was almost dragged ruthlessly from my hands. However I held on, and by degrees got the butt forward so as to throw the strain as much as possible upon the elasticity of the tamarach. This was no easy matter, and fearfully trying to hook and line. At length, however, I succeeded, and with the effort brought to the surface a noble fish. Being without a reel it was a cruel battle, a struggle for the mastery in which the possessor of the greatest amount of brute strength alone could gain the victory, provided none of my tackle parted. The biped succeeded, and the lithe, resplendently coloured denizen of this distant stream was forcibly abducted from his element.

My experience of the size of fish told me that this one was certainly over twelve pounds. In shape it was a perfect representative of the species known as *Salmo fontinalis*, but differed in colouring, for its flanks were marked on either side with five gigantic transverse bars, such as in the fry of the salmon are usually denominated thumb-marks.

Although I captured several more, this was the largest, and such was the avidity with which those cannibals bit—for the bait I continued to employ was a piece of one of their own race—that I came to the conclusion that the overcrowding of population here had placed food at such a premium, that all the inhabitants had ceased to be nice in their tastes.

All Englishmen know with what kindly feelings

and pleasurable sensations the robin is regarded by our countrymen. With the same affection the residents of America look upon the blue-bird. True, they have a songster which belongs to the thrush family, to which they give the name of robin, but it does not obtain the same sympathy as the little azure warbler. If we had blue-birds they would be the theme, *par excellence*, of nursery and children's story-books. To-day (the one succeeding my fishing experience) I have welcomed the first blue-bird I have seen this season, and the little darling was so tame that I almost believed he knew and appreciated my kindly feelings towards him.

Upon a dry limb of a shumach the blue-bird sat alone and warbled forth his sweet song, inviting a mate to join him in the cares of housekeeping. Again and again with renewed vigour he carolled out his dulcet strains; but he was alone, and no lady-love answered: not even any jealous rival of his race taunted him with want of success. He was, in this respect, a fit emblem of myself; but his solitude would not last long, for, unless a change in the weather took place, a day or two more would bring thousands of his species from the more hospitable sunny south, who, possibly quite as ardent but less venturous, wished to be assured that winter had departed ere they trusted themselves to this treacherous climate.

In build and size these birds much resemble the bullfinch, but they lack its defiant, impudent look.

Their manner possesses an air of conscious innocence, and timidity tinctured with confidence, that, even without the attraction of their beautiful plumage, would gain our love.

Of a migratory species, their summers are spent in similar and even much higher latitudes than my present position; but the blustering gales and cold weather of the autumnal equinox drive them south to such favoured regions as the blue grass slopes of Southern Kentucky and Tennessee, where they remain until the influence of balmy spring is again felt.

'Alabama' is, to my ear, one of the most melodious and expressive words. Let the reader repeat it, giving due length and stress to the vowels, and it will be found so attractive that it remains hovering on the lips, requiring scarcely more effort to give it utterance than a prolonged action of respiration. This melodious intonation means, in the tongue of those who were once inhabitants of the region to which it is given as a name, 'Here we rest.' The word was uttered by an exiled tribe, fleeing before the inroads of the grasping, unscrupulous, white invaders of the country, when they beheld the charms of this lovely region, and became aware of all its attractiveness. The strangers, in gratitude for the fortune which had brought them to such a place of rest, continued to call it Alabama. The Christian, however, soon followed upon the heels of the red sons of the continent, and now the country knows them no more, the only memento of them remaining being the sweet name taken from their vocabulary —a word more musical than any we have in our own tongue.

But it is not only the Indian that exclaimed 'Here we rest;' the blue-bird, the robin, the mocking-bird, and a hundred others, in their own language sigh out words of the same import: for Alabama is the southern limit of the migratory journeys of the majority of the feathered race, which, when they have entered this favoured region, are safe from the influences of the biting blasts of the north.

Could those poor, houseless, ragged, neglected urchins, whom I have seen in mammoth London, either sweeping crossings, or, fusee or match-box in hand, indefatigably soliciting the spoiled children of fortune to reward their labour or purchase their wares, migrate like the feathered race, how few would remain at home to expose their half-clad bodies to the pitiless blasts of our wet November days! They would rather be off to the radiant lands far beyond such climatic influences. But this privilege is reserved for the rich, who possess every luxury wealth can procure—shelter, clothing, and food, and can migrate from Norway to Southern Italy with the changes of the season. The poor, alas! we have always with us.

While passing over some open ground a rustling noise attracted my attention, but for some moments

I was unable to learn the cause. At length, as I was about to desist from my endeavour to discover it, I observed a pair of bright eyes watching me from a burrow excavated under a flat ledge of stone. At first I imagined it was a chip-monk, or hackee, the well-known and extremely pretty *Tamia* of the United States. To solve all doubts upon the subject I spent some time in endeavouring to dislodge the unknown creature, but my task was much more laborious than I imagined. At length perseverance was rewarded with success, and I secured the prize. It was a scarcely full-grown specimen of Hood's *Spermophilus*, the longitudinal bands and alternate brown and white spots of which made it most attractive to the eye. However, its temper appeared so irascible, and its disposition so vindictive, that although I had almost contemplated the cruelty of making it a pet, I changed my mind, and performed the kinder part of restoring it to liberty.

Saddling the mare one morning, I started on a journey of exploration for the country lying beyond the eastern ridge of hills. While ascending the high grounds at the back of my camp the surface of the soil was very rugged, but the descent on the reverse side again brought me to smoother ground. As far as the eye could reach extended a wintry-looking steppe, on which the only specimen of animal life at first discernible was a very hungry-looking grey wolf, who evidently was not favourably impressed with my appearance. Riding a few miles further, I descried in the distance a living object, which, on closer examination, turned out to be a wapiti; and as I wanted venison (yet did not care about alarming the camp by shooting the game in the neighbourhood) I determined to stalk this one. As the wind did not quite favour, I made a *détour* of several hundred yards, and at length reached the desired position for an advance up-wind. From the intervening ground being sufficiently irregular to favour my purpose, I got without difficulty within shooting distance, the facility with which I had made my approach astonishing me. A well-delivered shot terminated my labour, the deer dropping where it stood. On examination it turned out to be very low in flesh, and suffering from an ugly, unhealthy-looking wound across the hock. Its isolated position was thus accounted for; the injured limb preventing its remaining with its fleet-footed comrades.

The injury this animal was suffering from was, in my belief, caused by the canine tooth of a wolf; and if so, what a narrow escape it must have had, when the ferocious assailant was sufficiently close to leave upon his victim the impression of his tusks! So we see there are sometimes nearer slips between the cup and the lip, than that of a fox obtaining only the long feathers of a pheasant's tail, instead of the bird itself.

Occasionally in life we enjoy the most pleasurable sensations, not unfrequently produced by very slight causes. To-day, when returning home, fatigued from protracted exercise and disgusted from want of success, I perceived, on a mossy bank still wet from the moisture of the lately melted snow, a humble flower peeping out from under a withered fern-leaf. Its colour caught my eye, and in a moment more its shelter was carefully turned aside that I might the better examine its simple structure and the perfect blending of its various shades. Again and again I gazed upon this little treasure, till the flood-gates of my memory were opened, and a torrent of past episodes swamped my brain, for the modest flower was a violet. In this distant land it was almost more than unexpected to find a specimen of a family so treasured. Again and again I gazed upon it, drank in afresh its fragrant breath, and permitted my thoughts to wander off to other scenes. The memories associated with this flower were so tender that I could not pluck it, and by doing so doom it to wither and die before its time. I left with regret, but not with sorrow, the little charmer who had cheered my heart by recalling the treasured recollections of the past.

Next morning I made my start further north, as my animals had very much improved in flesh and spirits, and appeared capable of enduring considerable fatigue. The rest had done me good in more ways than one. My wardrobe was much improved; I had got rid of symptoms of fever and ague by drenching myself with a decoction made from the bark of the wild plum; and last,

F

though not least, I had added one pound of powder and three of bullets to my diminished stock of ammunition.

The way in which I obtained the latter requires an explanation. The squaw observed that I husbanded my ammunition, and asked the reason. I told her, and next day she brought me this present. At first I refused to accept it, and only did so when she consented to receive in return a guinea long worn as a watch-charm, a looking-glass, and a pocket-compass. Of the last I had two, but their value to me was inconsiderable, for I seldom consulted them—using the sun, moon, or stars in the open, and the mosses, the inclination of trees or shrubs when in cover, as my guides.

At sunset, having made all necessary preparations, the better to be able to get under way at an early hour, I paid a visit to my neighbour, not only to bid her adieu, but to obtain as much useful information respecting my route as it was in her power to give me. She was not in the least taken aback when I explained my intention, and we conversed in the most friendly manner. From her I learned that six long days' journey to the north-east would bring me to a fort where there were soldiers; that on the route there I should find game very scarce, and consequently few Indians, and these hostile in the extreme to the pale-face. Water, she also informed me, would be abundant at this season, though in autumn it is difficult to procure.

If I waited later, she added, I might possibly fall in with traders *en route* from the east to the homes of the Nez-percés and Fish Indians, living on the Pacific slopes. Although again and again the old lady repeated the name of the fort, I was unable to identify it with any of those whose exact locality I was ignorant of, though I was aware there were several on the tributaries of the Upper Missouri.

At length I bid my new friend adieu, and returned to my hut. On my way to my dormitory, and after I reached it, I regretted that so worthy and genuine a woman should possess so little regard for cleanliness and knowledge of those conventionalities of civilisation that are absolutely necessary to render feminine society attractive to a person of what may possibly be considered my fastidious taste. A nigger is generally deemed, and not without justice, a very odorous specimen of the human family; but the effluvium of a squaw is more peculiar, indescribable, sickening—strongly impregnated with the odour produced from bruised limbs or foliage of dwarf cedar.

In my young days, when wild romantic fancies floated through the brain, I had often imagined what a glorious thing it would be to expatriate myself, become adopted into an Indian tribe, fight my way through untold deeds of prowess to the position of brave or chief, ultimately marry a red princess, and succeed to the throne of her father.

Experience has rather cruelly knocked on the head such pre-conceived notions.

I was just about to depart into the land of dreams—for my pipe had got so low, that extra exertion of the lungs was necessary to keep it burning; and once I dropped that useful implement from my lips, it was very unusual for me to remain long awake—when I heard my mule give indications of being alarmed. In a moment I was on my feet, and as soon as I had got out from under my shelter in the night air, a voice addressed me. It was the squaw, who, for some purpose or other, had come at that untimely hour to pay me a visit, which courtesy required me to acknowledge with every expression of honour. The camp-fire, therefore, was again raked together, and after I had invited her to squat down beside me, I demanded the purport of what our feminine readers might consider a highly improper intrusion. The poor widow had no reserve in telling me. The simple truth was, fearing she would be lonely when I was gone, and seeing that the season was considerably advanced, there being every prospect of fur-trading commencing earlier than usual, she had made up her mind to go with me on the morrow. To such a proposition I could not say No. Her determination was asserted so frankly, without the least embarrassment, that I could not for a moment demur. I was indebted to her for many kindnesses, and she was a woman who could live alone upon her own resources; who could handle a rifle or set beaver-traps, and unquestionably belonged to that strong-minded type for which I had always entertained the highest respect. I had no alternative, therefore, but to agree to her proposal.

On the morrow all was ready. My mule, which had heretofore had nothing but his own carcass to carry, was, much to his disgust, assigned a load of skins. Even the dogs were turned into beasts of burthen, and most obstreperous ones they proved. A couple of long poles, similar to exaggerated shafts of a one-horse conveyance, were fastened to their sides, and on each of these was lashed a small pack. The squaw with her baby, straddled, not sidled, her own nag, while I mounted my mare, and thus the cavalcade started. Could any of those old friends who had been my constant companions when kid-gloves, neck-ties of various hues, and immaculate collars, formed my chief ambition, have seen me at that moment accompanied by my female fellow-traveller, they would have laughed heartily at the figure I presented. For ten days we pursued our journey, nothing breaking its dull monotony but the powerful voice of the papoose demanding, at rather frequent intervals for my repose, a renewal of his natural nutriment, or the howls of the dogs when flagellated by the squaw for some breach of discipline.

Large game was very scarce and wild, but as we were provided with a fair supply of comestibles, this was a matter of little importance. In many places snipe (*Scolopax Wilsoni*) were very abundant, but from various appearances it was evident that the present resting-place of these aquatic-loving long-bills was in summer a sun-baked barren. Wolves were numerous, but it would puzzle a person to know what they can obtain to live upon in a place so far from shelter, and where the cold was so severe that sleep was almost impossible. Suddenly jumping up in our vicinity, they brought the dogs into disgrace, for they appeared unable to control their desire to give chase. Such was their eagerness that they either disarranged their pack, or, knocking it off with the violence of their movements, scattered the contents. The fear of punishment had no deterring effect upon them; but if the wolves turned round and showed their tusks, which they not unfrequently did when they believed themselves sufficiently far from us to be out of danger, the dogs would sneak back to our heels thoroughly crest-fallen.

This night, immediately after sunset, the atmosphere was unusually rarefied; and away to the east I distinctly saw several white dots upon the slope of a distant elevation. Tents I supposed them to be, but the squaw corrected me by stating that they were waggons belonging to the pale-face; and when at night the darkness became sufficiently intense a fire could be clearly distinguished in the same direction. Once more then I was about to meet men of my own race, and I rejoiced at the prospect.

At an early hour on the morrow I saddled my mare, and leaving my mule, very much against his will, to the tender mercies of the squaw, started across the plain for the encampment of the traders. As the weather was thick and threatening, I had but a very limited view of the distance. However, I had taken by compass the bearings of their position last night, and had little fear of failing to fall across them on their march, or to strike their trail.

From the unusual disinclination which my mount evinced to rapid progression, and the efforts she would frequently make to halt, or turn round and look backwards, I saw that she much regretted separation from her old associate. I had probably proceeded about five miles when I heard a pattering of hoofs in the rear. The mare pricked her ears, and I turned hastily to the right about, not without fear that a brave of the Crow or Blackfeet tribes might be behind me. But a glance back dissipated that supposition, for I perceived my mule galloping as fast as Tam O'Shanter's good mare Meg did, on the occasion of her celebrated trial of speed against the witches and Cutty Sark at Alloway Brig. The poor animal rattled along, with the lariat-lines and hide-thongs, which had been employed for fastening on his load, floating in rear like the pennants of a homeward-bound frigate. His flanks were heaving and his nostrils distended, as, in a perfect lather of perspiration from fear and excitement, he rushed up to his associate, and testified by manner and voice the intense pleasure he felt at their reunion. This event was rather perplexing. I scarcely knew whether it would not be better to return, for I was certain that this son of an ass must have thrown off his load, and probably scattered it in every direction. Almost at the same instant up rushed the squaw, nearly as heated, though certainly in a different temper from the mule, which had preceded her. Without a moment's pause to take breath she rattled forth a long story of her misfortunes, interlarded with by no means complimentary addresses to the fugitive, of whose halter she had obtained possession. But when she attempted to lead him back all her efforts were unavailing, for the mule would not return without his companion. I was therefore forced to return with her, and afterwards to assist in gathering her scattered wealth, which was strewn far and wide.

At least a couple of hours were thus lost, and when I recommenced my journey to the waggons I was compelled to go with a woman and baby in tow. If she had been pretty, young, and attractive, it might possibly have been different, but to appear before my countrymen with a squaw without teeth, and her child strongly stamped with the peculiarities of the half-breed, was a very severe ordeal. However, there was no help for it; so I made a virtue of necessity, knowing full well I should get the credit, like many other unfortunates, in spite of all I could say to the contrary, of holding the respectable position of father.

I need not say I was much chagrined, and for a moment I almost thought I would once more turn my course towards the south-west.

The sun was about an hour high when we came up with the teamsters, who had already halted and released their cattle to feed. Consequently the whole cavalcade were in a comparative state of idleness, excepting those engaged in preparing the evening meal. Our advent naturally drew all the idlers together, to hear who we were and where we came from. When within speaking distance a volley of questions greeted us, and before I could edge in an answer, even sideways, a volley of laughter woke the echoes from the neighbouring hill-sides, repeated so often that I at last was constrained to join in; for, although it was at my own expense, I could not help seeing that the situation was intensely ludicrous.

Such proof of my good temper was fortunately in my favour, for they one and all came forward and gave me a hearty welcome. My animals were stripped of their trappings and provided with food, while I was received as the guest of the chief, Tom Morris by name. A bottle of choice old Bourbon-county whiskey was uncorked, and its contents disposed of in honour of my arrival.

That night, after enjoying a capital meal—a sumptuous one, when compared with my late primitive diet—we sat late. Tobacco and whiskey combined loosened my tongue, and all the principal portions of my adventures were narrated. The last I can remember before turning in for the night was my host saying, 'Come, Cap, that's all like enough, but the yarn about the squaw won't go down noways you like to fix it.' So others have since said. *N'importe;* the most incredulous I have ever found the most ignorant.

CHAPTER V.

WAGGONS ON THE WESTERN WILDS—SHOT AT A BUFFALO—BY THE CAMP FIRE—THE BOSS'S STORY.

BEFORE the opening for traffic of the Atlantic and Pacific Railroad all articles of trade suitable to the Indian market were brought into their territories by waggons. In fact, these conveyances played in Western wilds exactly the same part that camels do in Eastern deserts. In structure and size they very much resemble the ambulances of the military train, except that they are supplied with a cover of cotton-duck stretched upon elevated hoops of wood, sufficiently raised in the centre to admit of a man of moderate height standing upright on the floor of the waggon. When the vehicle is transformed into a dormitory at night, it is really a most acceptable shelter from the severe and sudden storms so common in this locality. Mules, horses, and oxen are all employed as beasts of draught; the first being the best, for they require less food, and can thrive upon what a horse will not eat. At the same time they are less liable to become footsore and fractious. Horned cattle also have some advantages to recommend them, such as great strength and wonderful patience; but, on the other hand, they are very slow.

As the lives of the Indian traders are constantly exposed to danger from the attacks of hostile or avaricious tribes, they are always well armed, and a mitigated system of military discipline is in constant use among them. At night the waggons are drawn together so as to form a stockade and enclosure for their cattle, and sentries are posted around them. Hunters and teamsters are all detailed to their respective duties, generally those they engage for, and the authority of the chief man is absolute. As really brave men are seldom quarrelsome, and these people are the essence of pluck, squabbles and disputes are not frequent among them. Moreover, there is in their dealings a kind of *bonhomie*, which goes so far as to make each welcome to the tobacco and personals of the other.

When, however, they do quarrel, they certainly 'go the whole hog,' for a duel to the death is often the result. As at home, a dusky fair one is generally the cause of these *contretemps*. O woman, woman! all over the earth you have much to answer for. Ages past it was so, and it is the same now: Delilahs and Samsons are as common as spiders and flies.

I had reason to consider myself in great luck, for it is a very unusual occurrence to find traders so far to the west thus early in the season. Formerly they did not leave the bounds of civilisation till the grass of the prairies was sufficiently advanced to feed their cattle, but as 'the early bird got the worm,' from the amount of competition that exists even in this business, it was found all-important to be first in arrival at the trading-post.

Mr. Morris, in his determination to be successful in the rivalry, had had many of his animals and supplies stored on the verge of civilisation during the winter; so that, as soon as travelling was practical, they were *en route*. Although the horses and mules were turned out regularly after the day's labour to pick up what vegetation they could obtain, they did not rely on this for food, as forage was carried in sufficient quantity to last till they reached their destination.

I turned out at an early hour next morning, feeling as fresh as a daisy. The weather continued very uninviting. A heavy haze was hanging over the earth, and the clouds appeared so overloaded with water, that the report of a gun, or other equally powerful concussion, promised to bring down an avalanche of rain.

After breakfast, while scanning the limited view of the surrounding country with the hope of seeing game, I could distinctly hear the deep lowing of a buffalo-bull. If my mare had not been too weak for the violent exercise necessary to run successfully this game, I should have gone in pursuit, for use could have been found for the flesh. However, I desisted, hoping that rest would soon restore my quadruped to a respectable condition.

Although the landscape was dismal and the weather such as invariably caused depression of spirits, I felt ten years younger than I really was, and anxious to go in for any kind of lark. Could this be attributed to the potation of whiskey of the previous night? If so, such results are rather different from those generally attributed to that potent spirit.

The old squaw appeared quite at home. She slept under one of the waggons last night, and looked as active and ready for the road as any of the party. My mule was apparently destined no longer to lead an idle life, for already he had her pack, which was formidable in bulk, upon his back. As I had no present use for his service, I did not object to this appropriation of my property, provided it did not lead to an attempt to raise a claim to ownership. 'Sufficient for the day, however, is the evil thereof.'

The waggons started at an hour after sunrise, each following in the track of its predecessor, while the teamsters cracked their whips, bandied jokes, sung snatches of songs, or whistled. They are a hardy, devil-may-care lot, with constitutions like water-spaniels. About noon, while with 'the boss' in front of the train, the mist lifted, and several buffaloes were seen feeding in the direction in which our route led. I expressed my regret to my host that my horse was in such an unserviceable state for a run, when he promptly offered me his own for the occasion. He was a powerful sixteen-hand nag, nearly thoroughbred, and in good condition. My saddle was soon transferred to his back, the girths were tightened, and I mounted.

Taking him well in hand I shook him into a gallop, but found, as might have been expected, that his mouth had been completely ruined by the constant use of the villainous Mexican bit, so much in vogue throughout the United States. However, the beast could go, and with satisfaction I found I was overhauling my game. A few minutes more and I ranged alongside, very much to the disgust and fear of my horse, who refused obstinately to take up such a position as I desired.

Wishing to do my work well, for I knew the eyes of all were upon me, and my reputation as a hunter would be damaged by a bungling performance, I delayed firing. However, a chance offering, I pressed the trigger, and my bullet entered low down and well back. The bull immediately charged, the horse cleverly avoiding his onset. Then the poor stricken creature slackened its pace into a walk, and ultimately halted, glaring at me from its little eyes smothered in hair, while glouts of blood soiled its lips and chin. Gradually its fore-legs straddled further and further apart to support its towering frame, then it swayed first to one side then to the other, making an unsuccessful effort to retain its footing, and, after a struggle, the monarch of the prairies was dead!

Continuing our journey we came to a watercourse, with a channel full to the brim. Anticipating difficulty in crossing, it was decided to halt for the night. Brushwood was abundant, and a few trees of large growth were visible; a promise of fuel for the camp-fires that is always acceptable.

When the day's march was over, and the labour necessary to make camp snug for the night had been completed, the traders assembled together, and, like sailors in a forecastle, spun yarns over their pipes; many of their tales being replete with adventures and romance, while their effect was seldom diminished by want of exaggeration.

The second evening I was with this waggon-train, the boss (*i.e.* the head-man), a highly educated and gentlemanly person, narrated the following to me and his partner. My knowledge of life and the locality induces me to give the story, as a specimen of those strange scenes which take place in new countries, where law has not had time to establish its powerful authority. The language is, of course, my own, yet the story was told so cleverly and graphically that I fear the change will not improve it:—

'I had been spending a few months in the land of gold, during which time I had visited the big trees, Mariposa county, the mines, Sacramento—in fact, done almost all that was worth doing, when I made up my mind to return eastward.

'With that purpose I took passage on board the "Nevada," one of the oldest of those magnificent floating palaces that ply between San Francisco and Panama, but, at the same time, far from the best of them. The day was beautiful on which I went on board, for the sun was as bright as ever gladdened a landscape, and all the passengers had a holiday appearance.

'Leaning on the bulwarks close to the gangway, about ten minutes before getting under way, taking observation of those who were to be my fellow-travellers, I was very much struck by a young lady, apparently not over seventeen, who, under the guardianship of a middle-aged, sinister, repulsive-looking man, came on board, and passed aft to the cabin; and as any number of boxes, of every size and calibre, accompanied them, at once I came to the conclusion that they were also passengers.

'Few see a really pretty woman accompanied by a vulgar or repulsive-looking man, without conjecturing how extraordinary is the *mésalliance*: at least, to speak for myself, I seldom do. It is a combination of sweet and sour, sunshine and storm, beauty and the beast: qualities so utterly dissimilar, that more than our ordinary interest is unavoidably awakened.

'The deep-toned, sonorous whistle had given warning to the dearest friends that the hour for parting had come. Elderly gentlemen and young ones again and again shook hands, and repeated their last words of instructions or good wishes; ladies kissed and rekissed each other, and again had a kiss and a hug; sailors rushed up and down, intent upon giant hawsers, as thick and far longer than boa-constrictors; the captain shouted unintelligible words, and the inferior officers answered in echo the monotonous "Ay, ay, sir;" the deck was nearly clear of interlopers, the ponderous paddle had possibly revolved half a circle, when another passenger, *minus* all luggage save a paper parcel which was thrown after him, by performing a variety of eccentric, decidedly monkeyish feats, swinging by his hands, and almost anything but holding on by his eyebrows, obtained a footing upon the ship.

'All were so much occupied with one thing and another, that few took any notice of this last arrival; but I, possibly having less to do—no friends to wave good-bye to, no sweetheart to send a parting kiss to—did; and, to my surprise, felt convinced I knew him. But either I was mistaken or a mutual recognition was not desired; for such an unembarrassed plainly-speaking expression of non-acquaintance was returned for my stare at him, that for once I felt satisfied my eyes had spoken to me falsely.

'When the City and Golden Gate had faded into the distance, and the towering, rugged, grand outline of hills had become less and less distinct, we had been under way some hours; yet those who had interested me most—the beauty and her protector, and the last arrival—I had not again seen. One meal had also passed, at which neither was present. I know not how it was, but, somehow or other, I could not help associating them together, though they were so different in every outward respect. People, however, will have fancies, generally possessed of as little substance as shadows.

'The Pacific Ocean in this part of the world, according to my experience, is well named. Our first night on board the sea might, without the slightest exaggeration, have been dubbed a mill-pond. Not a ripple broke the surface, except where a sleek, smooth, well-fed, jolly, India-rubber-looking porpoise tumbled over. Even the habitual long-rolling swell of the ocean was wanting, and our good ship, snorting out her pleasure in loud, sonorous grunts, at the gratification she felt that fine weather was accorded her, made good speed on her journey.

'A little after six bells had struck in the first watch I sauntered on deck, to enjoy my pipe, stretch my legs, and get a breather before turning in. The full moon, bright and large, shed a delightful romantic light; and, except the portion of the crew on duty, I was alone. What a night it was! a heavenly night, such as one never forgets, but associates in his mind with fairy-land or the spirit-world. I felt dull, however; for the scene was too lovely to be enjoyed in solitude. In fact I wished—but what was the use?—for some fair companion, whose arm would rest on mine, in whose eyes I could gaze, and in whose ear I could whisper all the promptings of my better nature. The unknown beauty would, moreover, hover before me. Is she maid or wife?

was a question I again and again asked myself, and determined to unravel in the morning by propitiating the stewardess.

'Not feeling inclined to sleep, I sauntered backwards and forwards, and at length stood by the stern-davits, watching the snow-white track of our wake, wondering what the fish thought of ships in general, and how many of them got bumped in the ribs by our stem, when a hand was laid on my shoulder. The owner of it was the last arrival.

'"Old fellow, it's me! Don't say a word. I saw you knew me when I came on board," he said, in an audible whisper. "I didn't want you or any one else to recognise me; so mum's the word. You were once my friend—prove that you are so still, by not taking notice of me. Good night. I can trust you, I guess." And before I had time to speak—almost to realise what had taken place—he had disappeared; and but for the noise of his boots descending the companion-ladder, I should almost have believed it all a dream.

'"Strange!" I murmured to myself. "What can this mystery mean?" I was certain it was he; but how, I asked myself, has he come here, and for what purpose? It cannot be more than a year since I left him in the Atlantic States.

'To go back to that time, I was then living in the State of Missouri. The Southern struggle was drawing to a close, and politicians were quarrelling, changing their coats, and becoming daily more intolerant. I was in want of a horse, and attended a sale in the nearest market-town to procure one. After examining several, I had all but decided on purchasing a nag that was being trotted up and down for my inspection. The brute was well bred, a little undersized, used its feet cleverly; but it showed an inclination to vice—a peculiarity I cared little about.

'At my elbow stood the person who had just left me. Before that time I had once or twice seen him in a neighbouring billiard-room, but had not taken sufficient interest in him to inquire who he was. Only three or four others were present, namely, the horse-dealer and his assistants, who were separated from me by something like a dozen yards. The word that would have transferred the animal to my possession was all but spoken, when Boyle, for that was his name, said, *sotto voce,* "Have nothing to do with him—in an hour at the billiard-room I will tell you why." And I followed his advice, rejected the mount, and soon after found my way to the billiard-room, where he was seated in a retired corner, evidently wrapped in thought.

'A more thorough specimen of the South-western States it would be difficult to find. Tall, thin, yet large-boned, bronzed in colour, with a piercing eye and aquiline nose, he appeared to me, as I afterwards found him to be, a man capable of strong friendships and dislikes, of perseverance and courage.

'Being each supplied with a "tod of Bourbon,"* he muttered the salutation, "How?"† and, without query from me, gave me the following information:—

'"I know you're Secesh at heart—I come from Arkansas, so guess you know what I be. Well, that 'ere horse is no account—not what he looks, for he's well put together; but he's balky, balky as be d—d. Touch him with the spur, and he'll sulk for a week. I have known him since John Morgan's people took him in Tennessee, and he's only here now because his last owner had to leave him in the raid they made across the Ohio."

'All this was true, as I afterwards learned, and it revealed to me that my new acquaintance, as I inferred from the precision of his story and the minuteness of the details into which he entered, was not only intimately acquainted with the supporters of the bonny Blue Flag, but had lately taken an active part among them.

'Not many days after the above occurrence, while snipe-shooting, I met Boyle engaged in the same amusement. A better shot I had seldom come across. At long ranges his heavy double-

---

* A glass of whisky.

† Copied from the Indians; doubtless originally their abbreviation for 'How are you?'

barrel unerringly dealt destruction. Our common love of field-sports drew us much together, and friendship was the natural result.

'I discovered by chance he was stranded for means, and consequently invited him to pay me a visit; which he did, passing the entire time, five weeks, in shooting or fishing, in both of which sports he was wondrously successful. At night he would amuse me and my visitors with his skill in performing sleight-of-hand tricks at cards, or by explaining and exposing the means that professional gamblers employ to swindle their victims.

'One day, breakfast had just been removed, my horse was at the door, and I only lingered to give some final orders about dinner, when Boyle joined me, giving the information that it was necessary for him to go to the next State. His business, he said, was important, and he could not perform it without the loan of a hundred dollars. Although I knew him to be a gambler, and one not very particular in the artifices he employed to obtain success at the gaming-table, I lent him the money, and we parted, for when I returned at sunset he was gone.

'It might have been eight o'clock, possibly later, while some farmers who had been disposing of stock were with me, when the third or fourth deal at poker having taken place, the house-dogs raised a disturbance more than usually loud and vindictive. The cause of their excitement was the appearance of several troopers, under command of a serjeant, who halted and dismounted at my door.

'The non-commissioned officer at once entered and informed me that he had come to arrest my friend Boyle, that the house was surrounded, and that it would be prudent on my part not to offer any impediment to him in the execution of his duty—a course which would certainly expose me to the displeasure of the authorities.

'I stated, of course, that Boyle was gone; but my assertion was not credited, and my domicile was searched unsuccessfully from cellar to roof-tree, much to the apparent disgust of Uncle Sam's myrmidons: for when they were satisfied that their expected prisoner had really taken his departure, they took their leave, not even deigning to say good-night or to return thanks for the brimming tods of my whisky to which they had helped themselves.

'A month passed, and Boyle was almost forgotten. One dark and gloomy night I was snoozing over the fire, painting in its glowing embers all kinds of memories of the past; fitful skuds of rain every now and then dashed against the windows, and I felt, as most men would feel in such circumstances, thankful for having a roof over my head, and that in such weather I was not knocking about at sea.

'A few minutes more and I should have been between the blankets, when I heard a gentle knock on the door. Answering it myself, I had no sooner opened it than out of the dark gloom of night entered a figure muffled in a large cloak, the stiff and heavy folds of which showed that it was saturated. Raising the candle to his face—for the man never spoke—I found to my surprise that it was Boyle.

'After following me into the sitting-room, he said, "I require to be cautious, and I can only remain an hour or so; but your servant, I presume, has gone to bed?"

'"What does that matter? if the black rascal dared, I'd——."

'Here he stopped me.

'"Much better as it is," he continued; "safer for both."

'Taking off his outer garment, I saw he was armed to the teeth; how many revolvers he had stuck in his belt, really it would be impossible to say. His appearance recalled most vividly to my recollection the representations of pirates I had seen on the stage. Of course I offered him refreshment, and when he had eaten and drunk till the inward man was perfectly satisfied, but not till then, did he explain to me the object of his unexpected visit.

'"I'm off for Dixie," he said; "at daybreak to-morrow I must be over the Southern lines. Thank God, no telegraphs run north and south in this part of the State, for there are at this moment a troop of dragoons on my track, and not over two hours have I the start of them, while my horse is clean beat. But I've got my plans all cut and dry. Uncle Sam don't catch me this hop, you bet, and there's none about here to tell tales, since that pesky cuss Charlie is snug in his roost; not even a dog-bark is to be feared, for my pets wouldn't bay one who had so often been good to them, and thus tell the neighbours that a stranger is about.

'" Old fellow, you stood by me once, you must do so again; my horse is in the woods by the tobacco-barn, he's clean give out; no wonder, for he has done a smart day's work: still, but for a sand-crack, I'd have made him do the rest. He's well bred, and he's kind as he's game; there's no better in the States, and he'll suit you to a dot. Well, he's yours, but I want a mount in exchange. I can't go on foot, so I'll just take your old mare Fanny; she han't got much longer to live anyhow, and she can go the pace when she warms up."

'Without demurral I acceded to his wish. Fanny was of little use, for from age and work she had become so groggy in front, that it took all the rider's attention to keep her on her pins, yet when well warmed she could go the pace, and jump or clamber over any ordinary kind of fence: whether or not she retained her legs on lighting was quite another question. Still I was fond of the little mare, for she had carried me well in many a hard day's work, and as my friend rose to bid adieu I spoke a kindly word in her behalf.

'Without considering the risk I was already running, I was about to accompany him to the stable; but Boyle refused to permit me. He had left his saddle at the stable-door; and he knew where the mare stood. It would be best, he said, for me not to compromise myself. After a firm grasp of the hand the door was closed, and, poor fellow, he was again out in the pitiless, pelting storm, the pursuers barely an hour behind him—men eager for his life, for they knew they could never take him alive. But what cared Boyle? He was devoted to his country; and in her service, like thousands of his fellows, he would make any sacrifice.

'If a stranger had been moving about my premises, every canine I possessed would have warned me; but they recognised their old friend, and with many caresses crowded around him. Throwing myself into my arm-chair, I sat and thought. The minutes appeared like hours till I heard the clatter of Fanny's feet announcing that my friend was in the saddle. By degrees the noise grew more indistinct, ultimately dying away, and I breathed more freely; but my respite was short, for soon afterwards a veteran hound of mine, deaf as a post from age, gave tongue, and I knew at once that the old scoundrel was following the trail of him with whom he had so often hunted. Nothing, I was aware, would call him back, for often he had practised the same trick on others, and I feared his deep mellow note would attract attention to the hard-riding horseman.

'Thirty-six hours afterwards the mare returned, and the hound with her, both appearing little the worse for their trip.

'Boyle's horse turned out what he was represented to be; certainly as good a steed as I ever crossed.

'Months had rolled on, when I received a letter enclosing one hundred dollars, stating that the sender was in Arkansas, that he feared he had killed my mare, and that the old hound had followed him to the river, where he had left the horse.

'For the next two or three days on board I occasionally saw him, but neither by word nor look did he suggest that we had ever met before. On each of these occasions he was gambling, while a whisky-bottle stood at his elbow beside a large sum of money, his adversary invariably being the repulsive stranger who accompanied the lady previously alluded to.

'My time was fully occupied, for she was constantly on deck. The captain had introduced us, and we talked over every subject we could think of. I learned that she was married, her companion being her husband. When they arrived in New York they intended to be very gay and happy; going to the opera and theatre, night after night, and to no end of parties and balls given in her honour by sundry rich relations.

'Within twenty-four hours after our introduction we were friends, and in as many more we were intimate; her husband never joined her at meals, or came near her—in fact, she might just as well have been without him,—possibly better.

'It was the third evening of our voyage. The moon was hidden by clouds, and a foggy haze rested on the water. The damp was so penetrating on deck, that I was compelled, for the lady's sake, to propose our retiring to the saloon.

'"But what can we do there?" she asked; adding, "I am so tired of playing cards, unless you know bézique."

'I confessed my ignorance of the game.

'"Oh! it's easily learned," she continued. "If you choose I will soon teach you, I have counters and cards below."

'The saloon was not crowded; we obtained a nice quiet corner near the stern, where compliments could be paid in sufficiently loud whispers to be certain they reached the ear they were intended for, but could not be overheard by others.

'We had been thus engaged an hour and a half, and the mysteries of common and royal marriages were commencing to be understood. Already I had marked a hundred for aces, and had almost held double bézique, when we were interrupted by the husband, who in a gruff, bearish manner, strode down the cabin to us, and ordered the lady to her room. To this command she at first demurred, when he seized her wrist, and whispered a few words in her ear. She then rose, and. bidding me good night retired with her liege lord.

'Seldom had I felt more savage, seldom more inclined to kick a man; but discretion whispered in my ear that I had better not. So I went on deck, and chewing the cud of passion with the end of my cigar, wished that really pretty women would remain single till I met them. That night our intimacy terminated, for until we reached port she never left her state-room. The tyrant husband meanwhile continued to gamble and to drink— the latter far from moderately. My old acquaintance was invariably his adversary. I fear I was grateful when I recalled to memory that Boyle was up to every *ruse* that ever gambler practised to pluck pigeons.

'At length the intermediate port of Acapulco was reached, and all longed to go on shore, as much as caged birds do to try their wings. Half an hour after the hawser had run out to the prescribed length the ship was deserted by her passengers, and I among the number was diving into the old streets, and searching through the intricacies of this diminutive, though not unattractive Mexican town.

'Acapulco, like all semi-tropical places, is far more attractive at a distance than it is within its precincts. The glaring white colour of the houses is then mellowed, the verandahs appear like perfect lounging-places, and the roofs composed of palm-leaves, so disorderly when closely inspected, recalls the comfortable shingled cottages of New England. But the bay is pretty, the waters being placid and blue. The shore-boats, though rather uncouth, are not altogether ungraceful; while the costumes of the occupants are varied with numerous brilliant colours. The town is skirted by a belt of green vegetation, and the high distant hills are soft and dreamy in their outline.

'We saw abundance of fruit, which our countrymen on such occasions would always find it safer to gaze at than indulge in. Several representatives of the military service of Mexico were walking about, whose arms, accoutrements, and clothing excited astonishment, if not admiration. The town done I wandered off, with the vain hope of finding some pretty lane or handsome homestead.

'After traversing half a mile of sandy waste— difficult walking from the looseness of the material— the prospect became more inviting. On each side of me was a high fence of prickly aloes. I was at the commencement of one of the paths leading to the hills. To avoid irregularities in the surface of the land it was very tortuous; and on turning a corner, to my surprise I met my fair fellow-traveller. With a smile of pleasure and with outstretched hand she welcomed me, saying archly, "We have not here to fear the violence of Monsieur; no, he is in Acapulco, playing. As usual, the stakes are very high; but it matters not, he always preferred gamblers' society to mine—an eccentricity of taste," she added, "I am glad of." Then, turning sharply to me, she exclaimed, "But you have lost your tongue. Where are you going? Possibly you have business, and I am an impediment?"

'If previously I had thought her beautiful, now she looked absolutely lovely; her colour heightened, her brilliant black eyes flashing rays of fire, while her mass of luxuriant, dark chestnut hair hung loosely. Her little hands, decorated with pink, shell-like nails, far superior as ornaments to any jewels, and holding her unemployed sunshade during her conversation, were every now and then raised impatiently to give emphasis to her language.

'Assuring her of the pleasure the interview afforded me, I told her how much I regretted the unpleasant termination to our game of bézique. Continuing our walk, we steadily increased the distance that intervened between us and town. I felt rather embarrassed, scarcely knowing how to act, believing that this interview if known would be regarded as intentional, and probably might embroil me in a quarrel, which must reflect unpleasantly on all concerned. The conversation commencing to flag, the lady at length complained of fatigue; and as she rested on the bank I stood in front, believing it better not to sit by her side. My formality evidently hurt her, for after a pause she exclaimed, "Why, sir, you have lost your manners! you are not half as pleasant a companion as I imagined you to be. Are you afraid? you need not be so. My husband is too great a craven to do you any harm, unless it were dark, and you were unarmed and unprepared."

'In delivering this speech she became so excited,

that I was obliged to try and soothe her, for her bosom heaved, and her colour came and went. After a few minutes she continued, "Is it not bad enough to be married to such a man, without becoming a stranger to society on his account? I will not long submit, and if he attempts to coerce me I will kill him!—yes, I would in a moment!" she repeated, as she saw me smile at her vehemence. "But listen, I will tell you my story. So you'll learn whether or not I have occasion to hate this man."

'"I am from the same city and of the same race as our General Beauregard. An Empress of France was descended from similar lineage. My father was wealthy, my mother has long been dead; but seven months have elapsed since I became a bride. It was in this way. This man, my husband, gambled with my father. The poor old gentleman lost the residue of what once had been a handsome fortune, for we have had to pay a heavy price for the war. Thus my father found himself a beggar, and committed forgery to raise funds for one final effort to redeem himself. Again he played, and again he lost; worse than all, he fell into this villain's power. The price to be paid for his safety was my hand. I made the sacrifice to save my broken-hearted parent's honour. The grave has now closed over him. I have no relations left to avenge the insults I daily received, for they died in our lost cause; the duty therefore devolves upon the representative of my house—myself, to vindicate its honour, and I will! See, Monsieur, I am not unable."

'And she produced a pistol, rising at the same moment to her feet. This revelation of her character so surprised me that I scarcely knew what to say. So we returned silently to Acapulco, she doubtlessly communing with her warring feelings.

'On reaching the landing-place, we entered a restaurant close to the quarantine office, where many of the passengers were lounging around. Madame called for a glass of wine and water, while I joined in conversation with an intelligent, gentlemanly person I had frequently spoken to during the passage. Moving towards the rear of the building we passed a door partially open, through which numbers were both going and coming. My companion inquired, "Have you been in there? the play has been very heavy." Answering in the negative, I received the information that Boyle and the husband of Madame had been closeted there since their arrival, that numerous heavy bets had been made on the issue, and that each of the gamblers was determined to ruin the other.

'On gaining entrance we found the room crowded. In the centre sat the players, and between them a card-table. Greenbacks to a large amount were piled beside each, and both appeared entirely absorbed in their occupation. So far money had changed hands, but for a few moments, to revert again to its original possessor. Luck seemed to be so evenly divided, that if they had desisted then my friend would have risen not over a few hundred dollars out of pocket.

'The next deal appeared to bring both good hands. Bet after bet was made, each placing thousands of dollars on the issue. The excitement became intense. The spectators were equally carried away with the infection. Each moment one or other was expected to be called upon to produce his hand, for they were playing poker, when Boyle rose, and looking his antagonist steadily in the face, pronounced in clear, measured words, "Sir, you are cheating." The other replied by a blow on his adversary's cheek, which Boyle did not resent, simply saying, "Enough,—we will settle our differences. You are armed; the courtyard will answer our purpose better—there are too many disinterested persons present to use our revolvers here." The other only answered, "Let it be so." The room was therefore at once deserted and they proceeded to the courtyard.

'Seconds were selected. Fortunately I was not observed, or I believe my acquaintance would have requested me to officiate; but he was in the hands of one who, judging from appearance, was worthy of the responsibility. Each disencumbered himself of his coat, and, revolver in hand, was placed at the wall, with his adversary opposite him, possibly twenty paces apart. Neither was to commence firing until they received the preconcerted signal; but as the crowd cleared away, Boyle, with a haughty, malicious scowl on his face, spoke to his antagonist,— .

'"You still do not remember me. Well, you cannot forget Harry Clifton, whom you swindled first and afterwards shot at St. Mary's. He was my pal. I am the person who hunted you to the coast. You know what you have to expect. I'm going to kill you if I can; while there's a bullet in my six-shooter, I'll aim it at your heart."

'With such *nonchalance* did many of the spectators regard the coming prospect of bloodshed, that betting on the result took place, the odds being generally in favour of the last speaker.

'Time was almost up, and each man, cool and collected, surveyed his opponent. Vindictive hatred was clearly stamped on their features, and they were even impatient at the delay necessary to clear the lookers-on out of the line of fire. At length the preconcerted signal was given, and simultaneously each of the duellists' pistols exploded. Boyle staggered with the report, while the hat of his antagonist moved several inches further back on his head. Willingly would I have gone to the former's assistance, but I was restrained by the information that they must have it out, and by threats that somebody would drill daylight in any person's carcass that interfered before their six-shooters were empty.

'From the right to the left hand Boyle unhurriedly changed his weapon. The time it took to do so was but a moment, but in that moment he received another shot. He still stood braced and firm, and, slowly raising the weapon to the level, he took what I knew was a deadly aim, for the movement, the attitude, and the hand were exactly similar to what I had seen him use when making practice I never saw excelled. During the short pause, how I prayed for the report! I feared the foe would fire before he pressed the trigger. At length came the report, and with it a yell full of vindictive hate from the unfortunate victim as he sprang into the air and fell lifeless upon the ground. The bullet had entered the left corner of his right eye, ranging upwards.

Boyle leant against a friend, and glouts of blood came from his lips, for he had been shot through the lungs at the first fire, and through the arm at the second. The dead was removed into the house—into the same room where ten minutes before he had sat a living man; while Boyle was taken forthwith on board ship, that he might immediately receive medical attention.

'And among all the passengers not one had spoken to the wife of the dead man. There she sat in the refreshment-room, and ate her lunch, and drank her glass of wine. I hovered round the door, hoping, trusting, almost praying that some one would reveal to her the circumstances that had just transpired; but no one took the trouble —no one appeared to care. At length she caught sight of me, and, with a playful but meaning wave of her handkerchief, beckoned me towards her. All eyes at once were upon us, so when I approached my first words were to beg she would take my arm, and come into the open air. Without demurral she did so; but my courage had fled, and quite fifteen minutes elapsed before I had recovered sufficient resolution to impart what I wished to say. The weather, the ship, the passengers, were each touched upon. At length, after sundry stammers, I commenced on the subject that had induced me to bring her out-doors.

‘ "You must not be alarmed," I said; ‘but something has happened that you should be informed of. No person appears inclined to tell you, so it devolves upon me. It is a very painful duty, but——"

‘ "I cannot imagine what you are driving at! What a staid, phlegmatic, cold, indifferent man! Are you going to propose an elopement—to miss the ship—to return to San Francisco? Go on, I say; come to the point; and do not keep me longer in suspense."

‘ With such a warning, what could I do? At last I did what probably would have been best from the first, viz. telling her in plain words that her husband was dead.

‘ With a most determined and stern look—one

so terrible, and yet so full of import—she turned, stopped, and looked me full in the face; muttering, almost in a whisper,—

' " I took you for a gentleman; can you lie to me ?"

'In a few minutes she was in possession of all the facts, and during their recital only uttered, "Thank God, I am saved from a great sin!" Then, turning to me with a fixed, rigid gaze, she said,—

' " I have a duty to perform, an important one— to attend to the obsequies of my nearest relation. Will you assist ?"

'During the night we got under way: a week more took us to the Isthmus. Daily I was with Boyle. From loss of blood he had suffered much; still, few appeared to have any doubt of his ultimate recovery: but in his transportation across to Aspinwall hemorrhage broke out afresh, and he, the second victim, as gallant a patriot as ever drew sabre or served country, now lies decaying among the damp mould, in sight of the blue waves of the Caribbean Sea, surrounded by thousands of his race.'*

'But the Creole beauty, what of her? whom did she marry? and where does she reside?' I asked.

---

* For every yard that the Isthmus railway is long, it is said that an Anglo-Saxon life was lost in its construction.

'In Georgia she can be found; rich, for much of her father's wealth has been recovered; still unmarried: yet the most beautiful and admired of a wide and aristocratic (as far as Republican ideas go) circle of friends.'

CHAPTER VI.

COON OR SHELL DRAKE CREEK—MUSK-RATS—THE SKUNK—RACOON HUNTING—STORY OF A SKUNK—A RECOLLECTION OF MINNESOTA—ANAS OBSCURA, BLACK DUCK—ALARM IN CAMP—PRAIRIE DOGS—FAITHFUL SENTINELS—UNWELCOME GUESTS—ANIMAL BAROMETER.

THE stream where we had halted was called, by some of the teamsters, Coon Creek; by others, Shell Drake Creek. The last name appeared to me the most suitable, for ducks of different species were to be seen in every direction. From the precipitousness of the banks, it was evident much time would be lost before the waggons succeeded in crossing; for an incline had to be cut on both sides, to enable them to get in and out of the water. The course had been searched above and below our encampment to find a more available place, but without success; for where the margin was not precipitous, the depth of water was greater. As it was, I feared some accident must happen even here, as in the transportation every wheel would necessarily be submerged over the hub.

However, these Missouri teamsters, having taken soundings, preferred making a trial to being detained for a decrease of the flood. If my opinion had been asked, I should have advised differently; but as there are no more skilled or practised waggoners in the world than these people, my tendering advice could only have been deemed presumptuous.

While debating in my mind how to spend the afternoon, Mr. Morris asked me if I was 'a good gunner;' *i.e.* clever at killing birds on the wing. Having answered him in the affirmative, we crossed to his 'store-waggon,' from which he produced his 'bird-gun' (smooth bore), with a large supply of ammunition, and requested me to 'try what hand I could make of the ducks,' as they would be better than buffalo and salt-junk for supper; and the boys wanted a good mess after being in the water all day.

While following the edge of the stream, intent on carrying out my host's wishes, I got several shots, the majority of which were at long range; but, as the gun was a hard hitter, and I succeeded in holding it straight, I had no reason to complain of want of success. From the quantity of wild-rice straw that floated in the eddies and among the wash of the stream, I supposed that this locality must fairly swarm with wild duck in autumn, as that grain is a very favourite food with nearly all aquatic fowls. The old residences of musk-rats (*Fiber zibethicus* of Cuvier) were also abundant; and while remaining at one stand, where the reeds were sufficiently high to afford me fair shelter, I observed a couple of these diminutive beavers gathering material for a new residence, for each year they build a fresh domicile.

As has generally been supposed, these animals are not entirely vegetable feeders, for, whenever it can be procured, they show a marked preference for animal diet, such as wild ducks' eggs and fresh-water mussels. They are slaughtered in immense quantities for their fur, which is much sought after, autumn and winter being the seasons chosen for their capture. Still there does not appear to be any visible diminution in their numbers, even within the limits of civilised communities.

From the constant industry of musk-rats, and their knowing and sagacious ways, they have ever been favourites with me; and although I know them to be guilty of certain tricks, like other vermin, still I should much like to see them introduced into England. About the size of a half-grown domestic cat, rather lighter in colour than our common brown rat, they are in all respects like the beaver; with this one noticeable exception, that their tail is flat perpendicularly, the beaver's horizontally.

About ten hours before sunset I turned my face homewards. My bag of game was so heavy that I had to leave the greater part of its contents till I returned with a horse, which I did about an hour afterwards. I was then none too soon, for short as my absence had been, it was long enough to enable a skunk (*Mephitis*) to discover its whereabouts. However, I succeeded in driving the ruffian off—no easy matter, nor altogether without danger.

This animal is about the length of a mature

male ferret, but of a fuller form and less active habit. It is found scattered over a very wide extent of country, ranging from the north of the Gulf of Mexico almost to the southern confines of the Hudson Bay Territory.

As might be expected in climates of such a diverse character, their habits, food, modes of life, and even the colour of their coat, vary much. Still all display that insatiable craving for blood so characteristic of the weasel family. They are a constant scourge to the settlers, whose poultry they destroy; and are no less obnoxious to sportsmen, being the implacable foes to all descriptions of game. In the more densely settled portions of the United States, where this animal is constantly hunted down and destroyed by the inhabitants, they have become comparatively scarce; but in the large forests of the west, more especially in those that margin rivers, it is no uncommon occurrence for the traveller to find numbers of them. When such is the case they do not seek to conceal themselves, or to avoid the attack directed against them, but seem to regard their enemy's presence with perfect indifference, often tempting the incautious and inexperienced traveller within reach, and without fail treating him to a sprinkling of their fetid secretion, the strength of which is so great, and its power to resist evaporation so unusual, that clothes which have once been contaminated by it are for ever after unfit for use. The distance at which this disgusting odour can be smelt is almost incredible to the stranger, and statements made by naturalists on this subject have been frequently disbelieved, thus calling the veracity of the most trustworthy into question.

When residing in the western part of the state of New York, I frequently formed one of a party organised to hunt racoons. Autumn is the season in which this sport is most successfully followed, for then Indian corn, melons, and sundry wild fruits are ripe,—attractions irresistible to the nocturnal animal that we were in pursuit of. The nights at this period of the year are particularly beautiful, more especially during what is termed the Hunters' Moon. The atmosphere, clear almost as day, is not disturbed by a breath of wind, and the damp exhalations proceeding from the soil are suspended over the surface of the ground like an immense piece of gossamer. The temperature is all that can be desired for out-door exercise, and from every wood and orchard migratory warblers, with plaintive swelling note, sigh out to the listener a warning that winter is approaching, or an intimation that soon they will depart for more favoured climes.

According to the abundance of the game we were more or less successful, and many were the miles we travelled, fatigue being unknown, so seductive was the fascination of the sport. Occasionally our dogs would find a skunk, and disregarding the experiences of the past, would make it their prey. Though they had been frequently flogged for killing these animals, they invariably forgot the punishment they had received, and repeated their fault, the result being that they became sick for some hours from the noxious stench they had inhaled, completely losing their powers of scent for days, and becoming so disagreeable to our olfactory organs, that for at least a month to come it was more pleasant to avoid their vicinity. I have passed at a distance of a mile from the spot where one of these fetid animals had been killed many hours after its life had become extinct, and the atmosphere was still impregnated far and wide with its nauseous effluvia.

When residing in the township of Oro, on the north-western margin of the charming waters of Lake Simcoe, I was the guest of an old gentleman, long an officer in the gallant 44th Regiment, and who had distinguished himself in Spain during the Peninsular War. He informed me that a skunk, which had decimated his stock of poultry, had taken up its residence under his house to be closer to the scene of its nightly forays. The loss occasioned by this unwelcome visitor was so great that it became absolutely necessary to accomplish its destruction. Traps skilfully set and carefully baited failing most signally to effect the desired end, it was at length determined to raise the flooring over the spot where the marauder's retreat was supposed to be, but the wrong planks were accidentally removed. In his impatience the old gentleman went on his hands and knees, and placed his head between the orifice in the floor to ascertain by ocular proof the exact position of the skunk's den; but scarcely had he reached the requisite position when he was saluted over the face, eyes, and shoulders with a perfect shower of odorous liquid, more powerful, but less pleasant, than any sold by perfumers. For hours afterwards he remained completely blind. His clothes were utterly destroyed, and although he shaved off all the hair that adorned his visage, and indulged in innumerable lavations, both hot and cold, it was days before he could divest his person of the obnoxious smell.

The distinct longitudinal markings of black and white which traverse the coat of this animal render it very attractive to the sight, so that it has been domesticated as a pet, but not before it has been deprived of the gland that secretes the objectionable liquid. In captivity it exhibits considerable sagacity, with much demonstrative affection for those whom it knows.

A skunk possessed by a friend of mine, who dwelt near Leavenworth, in the State of Kansas, was allowed unrestricted liberty. Day after day it would return from its wanderings with a partridge or young hare. It would answer its master's call with the readiness of a dog, sit erect to beg for food when the family were taking their meals, and in cold weather lie before the fire with a large cat, uttering frequently a murmuring noise, as an acknowledgment of gratitude for the luxury it enjoyed.

To the traveller, especially when he ventures beyond the regions to which civilisation has penetrated, and wanders in those unreclaimed lands where temporary residences of bark or boughs of trees are the only shelter obtainable, the skunks become a great plague, for during the night they will enter into these extemporised dwellings, and steal, eat, or gnaw whatever is found within reach; and if they should be detected and suddenly alarmed or disturbed, they will discharge their liquid defence right and left, making a change of quarters to the residents not only desirable but imperative.

Although it is not a generally acknowledged fact, skunks are aquatic, and betake themselves to the water if it becomes necessary for them to do so in order to obtain their food. I obtained this information, as many travellers and naturalists before me have discovered the phenomena of Nature, by having it thrust under my observation, at the very moment when I was least expecting any such addition to my store of knowledge.

In Minnesota, that charming Western State where wood and water appear equally divided, where winter is cold, but dry and pleasant, where summer possesses neither the fevered heat of the South, nor the changeable temperature of the Northern Atlantic seaboard, I was encamped with a companion on a small lake, picturesque as the fancy of the most imaginative artist could paint, and whose pellucid blue waters were margined with a belting of wild rice. The season was that at which wild fowl come from the North, retreating before the rapidly following Arctic gales, on their route to the lagoons and savannahs of the sunny South. Game was not only abundant but unusually tame. The day was such as nearly every sportsman can recall to mind, if he be so observant as to mark those peculiarities in the weather which have struck him as being fruitful of sport. On the occasion I speak of the sky was dark and unbroken by clouds, the wind was hushed into whispers, and the refraction of light made every object appear more than double its proper size. The atmosphere was surcharged with electricity, and all animal life was suffering under its lethargic influence.

My game-bag was full, containing more, in fact, than was absolutely necessary for culinary uses; but among its contents were several rare specimens of American aquatic fowls, the desire to possess specimens of which had induced me to be more than usually destructive of life and lavish of ammunition.

Determined not to throw away another shot, unless tempted by some unknown bird, and suffering much from the oppression of the close atmosphere, I sat down upon a boulder, and although half-dozing, still retained sight of a flock of black-duck (*Anas obscura*) which were floating on the surface, apparently asleep, and certainly unconscious of danger, although within sixty yards of my perch.

I

Now, these are goodly fowls to look at, larger and more robust than the mallard (*Anas boschas*); but tempting as the opportunity was, it would have been worse than sacrilege to deprive a specimen of this family of life. Happy in the thought that I could once in my life regard them without bloodthirsty intentions I relapsed, while still observing them, into an ambiguous state, difficult to distinguish between sleep and wakefulness.

But I was not the only spectator of the confiding broad-bills, apparently as listless as myself; for I was startled by the appearance of a head, which rose for a moment above the surface of the water. At the time I took it for that of a muskrat—a circumstance so common, that it made no impression on my mind; but the view I obtained was only momentary.

The poor ducks, floating with their heads nestled under their wings, remained almost stationary, unconscious of the fact that an enemy was near them, for there was neither current nor wind to move them over the surface of the lake. A cry of alarm, however, from one of the birds, accompanied by the rapid strokes of its wings, proved that one had been attacked. All save the stricken one, who fruitlessly struggled against his captor, took wing, leaving their unfortunate comrade to his fate; like man, too ready to forsake his bosom-friend in the hour of trial.

The poor bird continued to beat its wings in

vain efforts to escape, but its exertions soon became weaker, and at length entirely ceased. The variegated coat of the animal by which the poor bird had been slaughtered led me to believe that it was a skunk, but the distance was too great to be certain; and I determined, therefore, to intercept its progress to land. From an admirable hiding-place among the aquatic herbage, I gave the object of my stalk the contents of my gun when it was within twenty paces, and on picking up its carcass found that my supposition was correct.

As the last of the waggons and animals were being got over Corn Creek I joined them. There was scarcely a single member of the company that had not been in the water a great portion of the day. In consequence of this grog was served out, and as the weather was better, and we had every prospect of a dry night, the whole camp looked forward to a spree.

After all was made snug for the evening, Morris, his partner (who by the way was a most extraordinary man, knowing every place and person in the country, speaking about half-a-dozen languages, and glorying in the name of Rochefort, although his English was of the greatest purity), and myself, retired to the shelter of one of the waggons, where we passed the time pleasantly in playing at cards.

The night had already approached the small hours, and I had made up my mind that the present should be my last game of *écarté*, for Mr. Rochefort would turn up the king and hold the most extraordinary hand, when an alarm was heard in camp. Being informed that Indians were round us, and that they were about to make an attempt to stampede the cattle, our arms and ammunition were quickly laid hold of, and we sallied forth, to find each teamster, with rifle in hand, prepared for any emergency. A quarter of an hour passed, and not a sound disturbed the immense solitude, except the note of water reptiles and the occasional howl of some hungry wolf. We had almost come to the conclusion that the alarm was a false one, when an old man, whose duty appeared to be that of hunter, and whom I had previously remarked from his taciturnity and age, came up and proposed going out to 'prospect for the d——d Red Skins.' His request was granted, and he disappeared into the darkness. After the lapse of an hour he returned with the satisfactory information that the greenhorn (meaning the sentry) had taken some buffalo for Indians. In return for his trouble he received a dram of whisky, which, without comment, he gulped down as if it had no more strength than water.

Next morning the dawn broke clear, promising good weather. Buffalo were numerous in every direction, and we had the prospect of a long and agreeable day's march. About ten o'clock a few Indians, pronounced to be an offshoot of the Crow race, were seen upon the horizon. Either not liking our appearance, or too busily employed in their own affairs, they did not deign to pay us a visit. The old character of last night who had volunteered to find out the cause of the alarm, and who was familiarly known as 'the Old Man,' rode ahead, and in the course of the afternoon killed a buffalo bull, which was beyond comparison the largest specimen of the kind I had yet seen, but so low in flesh as to be quite worthless for food. Prairie dogs (*Arctomys ludivicianus*) were numerous, although not in such numbers as I have seen them further south.

In some sections of the country the ground is so honeycombed by the holes of these little animals, that it is almost impossible to ride faster than a walk without coming to grief in their subterranean passages, or over the *débris* which they pile upon the surface. Prairie dogs—for by this name these animals are more generally known—are perfect characters in their way—Dutch burgomasters among the animal creation. Phlegmatic, cautious, acute, and provident, they take life very easy, appear much addicted to good living, and have a great sense of their own importance. At stated hours they come forth from their retreats, and pay visits to their neighbours. They do not appear to have any predilection for exercise, but, when taking it, exert themselves with so much energy that the beholder cannot help wondering at the activity displayed by such small and pudgy bodies. They live in communities like good citizens, each one displaying a great regard for the safety and lives of his fellows. On hearing the slightest unfamiliar or suspicious sound, warning is communicated at once to all of their race within hearing; and if one is shot, the last act of its life—a purpose that even the paroxysms of death do not prevent—is to dive headforemost into the nearest burrow, where, if incapable of further progress, it is lugged off by its fellows into some of the numerous deeply excavated passages. In their wild state they will, if captured, bite and scratch with unconquerable ferocity; but if obtained young, they are easily tamed, and become rather stupid pets, with little more to make them attractive than a guinea-pig. Their food consists entirely of vegetable substances, and it has always been a matter of wonder how they manage to procure sufficient for such large colonies as are occasionally to be found, the population appearing to confine themselves strictly within the limits of the surface broken by their burrows.

Although I have never witnessed guard-mounting among these curious little animals, such a ceremony very possibly takes place underground, for sentries are scattered at regular intervals all over their works, and faithfully these miniature soldiers perform their duty. As the Americans would express it, 'they are all there.' And so watchful are they, that it is almost impossible for an unknown or dangerous animal to approach them without exciting their attention, when the shrill whistle of alarm is sounded and re-echoed from one guardian to another, till the whole community is on the *qui vive!*

Even in a state of rest their nervous little tails keep twitching, a movement possibly adopted to keep the watchmen wakeful when at their post.

This species of marmot is so susceptible to atmospheric influences that I have found them superior to a barometer as indicators of a change of weather. Before a storm they are unusually demonstrative, constantly going from earth to earth, rushing up to one another, apparently exchanging their thoughts, and then dashing off again. Sometimes they may be seen at the entrance of their burrows, taking a survey of the clouds and horizon, and then disappearing with the same unaccountable impetuosity. Their residences are never free from the presence of two guests, who, I am inclined to believe, are far from welcome, and who render their life less pleasant than it might otherwise be ; the first are rattlesnakes, the second the small burrowing owl. These gentry attach themselves to the prairie dog, because they find a shelter and nest ready to hand without the trouble of employing their brains on planning, or their hands on construction. The snakes, however, I fear, repay the benefits they receive by the basest ingratitude, and many a poor little prairie dog is sacrificed to their insatiable appetite.

There may possibly be some exaggeration in this account, but it is certain that, wherever the prairie dog fixes his dwelling, there the rattlesnake and the burrowing owl are sure to be found.

CHAPTER VII.

AN INDIAN MOTHER—DEATH OF THE PAPOOSE—BID ADIEU TO THE TRADERS—VOLUNTEER GUIDE—HIS HISTORY—EXCITING ADVENTURE—ENCOUNTER WITH THE GREY WOLF OF THE NORTH—A TRAPPER'S COURTING—DREADFUL TRAGEDY—CONCLUSION OF THE OLD MAN'S STORY.

THIS evening we reached an admirable camping-ground, well supplied with small timber, the most prominent among which was the soft maple and black ash. The night, however, closed in dreary and inhospitable, the thermometer having fallen, accompanied by large, ominous drops of rain, which continued increasing till midnight, when such a deluge descended that the camp fires were extinguished, and even under the waggon covers not a dry spot could be found. Having been so long accustomed to exposure and hardship, this would not have prevented my sleeping, but unfortunately the squaw's baby, which had not been well, suddenly became worse. The mother, alarmed, sought me out with the child in her arms; for although she did not constantly remain tied to my skirts, she came to me for protection and assistance on every indication of trouble. The little invalid, who was evidently suffering from a complaint that much resembled cholera, endured the most terrible griping pains, during the paroxysms of which his little body was almost doubled in two, while every writhe of his tortured frame brought the large crystal tears into his mother's eyes. It was evident that the disease had got such possession of the poor child that only a powerful medicine could give relief. I therefore searched the trunk that bore the name of medicine-chest, and found some essence of ginger, which with four or five drops of laudanum, diluted with water, I administered, applying at the same time a mustard poultice to the sufferer's stomach. The poor woman, with the most perfect confidence in my good intentions, sat by, watching with anxious eye all I did. For half-an-hour I thought I should succeed in effecting a cure, but a fresh paroxysm, far more severe than those that had preceded, took place, and from that moment the little sufferer gradually sunk, his spirit going so slowly and peacefully to the source from whence it was derived, that I was ignorant of the moment when it had departed. When the poor mother became aware that her child was dead, a loud wail of anguish burst from her lips; but when I told her that all was for the best, that her progeny had gone to the great hunting-ground, where he would be ever happy, where he would be ready to welcome her, with an effort almost super-human she controlled herself, and relapsed into a moody silence, still pressing closer to her breast the inanimate form of her darling papoose.

With her permission, next morning I dug a tiny grave at the root of a spreading elm, and with no witnesses but ourselves deposited deep in mother-earth the remains of the little half-breed. Over the grave I placed a rude cross, hewn from the green timber with my hunting-knife. She watched me silently, and when I had concluded asked in mournful tones, 'What for dat?' I answered sadly, for I felt keenly grieved for the poor parent, 'That is a mark to indicate that here rests the body of one of the Great Spirit's children.'

In our ride to overtake the traders, who had gone on, not a word was spoken. The mother's thoughts were with her child, mine far away across the broad bosom of the tempestuous Atlantic.

That evening the waggons were joined by a party of Indians, an offshoot from the Crow tribe, all miserably mounted, and filthy in the extreme. From them we learned that a party of traders were in advance of us, and were hurrying forward as rapidly as possible to the south-west. Of the correctness of their statements there could be no doubt, for a severe cross-examination failed to furnish grounds for doubt. After they were ordered outside our *coralle*, which was not till dark, Morris and his partner held a consultation, at which I was present. The result was a determination to change their course on the morrow to the south-west, giving up their original intention of visiting a party of trappers who were supposed to be hunting about 120 miles to the north-west, and who, report said, had collected a large pack of peltries. They intended, however, to send one of their party to see these people, if a volunteer could be procured, to give them information of their whereabouts, in case they desired to trade away their furs.

To return south-west, almost the direction in which I had come, did not suit my purpose, as I wished to gain the Missouri, and, if possible, the Saskatchewan, a country of which as yet very little is known, and from which, through Lake Winnipeg and the Lake of the Woods, I hoped to reach Lake Superior before winter. I determined, therefore, if a volunteer was found, that I would join him; if not, to proceed alone.

The Indians who were in our neighbourhood had been civil enough, though their good conduct might be accounted for by the fact that they were in the presence of a numerically greater force, all of whom were well armed and experienced in Indian treachery. If I went, therefore, it would be advisable for me to start during the night, so that when day broke I should be far beyond the range of their vision.

When I communicated my intention to Mr. Morris, he would have dissuaded me if possible; but when he found I was resolved on my course he desisted. A volunteer was soon found for their service—no other than 'the old man'—and in a moment he and I had agreed to travel together.

A little after midnight we started. The night was dry overhead, but very dark, and for a couple of hours we plodded northward; the horses almost uncertain, from the perfect want of light, on what they placed their feet. At length the moon rose, and soon after the sun, but even by the aid of that luminary we failed to distinguish the white covers of the waggons, from the good speed we had made.

I could not find the squaw to bid her adieu before leaving. She evidently was with her countrymen, who were encamped to the south, a short distance from our waggons. However, I left her many kind messages, and obtained a promise from Mr. Morris, that, as I required to take my mule, he would order her load to be carried until she thought fit to sell it, or leave his company. Nor am I ashamed to acknowledge that it was with regret I left this daughter of a primitive race without having it in my power to do her some service that might benefit her in after-life.

Next day I and my guide halted all day in a ravine. Game was abundant, but as we did not require supplies it remained undisturbed. A more taciturn companion than my present one I do not think I ever met with. During the entire day he did not speak half-a-dozen words. At last, during our evening meal, after imbibing a couple of bumpers from my bottle, such mighty ones as half emptied it, he became loquacious.

The loss of the whisky I certainly regretted, but

hoped it would be the means of worming out this man's history, for I felt convinced it was no usual one. After trying many expedients I got him on the track I desired, and he told me his story. I commit it to these pages, not only because it illustrates his remarkable character, but because the incidents of his history are such as were once common in those regions which are situated on the verge of civilisation :—

'I was born away down east, in Maine. My home was not far from Bethel, Oxford County, in those days a small place, for it had then scarcely over a dozen houses all told; but folks tell me now that it's a prosperous big town. When I was a boy you could not find a school in every township as now, so I was reared without learning to read or write. When I got big enough to use a handspike and drive a yoke of cattle, the old man, my father, took me along with him every winter, for he always spent that period in the woods, engaged in the lumber business. I could soon handle an axe with the best of the gang, and cut as smooth a chip as ever was knocked out of pine-log; so I got men's wages, and thought myself " no small punkins."

'The first adventure I remember to have met with was shooting a bear—for, like most lads reared in the woods, I was a plumb-centre shot. It was in this way. I was out looking for moose, and they were plenty then in those parts. The day before I had tracked the biggest kind of one, but as it was late, and he had taken to a tamarack swamp, I gave him up. Before sunrise the next day I was on the ground again. It was the fall of the year, and the rutting season had commenced. In an opening covered with spikes* I took my post. My birch-back horn soon echoed over the unpeopled waste; and long and silently I waited for a response. At length the delay told upon my patience, and I would have quitted my station, but that the faintest sound caught my ear. At first I thought it might be a loon,† but again it was repeated more distinctly, and evidently closer, leaving no further doubt upon my mind that it emanated from the quarry I sought.

'The approach of moose to the call of the hunter is often slow and tedious. They are so suspicious, especially old ones, that they see or imagine danger on every side. Patience and perseverance are great helps at all times and in all employments—in hunting more especially. While listening to hear the game again, in response to my call another moose spoke from quite a different direction. Here was a piece of luck! If neither winded me, I was most certain to get more moose beef than would feed the camp, and a good few dollars for the hides. Again my call was placed to my lips, and again the answering voice of both deer reverberated through the woods. In ten minutes more, the tallest bull, with

---

* *Anglicè*, dead pine-trees that have lost all their minor branches.
† Great Northern diver.

the heaviest head of horns I had ever looked on, trotted into the open, not over forty yards off from me. The silver head on my rifle-barrel was almost plump on his shoulder, when, with a crash that made the saplings splinter, the second male rushed on to the ground. The first was tall, but ragged-looking —an old rake, who devoted more time to courting and love-making than was good for his health. The second, though scarce as high, was far more chunky, and would have weighed a good hundredweight over the other, or I am no judge of size, particularly of moose. The two rivals approached each other— for they both thought it was a cow of their own race they were going to meet—stopped, stared, and with a grunt of defiance rushed together.

'Hard and fast the battle raged, first on their feet, then on their knees, the two combatants struggling with an all-powerful and vindictive hate. Around them the brush and saplings were trodden down, and the vegetation scattered around. Their determination, their courage, and their endurance of punishment were so great, that the most apathetic could scarce have surveyed the scene without becoming spellbound. At length their tongues hung from their mouths, their flanks heaved from excessive exertion, and their dark brown coats were disfigured with mire. A halt, as if a respite for obtaining breath or renewed strength, took place, and as the heavier of the two bulls was towards me, the opportunity was not to be lost; so I pitched my rifle to my shoulder, and, with its report a gallant hero fell to rise no more, while his now inanimate remains were gored without any power of resistance by his late antagonist. My ramrod had, however, just sent a fresh bullet home, and I had a good prospect of killing the remaining moose, when he winded me, threw his wide-spreading antlers on his back, took a fresh sniff of the tainted air, and broke into a trot so rapid that ere my chilled fingers could place a cap on the nipple, the quarry had disappeared into the neighbouring timber. Securing the tit-bits of the animal I had killed, I returned to camp to bring a yoke of cattle and sled to transport the result of my morning's labour home. I might have been gone a couple of hours—possibly more, when on my return I found one of the largest, roughest, and wickedest-looking bears I had ever set eyes on, coolly licking the shot-hole, and other portions of the carcass of my game, wherever blood flowed from it. So suddenly did I come upon the intruder, that both the steers and myself were within twenty yards before we saw him. The former were so terrified when Bruin turned up his thin lips and exhibited his white tusks, plainly indicating that he intended disputing possession, that both wheeled to the right-about and bolted along the back tract with a velocity that one could scarcely have given them credit for when yoked, and dragging a sleigh at their heels. I was terribly riled, and my dander was fairly up. The departure of the steers helped to make me more savage, and consequently more determined; so

K

I let the thief know who was master. Guns in those days were not as good as they are now, for a miss-fire was far from uncommon; but I had a fresh load in my piece, for, ten minutes before, I had knocked over a Canada partridge that was roosting in a spruce tree I passed immediately after leaving camp. If I had turned tail and made tracks, I could have done so without risk; but give up my moose-meat, and have my hide destroyed, the value of which I almost felt already in my pocket, was more than could be expected from human nature. Well, I went in determined to win, and scarcely had I ever a tougher job since I was born. I aimed for the horse-shoe on the bear's breast, but shot too high, for, instead of dropping the beast, he came right at me. I had not the ghost of a chance to load again, so I clubbed my gun, and gave him the full weight of it over the head, smashing its stock into splinters. Although this halted him for a few moments, it was more from feeling stunned than disinclined to continue the battle. He rushed at me a second time. The gun-barrel, which alone remained in my hands, proved a good weapon: for over five minutes I kept the vermin off, till both became weak with exertion and excitement. At length, when trying to deal a heavier blow, I tripped over a limb, and in a moment the black fiend had me by the shoulder, his nostrils squirting out jets of fire upon my cheek. Some folks would have thought all was up with me, but I didn't. The blood-letting which I suffered seemed to bring me to, and as we rolled on the ground together I remembered my butcher-knife which hung in my belt. If I could only get at it there was yet time to turn the tide of battle. I made several efforts for this purpose, but I was doubled up so that my hand could not reach it. At length I seized it, and the broad, flat, long blade was never drawn with greater pleasure. The touch of the heft as I laid my hand upon it was more welcome than the shake of a long-lost chum's hand ; and it stood a friend to me, for it saved my life. The better to free my arm for use, I made a determined struggle. The foe bit deeper into my poor shoulder, at the same time drawing his paw across my face, but the effort did my work, and I buried the knife to the handle in the stomach of the savage. Again and again I repeated the blows, but human nature could stand no more, and I fainted.

'The sun was gilding with his last rays the scarlet leaves of the maple when I awoke, as if from a fearful dream. I felt stiff and sore, and the blood still trickled from my shoulder. Dead as a stone, lying partially on me, was the cause of my present helpless condition. I lay there all that night, and it was cold, bitter cold. Day at length broke, but what was the value of its return without human aid ? I was lost ; left to die a far worse death than the one I had escaped. Again and again I made efforts to rise, but I was paralysed. I attempted then to scream, when nothing but a guttural rattle proceeded from my parched throat. I thought my last day was come, and I gave way, like a child as I was, to a burst of petulant impatience at the hopelessness of my position. My late exertion and weakness again brought on faintness, and I dreamed of home and the dear mother so long gone to the spirit-land. Pain had left me, and I was almost reconciled to die, when a deep voice, driving cattle, "Gee, Buck," "Haw, Bright," struck upon my ear. In a few moments after, one of the teamsters from the lumber camp was at my side. My absence during the night had alarmed all, and this man had taken my back-sled track, trusting through that means to find my whereabouts. It was many a month before I was fit for much. Youth and a good constitution carried me, however, through, but the scars I shall bear as mementos till my dying day.

'You have not much to do with wild beasts in your land; so I'll just tell you another close shave I had, where luck and presence of mind carried me through, when nothing else could have saved me.

'It was little over two years after the bear mauled me, and I was again settled with a party of lumbermen upon the upper waters of the Penobscot River. The fall had glided on into winter, the birds had migrated to warmer countries, and the woods were deserted, except by the snow-bird, cross-bill, or noisy woodpecker, for heavy snow had set in, and all the country was covered with it as with a shroud. Still, the frost had not been sufficiently severe to freeze the river, and our work was almost suspended in consequence. But at length the looked-for frost came, and with it that clear, bright weather that makes a northern winter so enjoyable. After dinner I buckled on my skates, and followed upwards the edge of the stream to discover new fishing-grounds, for I was but a comparative stranger in the neighbourhood. You know the feelings that actuate the schoolboy when released from control, and he has the whole day before him for pleasure or adventure; or of the colt when he is relieved from the confining harness, and is turned out into the pasture-field. Similar sensations I had as mile after mile fled by, and distant objects, never seen before, were passed and left far behind. From the right entered the parent river, a sullen, deep-looking brook. Over its surface many a giant pine-tree leant, and in places spruce and birch came in contact at their summits, shutting out the light of heaven, and making a retreat attractive from its sombre solitude. A child of the forest I may call myself; was it to be wondered, then, that this weird-like retreat had an attractive, an all-powerful fascination, that induced me to penetrate its darkest recesses, and seek to learn more of the almost stagnant flowing rivulet?

'The ice was smooth on the Penobscot, and here it was, if possible, more so; for no breeze could reach the surface of the water, so dense was the dark green net-work of cedar and hemlock that formed its marginal walls. Happily I sped on; bend after

bend, and point after point, was reached and passed.
I shouted aloud with a spirit of bravado, the echoes
answering back with mocking, jeering distinctness,
supernatural in their intonation, till the lengthening
and greater density of the shadows warned me that
night approached rapidly. Buckling the strap of
my skate tighter, for it had become loose through
the protracted strain, I almost flew as I retraced
my steps, for I regretted the curtailment of time,
and was eager to make the most of what was
remaining. Possibly a growing horror of passing
the night where the solitude was the most intense
I had ever experienced, gave me wings. At any
rate my retreat was infinitely more swift than my
ascent. A mile more would carry me out of the
swamp and leaf-bound watercourse. Already, in
imagination, the broad expanse of the receiving river
was in sight, when a yell so wild and unearthly
that my blood became cold and stagnated in my
extremities, struck upon my ear. The dweller in
cities or the foreigner might have thought that it
emanated from a fury expelled from the regions of
the wicked one; but not a moment was I in doubt
—it was the voice of the dreaded grey wolf of the
North. You know the cayotte and prairie-wolf;
they are no more to be compared with these fiends
than a terrier is with a bloodhound. In size the grey
wolf is double that of the others, in speed he is
almost a match for the fastest horse; their sense of
smell is so acute that they trace their prey almost

entirely with the nose. Their bloodthirsty instincts are insatiable. Woe be to the farmer in whose vicinity one of these animals takes up its residence ; for if it should gain access to his fold, not a member of his flock would be left alive. There is but one animal in the forest that is able to cope with him, and that is the adult bull-moose ; but when age and the decrepitude of years have weakened his frame, he must also succumb before this scourge of the northern forest lands.

'When I tell you this, can you be surprised that fear lent me wings, and that every muscle and every sinew was strained to the utmost tension in a race in which life was the reward? Trees, stumps, and fallen timber were passed. All was dead silence, save the sound caused by the grating of my skate. My ear anxiously listened for further indications of the proximity of the dreaded foe, while the sole response thus far it had received was the impetuous palpitation of my heart, caused by the unaccustomed severity of the exercise and the increased velocity of the circulation of my blood. Despair had not taken possession of me, though hope had but feeble grounds to exist upon : but the further I advanced it increased ; for, could I but gain the expanse of the wider river, I felt the prospect of escape more probable, as by pursuing my course down its centre I should at least be free from surprise. A couple of hundred yards more and it would have been reached, when, distinctly on right and left, I heard the panting as of a blown hound, and the snapping of dried diminutive branches—doubtless caused by the progress of large animals through the underbrush.

'We all know their speed must be infinitely greater than mine, even when on skates, but their advance was doubtless retarded by their selection of the wood, while mine was clear and uninterrupted. Apparently the ice was not the footing my pursuers preferred, or possibly they intended heading me off, or springing upon me if they could obtain a sufficient lead, or a suitable position.

'Thoughts like these passed far more rapidly than words can describe. A few strides more must have brought me to the open ice, when not one, but three, deep prolonged howls echoed through the uninhabited solitude. These resembled that of the foiled but bloodthirsty hound, only differing in power, which was greater, and in a more thorough vindictiveness of tone.

'These notes of warning acted as a stimulus to renewed exertion, corroborating the impression I had formed as to the foes I had to deal with. Like the tired horse making a last exertion to reach the goal, I rushed on with more rapid strides, which ultimately bore me out upon the clear uninterrupted bosom of the Penobscot. With my exit into the comparatively open locality, courage, strength, and perseverance returned; though the fiends, disappointed of their prey, no longer hesitated to take the ice, but dashed after me in hot pursuit. Before half a mile was traversed I found they had the advantage of me in speed. In half that distance further they were close behind, and a few strides more must enable them to lay hold of me and pull me down. I almost imagined I felt their hot breath and their panting respiration, while the dull thud of their paws coming in contact with the ice struck ominously on my ear. Would their impetus cause them to overshoot their object if I suddenly turned? The idea flashed across my brain like a ray of hope. I knew their footing on such a surface was far from secure. Many a time I had seen dogs fall or slide along when, under similar circumstances, they wished to stop their velocity or suddenly turn; but if I was to practise this trick it must be attempted immediately, for I knew, as if by intuition, not daring to turn to look, that the fangs of one could not be many inches from my person. In a moment I shot off to the left, while my foes, with headlong impetus, slid or fell to the ground in their exertions to turn or halt. I then retraced my course at a measured pace, so as to regain both wind and strength. But I was not long left in peace, for my eager pursuers were soon again in my wake. In a short time they were so close to me that they believed themselves almost in possession of their prey, when the same *ruse* was once more successfully performed, and I resumed my original course with redoubled vigour. Twice more had I to adopt this plan, till at length I came in sight of our log-hut, where my companions were busy with their respective evening duties.

'Their familiar voices and the cheery click of their axes broke most welcomely on my ear, the assurance that in a few moments more help would be at hand imparting fresh strength to my almost exhausted frame. The skulking scoundrels, however, knew that they were beaten, for they halted, gave utterance to a few howls of disappointment, then slowly crossed to the river, and entered a neighbouring dense cedar-swamp. It was as narrow an escape as I ever wish to have—a narrower one I could not even wish my foes.

'Perhaps a year or so after that I lost the old man, who from age had become much impaired in activity. In trying to shift a log his handspike broke, and the stick of timber rolling back crushed him to death.

'Game ceased to be plenty in Maine—not that the State was becoming much more thickly settled, but strangers would come from far and near to hunt it. The timber business, too, got bad, for timber fell to one half its former price; and as I had no folks remaining of my own blood, I made up my mind to come out West, where I had heard that deer, and even buffalo, were to be had for the seeking.

'The rich often think that, in comparison with themselves, the poor and unlettered have no delicacy of feelings, that poverty blunts the finer sentiments, and that ignorance produces selfish and narrow prejudices. I have had opportunities of forming a different judgment. The morning I bid adieu to the old shanty — the common slab-shed in which I was born, where my mother lived, and where the old man had taught me to handle the axe and rifle — I felt like a villain that had no right to live for deserting the old homestead. When I looked up at the familiar little cedar-bird singing his morning song from the top of a spruce that grew against our gable, the tears ran down my cheeks; but I knew it was for the best, and, with the exception of a parting glance as I commenced to dip beneath the brow of a hill that would soon hide all from sight, I never turned round till many a long mile lay between me and my birthplace.

'But in those days travelling was not as it is now. It took as many days then as hours now to come from Boston to St. Louis. At times I walked, but often got a lift in a waggon, and what between hunting and doing an odd day's work I reached St. Jo's, then the starting-point of all the fur-traders. From there I got to Fort Leavenworth, and where the town now stands many a deer I have tumbled in his tracks. Here I made the acquaintance of a Yorker, going some fifty miles further on to squat. Feeling kind of lonesome, I joined in, and we both started together. The place we fixed on for our location was half prairie, half timber land, and in a month we had a snug house up, and three or four acres planted with corn.

'As the season was summer, and there was little or nothing to do, I started along the bottom land to look for game. A few miles brought me to a clearing, in which there was a shanty. Before this I had not known that neighbours were so close. As I was thirsty, I thought I'd go to the house and borrow a dipper to get a drink from their well, but nobody was inside. I looked about, and in a small tobacco-patch observed a young girl topping and trimming the plants. Before I got to her she raised her head, and, from her look, I could see that she was scared at my presence.

'In the old State where I came from the women are comely. I have seen in my time a heap of good-looking girls, but never any that could compare with this one. When she heard my errand she appeared satisfied, and procured me the dish. While I drank—and I know I made as long a job of it as I could—I got a good look at her, and my heart was none the better for the same. She might, however, be a married woman; but I soon solved that point, for I asked her, at the same time assuming an air of indifference, whether her husband was soon expected back. "My father is," she replied. I told her where I lived, adding, that I would like to meet the old man. So I sat upon the fence rails, and talked to her about everything but the one that was nearest my heart.

'But at last the old man did come. Long before he appeared I could hear the grating of his waggon-wheels; and, blow me if I can tell why, I felt kind of all-overish, half afraid and half modest. So I would have sneaked off, but that I thought the young woman might think such conduct strange. I sat still, therefore, on the fence, whittling away at a stick, and a stranger to have looked at me would have thought me at my own diggings, not in another's, with courting notions in my heart. But I was not long kept waiting. The old man came, and although I heard him I never turned to the left or right, but pretended not to know he was there. At last he spoke, and that in a tone so sharp, and cross, and loud, that with a hop, caused I almost believe by fright, I tumbled off my perch. As soon as I could dust myself a bit, I turned up and looked him in the face; I could see from the corners of his mouth that he was kind of tickled at what had taken place. So, thinking it was but right to put the best face possible on the matter, I told him we were neighbours, and that I had come out for a hunt; but never saying a word about what had kept me there. I put that off by telling him, that, being a stranger, I hoped he'd give me some directions that would enable me to find my way back. While I was telling him this, he examined me all over with his eyes. There was not a button on my coat, or a bit of tobacco in the corners of my pockets, he did not see. The look, however, seemed to satisfy him, for he asked me to come into the shanty, where he gave me a glass of peach brandy, and we both lit our pipes and smoked together. After that he put me a mile on my road, and we parted as neighbours ought to part.

'From that time it was extraordinary, but all the game was to be found between his homestead and mine—at least I invariably hunted in that direction. And I always got more than I wanted, for my appetite seemed to have fallen off lately. So, not to waste good food, I never passed without leaving some at the old man's shanty. But as he was always in the way, I never could get to have a word with Angey alone.

'In this way did time pass for three or four months. The corn had been gathered, and winter was pretty close at hand. Turkeys were plentiful down in the bottom lands, for there had been a heavy fall of mast that year.

'I took my rifle after breakfast, and went to look for game. Before an hour was over I had killed a pair of splendid gobblers, one of which I hung in a fork of a tree, while with the other I turned my steps towards my neighbour's shanty. As I approached the house, I saw Angey busy husking corn. She sat out on the stoop, and the house-dog lay at her feet. By this time he knew me well, and never uttered a growl or bark as I approached. When I was close by, I stood, unseen, looking at her. If before I thought her pretty, now I thought her perfection.

Her dark hair hung loose down her back, and her arms, which were beautifully shaped, were bare to the elbows. As she stooped forward at her occupation, a disengaged lock would fall over her face, and she would raise her white hand to throw it back into its place. At last I drew near, and spoke to her. She rose with a little start, and her brunette complexion was suffused with a deep blush, which even passed down her neck. She soon recovered her composure, however, and long I sat and talked to her. As the old man was gone for the day, there was no chance of interruption, and though time was flying fast, not a word of love could I say. Whatever direction our talk took, not a chance occurred to speak of what was next my heart.

'At length, among the ears of corn she shelled there came a red one. Says I, "Angey, were you ever at a husking-bee? they are common down where I come from."

'"No," she answered; "but I have heard tell of them."

'"Well, do you know," continued I, "what happens to those who get a red ear of corn?"

'She shook her head, to imply that she did not, so I continued, "When a young woman gets a red head of corn when husking, whoever is her sweetheart has the privilege of kissing her. If a young man gets one, he has the right to kiss his sweetheart.'

'"So the young women get kissed any way," said Angey.

'"Yes," said I; and for the life of me, not caring if I was to be hung for it, I got up, put my arms round her neck, and kissed her. Not a word of objection did she say, nor did she repulse me. So I kissed her again and again, and how much longer I would have continued doing so I cannot say, when a rough hand was placed on my shoulder, and a harsh half-oath, half-exclamation, reminded me that I was still in this world.

'The old man was mad. He stamped and swore, and ordered me off his place. Not a word could I get in; he would not listen to me. At length I thought he would have struck me—I half believe it was his intention to do so, but Angey came in between us, threw herself at her father's feet, and begged that he would forgive me. This calmed him down a little, but when she added that she was as much to blame as me, if not more, he changed entirely, and, collecting himself with an effort, asked, "Do you, my daughter, mean to say that you love this stranger? that you could leave me, and go and live with him?"

'His daughter answered, "I do love him, but it shall not part me from you."

'Again I would have spoken, and again was ordered to go. Angey beckoned me to obey, but as I turned slowly round and moodily retraced my steps towards home, the old man called after me, "To-morrow, at noon, I will come and see you."

'All that night I sat up over the fire. Sleep

I could not, and in every blaze, every glowing ember, I could see Angey's face; by the wind that sighed through the timber I could hear repeated, " I do love him."

'The father came. His face showed that he also had suffered. "You can speak now," he said. And I did speak. The words flowed fast, and he listened patiently. When I came to the end he held out his hand, and said, "All is perhaps for the best. My stay in this world I have no right to expect will be long, and but for you my girl might have been left alone."

'So we went to the fort at Leavenworth and were married. The old man and I got on first-rate. I built a new house; the world prospered with us, and I was happy as the day was long.

'But trouble was not far off; the Indians were on the war-path. Already they had committed several depredations, and fear was entertained that they might still come further into the settlements.

'My father-in-law knew them well. He had once been a trader, and had on several occasions received severe treatment at their hands. He had retaliated, taken the law into his hands, and revenged himself. On account of this he feared their coming; not that he dreaded the result for himself, for a braver man could not be found, but in case they should destroy his dwelling or injure his child.

'His wife, the mother of mine, had perished by their means. This was sufficient cause to make the bravest heart nervous when others as loved and as defenceless were in similar danger. His wrongs and sufferings had prompted an eager desire for retaliation. But our grounds for apprehension at that time were unnecessary. A strong force of United States dragoons, assisted by a number of volunteers recruited among the neighbouring farmers, soon brought the Red-skins to their senses, and drove them back to their Indian country.

'After the lapse of some months, it being the season to lay in a stock of buffalo meat, my father-in-law and self determined to visit a range that these animals frequented at that season of the year. Our absence would probably last over some days, but as my wife previous to her marriage had been left alone for much longer periods, we parted with each other without her expressing any fear, or even evincing the slightest nervousness. Of the two I believe I felt the ordeal most, and as I turned in my saddle to wave a last adieu to her ere the timber shut my homestead from my sight, a sense of loneliness, almost amounting to dread, stole over me. Even the old man observed it, and chaffed me at what he was pleased to designate my calfishness. His reproof was submitted to without remonstrance, for I knew it was merited. Still, a presentiment of evil persistently intruded itself on my mind—that inexplicable feeling that I have found so often to be the forerunner of misfortune. I could not shake it off. From the hour we left our home all appeared to go wrong; the first night it rained in torrents, and our encampment was so situated that there was no protection for man or beast. Worse than all, a portion of our ammunition became so saturated as to be entirely useless.

'The next day we entered our hunting range. Mile after mile we traversed the lonely prairie. All appeared still as death. Even the wild fowl and birds of prey had forsaken it, as man would a plague-stricken city. Again, at night, the rain descended with such violence that it seemed to threaten a deluge. The discomfort I experienced, the want of success in our expedition, and the prospect of having to remain longer than we at first proposed, all tended to keep me in a depressed state of spirits.

'The third day was as unsuccessful as the preceding ones. We saw game, but so wild that it was impossible to get within shooting distance. I proposed an immediate return to my father-in-law. He refused to listen to such a course, without at least trying our luck upon the morrow. That day broke bright and cheerful,—an omen we accepted as a good one. Nevertheless, at night we had to go supperless to sleep, for our stock of provisions had become exhausted, and no game had been killed.

'Our journey home was tedious in the extreme. The ground in many parts was so heavy, in consequence of the saturation it had received from the late rains, that our horses, for miles, sunk at every step over their fetlocks. However, we got on; and at last only a few miles separated us from our home. With each advancing step my spirits rose, for soon I hoped to clasp to my bosom my first and only love. Over a distant margin of trees, that denoted the boundary between forest and prairie-land, in the direction in which our house was situated, my father-in-law called my attention to what might be haze, or possibly smoke: such is so common in the fall of the year, or when squatters are clearing new land, that I scarcely deemed it worthy of notice. The ground being here firmer, and our horses probably conscious that the sooner we got home the sooner they would be fed, moved forward with quickened pace. The nearer we approached, the denser became the smoke; and, from the direction, no doubt remained upon our minds that it must originate in the immediate vicinity of our dwelling. Still, any fear that it was our house never occurred. The horses, unpushed, pursued their own gait; and at length the wood was entered, the clearing broke into view, and, to my dismay, volumes of smoke were issuing through our shingle roof. With slack rein and spurs driven well home, we both dashed forward. A couple of hundred yards had but to be traversed, when the head, arm, and shoulder of a woman appeared through the window. A couple of rifle reports instantaneously followed, and my wife (for it was she), throwing her hands over her head, disappeared.

' "Indians, by Heaven!" exclaimed my father-in-law; and both of us rushed forward with redoubled vigour burning with hatred, and lusting for revenge. Each of our rifles did its work upon the assassins, and I brained a third with my tomahawk. The remainder fled, while we hastened to the burning house. The door was closed, fastened on the outside. In a moment I burst it from its hinges, and rushed into the room through fire and smoke. In front of the window I tripped over a body. Clasping it in my arms, I attempted to regain the door. Smothered with smoke, and gasping for breath, I should have failed, but that the hand of the stalwart old man drew me and my burden into the open air. It was an act of Providence; for, with half a minute's delay, my rescue would have been impossible,—the air admitted through the shattered door immediately afterwards causing the whole building to burst into flames.

'More stunned than hurt, I soon revived; but, believe me, if at that moment I had had a choice between life and death, the latter would have been preferred, —for my wife was dead. A rifle-bullet had pierced her heart, and another had penetrated her head, fearfully disfiguring a face which my eye had never rested upon without deeming it more perfect than even imagination could conceive.

'That night was the most bitter I ever spent. I had been so little familiarised with death, that I felt almost as if deprived of reason. I appealed to Heaven, and disputed its justice in depriving me of her I loved. The old father, bowed down with care, submitted to his loss, only vowing that his revenge would be commensurate with the injury received.

'The next evening, as the sun set red and fiery in the western heavens, tinging the clouds with a blood-like margin, we deposited my wife in her lowly bed,—under the hickory beneath which she loved so much to seek for shelter from the noon-day heat. That tree still flourishes, green and vigorous—for I was there only a few years since; but the little mound that marked her resting-place has disappeared: in my heart alone is her memory preserved.

'Vowing vengeance against the savage, and determined that our revenge should not be satisfied till death terminated our careers, we both started for the Indian country, resolved—like the panther—to dog every Red-skin we met, and, with a barbarity equal to their own, satiate our passions.

'The old man and I wandered for many a day, he growing from hour to hour more moody and silent, eating but to live, and living but to gratify his revenge. The year glided on; and as his hate increased against the savage he grew thinner, his strength gradually failed, and he became less capable of carrying out his purpose. That he was not destined long to survive his daughter, whose name was ever upon his lips, hourly became more apparent.

'On the Yellowstone River there is a branch. At the time of which I speak beavers were plentiful there. It lay some distance from any regularly frequented war-trail. The old man and I used to consider it our holiday retreat. We had been there about a week, and I was footing down the bed of the watercourse, setting traps, while the old man tramped along the margin, carrying our surplus effects on his back. At length, when all were set, and I had left the water, my father-in-law, without moving a feature or raising his voice, told me that Indians were following us. "I know it," he said; "for the wild ducks above, almost at that bend, are swimming down stream. It's not a brute beast would make them do that."

'With a demeanour as if conscious of security we returned to our camp. All was as we had left it; but a broken eagle's feather, part of the head-dress of an Indian, lay near the dead fire; proof that during our absence Red-skins had been about. On further examination, a young man's foot-prints were discernible,—for the distance between each impression was wide, while the deepest part of the track was formed by the toes, denoting the elasticity of youth. An old brave, or chief, would have known too much to leave such a sign; the younger ones, from ignorance or recklessness, might be guilty of oversight.

'As it would be difficult to surprise us by day, we performed our usual camp avocations, laying our plans for future action. Darkness at length set in. The fire was purposely left unreplenished. But, as soon as the gloom prevented our actions being perceived, we stripped off our hunting-shirts, stretched them on rods, placed our caps on their supposed heads, and deposited these figures in such a way as to bear the greatest resemblance to ourselves reclining in rest. We then piled some fuel on the fire—damp, decayed wood, that would make at best only a fitful blaze, not burn with too great brightness.

'Having thus far uninterruptedly carried out our purpose, we crawled from the scene on all-fours, traversed a distance of a couple of hundred yards, made a *détour* round the camp, and gained a position to leeward, where we could see the dummies and watch the success of our plot.

'At length the fire commenced to flicker, and in an hour or so the light it emitted caused the figures to be seen indistinctly, yet sufficiently to shoot at. The report of three guns fired close to us soon after broke the silence of the night. One of our inanimate representatives fell forward (for they were purposely insecurely stationed, and the thick buckskin hunting-shirt, as it yielded, was carried to the ground by the force of the bullets). The Red-skins rushed out, tomahawk in hand, to finish, as they supposed, their work more thoroughly. Scarcely had they gained our decoy sufficiently near to learn how they had been tricked, when our turn to shoot came. We both fired, and rushed from our ambush on our foes. Two lay apparently dead, the third I pursued till I found it useless. The fire had burned up brighter, and by its lurid glare I saw, as I returned, two figures struggling. I hastened to the conflict; but it was too late. One of the savages had only been stunned; and, on regaining consciousness, had had a fearful fight with the old man. The latter lay dead, stabbed through the heart; the former was rapidly going to his last account.

'A few months after I returned to the settlements, and wandered about them reckless and dispirited. Life ceased to have any attractions for me; and the merry voices of women and children palled upon my ear. Again I sought the Indian country; to return, after a time, to civilisation. But happiness was gone; for I thought incessantly of the one who was gone.

'The frost of the winter of life has grizzled my head and beard. The season of my migration to the other world is rapidly approaching. But when the time for that journey comes, if I knew that this poor carcass would be laid under that hickory-tree on the banks of muddy old Missouri, this "old man" would be satisfied.'

CHAPTER VIII.

ECCENTRICITIES OF CATTLE — RED-HEADED WOODPECKERS — STRANGE CAPERS OF AN OLD DOE — RATTLESNAKE KILLED BY A DEER — THE BOBOLINK, OR REED-BIRD — TRAIL OF INDIANS — ATTEMPT TO BURN A BEAR OUT OF A CAVE — ROUGHED GROUSE — OBSTINATE COURAGE OF MY OLD GUIDE.

As the night slowly darkened, and the landscape became obscure, we started northward, moralising over the question whether any one goes through this earthly pilgrimage without trials. The old man's story was a sad one; but he had obtained retribution for his wrongs. Was he to be blamed for seeking it? Possibly the extremely good may think so, and be correct in their judgment. Yet if I, with the benefits resulting from education, had been placed in his position, I fear I should have done likewise. You can no more mould all men into one common pattern, than you can make china, porcelain, and common delf out of the same clay.

At daybreak we halted, tired and hungry. Having eaten a little, I slept till after mid-day. Determined to remain here for the night, that I might again be able to travel by day, I wandered off into the brush, to observe the animals in the neighbourhood, and to be alone.

Have you ever observed, previous to a change in the weather, cattle performing a variety of awkward yet amusing evolutions, the purposes of which were quite unaccountable? I frequently have; and to-day witnessed a somewhat similar performance, and had the good fortune also to discover the cause for these eccentricities.

From a bend in some low ground, which turned off to the south for more than a mile, I resolved to walk due east, where I hoped my progress would be less impeded. For some yards my steps were much harassed by a thick growth of under-brush, which after a struggle, and no small amount of exertion, I traversed. From here the brush became more and more open, till at length the bushes were so far apart as to encourage a close growth of short grass. It had been so long since I had seen such grass—for in this land it either does not grow, or it is longer and stiffer than meadow-hay, and matted together—that I felt the greatest pleasure in traversing its velvety surface; and while doing so, visions of numerous croquet-grounds I know well—Richmond, Kensington, and other places celebrated in the calendar of my memory for turf—floated before me. After traversing several acres, I was attracted out of my course by a pair of red-headed woodpeckers, who were most assiduously plying their avocation on the dead limb of a gnarled old tree. These birds have always been prime favourites with me, for they are the most indefatigable little labourers, gifted with a great amount of cunning; while their plumage is most attractive, being of a bright white and black, with the hackle-feathers of the crown of the deepest scarlet colour. Hammer! hammer! hammer! went this pair of worthies, who every few moments quitted their perch to rush round to the reverse side of the limb, to secure such of their prey as had there made their egress with a view to escape. So strong are the blows these birds strike with their bills, that, on a calm day, they can be heard for almost a mile. Their exertions are so violent, that one is struck with surprise that they do not dislocate their necks with the power of the blows they strike.

Woodpeckers of many species are common throughout this country, but none are so numerous as those of which I speak. Every dead limb and decayed piece of timber tell of their industry, for their surfaces are found penetrated with holes in all directions, almost similar to those made with a gimlet. The amount of service these birds do in destroying insects is incalculable; and there is little doubt that they might be most advantageously introduced into England. There is an erroneous impression, however, common throughout the United States, that woodpeckers destroy timber; but, after a great deal of close observation, I never was able to discover a single instance of their boring into any trees which were not dead and partially decayed.

For possibly a quarter of an hour I was thus engaged, when my attention was attracted by the indistinct outline of an animal at some distance. Availing myself of the shelter afforded me by an intervening tree, I advanced sufficiently close to the unknown creature to find that it was a deer, with several companions. As they were huddled together, and their heads all pointed in the same direction, my knowledge of the habits of these animals at once told me they were alarmed. What was the cause of their fear I could not tell, but I determined to find out by remaining concealed. At length the largest of the deer, evidently an old doe, left the remainder of the family, advanced a few steps, and, with a spring into the air, dropped on the ground with her four feet pressed closely together. This manœuvre was repeated again and again, with the greatest celerity; the old lady bounding up and down like an India-rubber ball. Although there was little or no grace in her movements, they provoked admiration among her friends, who, without evincing the smallest symptoms of impatience, or being tempted to feed even by the verdant grass on which they stood, centred all their attention on the eccentric capers of the doe. Not requiring venison, I came forth from my shelter, and the timid creatures trotted off, stopped, moved on a few more paces, and ultimately disappeared. On reaching the spot where the pantomimic performance had been carried on, I found a large yellow rattlesnake, so much contused that it was almost unable to crawl. After despatching the reptile, which was so exhausted that it could not raise its head, I found that it had suffered severely, the scales being in several places torn off its body, and its vertebræ near the vent broken.

I have heard backwoodsmen say that deer would kill snakes, but before my experience of to-day I did not believe it, for their mode of procedure I was unacquainted with. The ocular demonstration, however, I had just enjoyed, prevented my being further sceptical on this point. The sharpness of a deer's hoof, and the precision with which it uses it, render its foot a more dangerous weapon even than its horns.

Soon after I joined my companion, who was stretched near the fire, which he had already lit for cooking our evening meal. It was a dry clear night, a most welcome change from the previously bad weather. The owls, however, never ceased hooting—an indication that more wet was in store.

The country through which we passed this day improved in appearance, for vegetation was much more plentiful. Deer also were becoming numerous, but we had lost sight of buffalo. The old man said that, with luck, we should see the Missouri in three days more. I sincerely hoped so, as I was beginning to believe my search for it rather a wild-goose chase.

The first Bobolink (*Emberiza oryzivora*) that I

had observed this season welcomed our appearance by carolling forth the sweet notes from which it derives its name.

From being migratory, and changing its plumage during the time of its periodical journeys, arise, doubtless, the number of appellations by which this diminutive songster is known. In the rice-fields of Carolina it is a Rice Bunting; in the marshes of the Delaware, a Reed-bird; and in New England, a Bobolink. But widely different as are its names, its habits are equally so. In the southern and central countries it is gregarious; in the less hospitable and more temperate, it is seldom seen otherwise than in pairs. To some extent this difference may be accounted for by the fact that when it breeds in the North the nurturing of a family requires undivided attention; whereas in the South, where this little beauty appears to have nothing else to do but to enjoy itself, it assembles in flocks, either from a love of sociability, or for protection against birds of prey, its instinct suggesting to it that 'unity is strength.'

The reed-bird is very much like the linnet in shape. It is about seven and a half inches long, and twelve inches across the extended wings. The colour of the male bird in spring is very much more brilliant than later in the season. The back, wing-coverts, and tail, vary from russet-brown to black; the tail-coverts, scapulars, and rump, are pure white; the lowest parts of the body are of a lead colour. They use their tails in a similar manner to the housemartins, each feather being pointed, and very hard at its termination. Although so insignificant in size, these birds are as much sought after by the epicure as their Oriental relations, the rice-birds of China, or their Transatlantic cousins, the ortolans; and as I have had the fortune to eat specimens of each in their respective homes, and at the season when they are supposed to have attained perfection, I believe myself justified in offering an opinion on their respective table merits. All three, in my judgment, are so much alike, after passing through the cook's hands, that it would be impossible to make any distinction between them.

In a carefully constructed nest, situated on the ground in a meadow, or among the short herbage on the margin of a stream, they deposit their eggs, generally five in number, and of a bluish shade, irregularly blotched with chocolate colour, and there they rear their progeny. As the season advances, and the lengthening night proclaims the approach of cold and storm, they assemble in coteries, which keep augmenting as they proceed southward, till these flocks assume such gigantic proportions, that a flitting, ever-varying light is reflected from their backs when on the wing; the effect being so curious, that the observer might imagine he was contemplating some of the phenomena presented in a gigantic kaleidoscope.

The weather still continued variable, and although our horses were commencing to evince most unmistakably the result of hard work and short commons, it was considered desirable to push forward. The country was becoming more park-like. Timbered and open land were in about equal proportions, recalling to memory parts of the splendid State of Kansas. This new characteristic was particularly pleasing to me, as it indicated proximity to a large water-course — doubtless the long-looked-for Missouri. Away to the north-west could be seen occasionally the outline of some high and irregular hills, one of which, from its decapitated appearance at the summit, recalled to mind Mount Fusiama, in Japan.

Game, both deer and buffalo, being abundant and tame, we had felt tolerably free from the fear of meeting Indians. On traversing a water-course, however, we observed the most convincing proofs that the slightest neglect of caution might embroil us in trouble; for, on its sandy margin, horse-tracks were in such numbers that we could not doubt a large body of Red-skins had lately been there. The direction of their trail pointed towards the south-west, but all our efforts to discover their whereabouts were fruitless.

When we halted for the night, we resolved to do without a fire, although the weather was cold. After dark, many miles off, we distinguished a redness in the heavens in the direction we believed the Indians had gone. This illumination, we felt certain, was caused by their camp-fires. Believing

M

that sufficient space intervened between us to prevent these astute individuals noticing the trifling glare that would result from our diminutive flame, we lighted a fire, and soon had the wherewith to commence cooking.

From our horses being restless all night, we did not enjoy much sleep. Twice I had to go to them, to prevent their breaking away; but this long night, like others, came to an end. All, however, were so little refreshed at its termination, that we determined to remain where we were for twenty-four hours longer. After our morning meal, 'the old man,' rifle in hand, went out 'to prospect,' as he called it, for Indians. As I had various little duties to perform, such as washing and mending my apparel, I remained to keep camp.

When my companion again joined me, he was in an unusual state of excitement, having seen a very large bear enter a cave situated in a neighbouring ravine. Right or wrong, with perfect disregard for consequences, he had determined to have the pelt of this 'tarnation crittur.'

I knew the old man's character too well not to be aware that any opposition on my part would only make him the more obstinate in carrying out his schemes; so, making a virtue of necessity, I was therefore compelled to submit to his caprice, or sever partnership with him — an alternative that could only be regarded with dread.

He washed out his rifle silently, without even a whistle; and on his countenance there was a frown, while the corners of his mouth looked more drawn down than usual. His conversational powers, which were always extremely limited, appeared to have deserted him altogether; and all his actions were slow and measured. I verily believe that while one of these fits was on him he would have walked into the very jaws of death rather than renounce his purpose, or admit himself to be in the smallest degree wrong.

I had already had some experience of the difficulty of getting a bear out of a cave; an adventure which through the merest chance did not terminate with the death of one of my friends engaged with me in the undertaking. Bruin, when in the shelter of his cavern-retreat, generally defies all attempts made for his destruction, and often retaliates with fearful interest upon his aggressors. Any lad who knows how to handle a gun, and keep cool, may shoot a bear in the open, but to grope your way into the dark recesses of a cavern—the height, width, surface, and length of which you know nothing about—and there struggle to the death with an animal of almost unequalled strength, is an act of rashness that nearly amounts to madness. In such a case, a miss or hang-fire must result in serious consequences to the aggressor. I therefore sat down to wash out my gun, and while preparing a limb of brush for a wash-rod, I saw, as I cast an occasional furtive glance at my companion, that my proceedings did not please him, and that before long he would let his tongue loose.

'Your gun ain't dirty, is it?' he asked.

'No, not very,' I replied.

'Then what are you swabbing her out for?' he continued, after a grunt, and a pause.

'To prevent a miss-fire,' I answered.

This reply was received with a couple of grunts, and a longer silence.

'I guess you'll be here when I git back?' he said by way of question.

'No; for I'm going with you,' emphatically I uttered.

'No need; guess I can take care of myself. Calculate I knew how to kill a bear, before ever I seen you,' he continued.

'Highly possible!' I pronounced, in a nonchalant manner, and the conversation ceased—both being as cross with each other as a brace of jealous rivals.

I knew I had to watch the old man, or to a moral certainty he would slip away from me. At length he got up, stretched himself, gave a grunt, and exclaimed—'I'm off.' Possibly without the stretch, certainly without the grunt,—I followed at his heels.

We traversed some broken land, edged with dead fir-trees, skirting a very spongy piece of morass that shelved off into a diminutive lake; then turned to the right, up a ravine, down the centre of which rushed a brook. Dwarf birch-trees and hemlocks hung over the water in places, damming back the light, or forming a screen which concealed shaded retreats.

Turning from the rivulet, we clambered up the side of the ravine for a few hundred feet, the trees becoming fewer and smaller as we ascended. In an indentation in the ground—which looked as if it were formed by a giant, with a crowbar, who had pried out an immense boulder—was an orifice large enough for a man to crawl into. Some *débris* of animal matter, plenty of old bleached-looking brown hair, and a musky odour—such as one gets a whiff of occasionally at the 'Zoo,'—were sufficient to indicate Bruin's residence without the sight of his name on a brass plate over the door. How many of these formidable animals might there be in this retreat? Any number, from one to half-a-dozen! From my knowledge of the appearance and habits of the animal, I should say the latter number was not improbable; and I expressed myself to that effect to my companion. 'Like enough,' said the old man.

Our plan of operations was first to endeavour to smoke the brutes out. If the floor of the cave ascended, this could be accomplished easily enough, for the smoke would circulate throughout its entire limits, and force them to bolt, when their destruction could be effected with despatch, and without danger; but if the floor of the cavern was deeper than the entrance, the lightness of the smoke would prevent its descending beneath the level of the fire, and the animals would be free from its noxious influences.

For half an hour we both toiled collecting all

the inflammable material within reach. Several birches were stripped of their handsome, silvery, paper-like bark, and a quantity of decayed wood was collected. During this operation we did not dare to wander far from our arms, for our prey might be abroad, or, if in his dwelling, might sally forth, not with the intention of fighting, but of avoiding the enemy.

Having gathered sufficient dried vegetable matter for our purpose, we formed torches out of birch-bark, with which we fired the heap.

The bright flames soon leaped aloft; damp wood and turf being piled on when they ceased to imperil the life of the blaze. The glowing embers were then shoved back into the orifice by aid of poles, and when this portion of our work was performed, the opening was partially closed.

When a boy, I had often resorted to smoke as a means of bolting a recusant ferret, but I do not think I can state with great success. The rabbit-burrow was at first watched silently, that the truants might not be aware of our presence, and prevented coming forth; but impatience from delay generally loosened our tongues, and we vented our spleen at the loss of time. So it was with us in the present case. For half an hour not a word was spoken; then, broken sentences, meaning looks, monosyllabic answers, afterwards a drooping conversation succeeded, followed ultimately by the removal of all restraint on our tongues, when we freely expressed doubts whether there was anything inside to come forth.

That such was possible, could not be doubted; but it was extremely improbable. The old man had seen the bear enter in the morning, when, doubtless, its stomach was full, after its nocturnal rambles; and, from his not having approached its den, and kept out of its view, while he paid particular attention that the animal should not get his wind, the odds were all in our favour that Bruin was inside and previous to our advent in the arms of Morpheus.

On removing the smouldering fire, and the *débris* by which the mouth of the cavern was choked up, the smoke rolled out in volumes; but, in attempting to pry into the interior, we got nearly suffocated. The den for the present was inaccessible. As more than an hour's delay did not improve matters, it was agreed to scarify the soil and ashes at the mouth of the cave, so that the trail of any animal entering or leaving would be distinctly shown. Having completed this process to our satisfaction, we bent our steps to camp in a more companionable frame of mind.

The sun was about two hours high next morning when we started again for the cave. The day was warm and pleasant. From the brush we flushed a young family of roughed grouse (*Tetrao umbellus*), which were already half-grown. The stupid birds took to a tree, and with outstretched necks gazed with wonder and curiosity at us.

On inspecting most carefully the entrance of the cave, we found, to our common surprise, two distinct tracks—one in, and the other out. What did this indicate?—a question which it required some knowledge of venerie to decide. Were these marks caused by the egress of the original occupant, or had a stranger paid the place a visit, and finding it untenantable from the smoke, at once departed? As the footprints in both directions exactly tallied in length and breadth, we unanimously came to the latter conclusion.

Having failed so thoroughly in carrying out our project by means of smoke, it was apparent that some other method had to be adopted; and although the old man had not said a word, I knew from the expression of his face that he was determined to investigate the cavern from end to end, and, if need be, fight its tenant in its recess.

I know I am not a coward, for I can scarcely recall any occasion on which I experienced the sensation of fear; but I was not prepared for such a course as this, which appeared to me, not bravery, but sheer recklessness. I was aware, however, that I might as well attempt to stem the current of Niagara as alter his purpose. Still I considered it my duty to make a trial, and pointed out the risk. A look from him told me that my solicitations were useless, and that a further repetition of them would probably lead to open hostilities between us. I felt, however, that his determination placed me in a not very enviable position; for if a fight took place in the interior of the cavern between my companion and its occupant, it would be impossible for me in that probably contracted space, involved in darkness, to render him any assistance.

With two or three pieces of birch-bark a couple of feet long, rolled up so as to look like brown piping, shoved into the bosom of his hunting-shirt, and a torch of the same material in his hand, his hunting-knife loosened in its sheath, and his rifle ready for action, the obstinate old fellow—for such I considered him—disappeared on all-fours into darkness. For some minutes I could hear his advance, and knew his position by the light he carried; but this soon ceased, concealed by some turning, or obscured by the darkness. The only service I could render now, was that of preventing any new enemy from attacking my adventurous companion in rear. The anxiety and suspense which I suffered was intense. A cedar-bird, which twittered from a bough, gave me such a start as to send my heart into my mouth. At one moment I thought I heard a groan; afterwards a cracking sound;—but an over-wrought anxiety deceived my ears.

There is generally a charm about mystery, but there was none in the present case. Nothing could equal my impatience,—when, first one mocassin, then another, afterwards leggings, and ultimately a body, slowly made their appearance from the cave. I shook with laughter, while the old fellow held out to me a handful of hair,—for his appearance had considerably changed; for his face, as well as the greasy brown hunting-shirt which he wore, was completely blackened by the smoke of his torch.

But Bruin was disposed of,—smoked to death. The old fellow, however, acknowledged, with evident grief and disappointment, that from the contracted proportions of the interior, the carcass could neither be removed nor skinned. As the cave was not long, he returned into its depths for a few pounds of the meat, which, when exhibited in daylight, looked anything but appetising, from the ashes and mould which had become attached to it.

CHAPTER IX.

ANTELOPES — THE GARTER-SNAKE — THE JAW AND TEETH OF SNAKES — KILDEES — SPRIG-TAIL OR PHEASANT-DUCKS — ZEAL IN THE STUDY OF NATURAL HISTORY — SPOOR OF THE BEAR — A DAINTY MARAUDER — THE VARIEGATED HARE — THE MISSOURI — ENCAMPMENT OF TRAPPERS.

NEXT morning we were *en route* at an early hour. Rest having done the nags good, we progressed right merrily. Several antelopes (*Antilocapra*) were in view all day, but would not permit our coming within range; neither had we time to lose in stalking them.

In summer, these animals are immensely abundant all about this neighbourhood; but, when the cold weather approaches, they usually shift much further to the southward. At the same time it is no uncommon thing for them to be captured in the snow-drifts by the Indians. So great is their speed, that the swiftest horse or greyhound would be nowhere in pursuit of them.

Curiosity appears to be their besetting fault; in the indulgence of which they often become the prey of the rifle-ball. The sportsman, well aware of this marked feature in their character, by remaining to leeward, and waving a piece of bright rag, or anything with the appearance of which they are unfamiliar, frequently induces them to come within range of his rifle. Towards the afternoon, when we struck the margin of a diminutive water-course flowing to the north, I felt convinced that the little stream was a tributary of the long-looked-for river Missouri.

While searching for the nest of a wild duck that flushed within a few yards of me, a protracted noise, between a croak and a squeak, attracted my attention. After endeavouring to determine the exact spot from which the sound emanated, I discovered that it proceeded from an unfortunate frog which the fates had cast within reach of a large garter-snake. As this variety of serpent is not poisonous, I made it a captive without hesitation, and carried it home. During this operation it never left hold of its prey; and when it was shaken out of my bag beside the camp-fire, poor froggy had disappeared down its capacious throat. Anxious to become thoroughly conversant with the habits of snakes, I retained the captive for some time. At first he exhibited the greatest disinclination to feed, but at length the cravings of appetite compelled him to take his food. Selecting a large frog, I placed it within the temporary cage in which the serpent was inclosed.

When the frog became conscious of its proximity to its deadly foe, it appeared to lose all power of making any effort to escape. The serpent approached to seize the victim, and in an instant after it had reached striking-distance, this was accomplished. When the poor frog felt the snake's teeth imbedded in one of its limbs, it made no attempt to escape, but uttered the most plaintive cries. By degrees, slowly but steadily, the whole limb was absorbed into the reptile's throat, the process being so strong and regular that the other hind-leg was forced forward against and parallel with the body. Although the carcass of the frog appeared to be of greater width than the head of the snake, it continued gradually to disappear. While the victim's head was being drawn in, the unfortunate animal uttered a low protracted wail, as if sorrowfully bidding adieu to this world. The snake closed its mouth, and the frog was entombed in its stomach.

In a quarter of an hour afterwards, upon opening the serpent, the frog was found still alive; and, though its skin was scarified, I do not believe it had received any wound likely to cause death.

As many of my readers are not students of science, I may mention, in explanation of this operation, that, at the apex of each jaw, there is a muscular substance capable of considerable expansion. This substance, while it admits of enlargement, also permits the side of each jaw to act independently of the other, so that the victim is held fast by one side of the mouth, while the other side of it is moved forward in advance in order to obtain a new hold,—a process which is repeated till the entire carcass has been absorbed. The teeth, therefore, are not used to masticate, but to assist in swallowing,—a fact which is proved by the circumstance that the frog was found alive after having been fifteen minutes in the reptile's stomach. From the position and shape of a snake's teeth, I am very much inclined to believe, that, if so disposed, it could not eject a large prey from its mouth after once having obtained a good hold of it, more especially if it were of sufficient size to cause the least expansion of the jaws.

At sunset we saw in the distance a yellow line of light, and beyond it a dark fringe of trees—indications of our approach to the mighty Missouri. A violent storm of rain came on during the night; and our horses, which were very gaunt, looked most wretched. We determined, therefore, not to make a renewal of our journey without a day's rest; and, as our arms required cleaning, and our clothing and mocassins would be better of some repairs, we had sufficient grounds for this delay.

Previous to taking my morning meal, I went up to a pool I had observed the previous evening, to enjoy the luxury of a swim. Although, after divesting myself of my clothes, the atmosphere felt very chill—almost so much so as to cause me to postpone my intention—I screwed up my courage with an effort, and took a header off the bank into deep water. Ere I had taken a few strokes, I felt immensely benefited. The opposite bank reached, I instantly returned, considering after being five minutes in the water, I had had enough;—for nothing is so weakening as a protracted stay on such an occasion.

At the mouth of the pool in which I had bathed, there was a point of sand, on which I saw several kildees, a species of plover, and, being desirous to note some of their peculiarities, I approached as close as these pretty little birds would permit, without their being driven to take wing. I remained thus for a few minutes, giving all my attention to their peculiarities, as, with swift, energetic movements, they captured those unfortunate water-insects that came within their reach.

Their call, consisting of two notes, kil-dee, from which their name is derived, is continuously repeated every few moments—not even the important duty of obtaining their morning repast being any check upon their loquacity. A party of old women over their loved cup of tea could not be more garrulous.

The shrill whistle of wings called off my attention, and I observed a pair of pintail duck (*Anas acuta*) rapidly winging their way to fresh feeding-grounds. Sprigtail, or pheasant-duck,—for by all these names is this species known—is an elegant-shaped, long-bodied bird, capable of sustaining the fatigue of very protracted flights. To the dwellers of the North, it is frequently the first harbinger who proclaims the advent of Spring, and is therefore a welcome visitor. It would scarcely be wrong to hint that its excellence on the table has also, perhaps, something to do with its popularity.

It is found widely spread through both Northern Europe and America. As these ducks are very shy, it is seldom that the sportsman is successful in killing them in great numbers. Of one thing, however, he may be certain, that the more severe the weather the greater will be the probability of his success when out in their pursuit.

In the north-western portion of Illinois, there is an extensive stretch of wild land, which has not presented sufficient attractions to induce the emigrant, or the tiller of the soil, to undertake its conversion into corn-fields and pasture-lands. One reason for this apparent remissness doubtless is, that it lies so low that drainage could not be accomplished without an outlay far greater than is generally within the means of the precursors of civilisation—for even the American squatter, capable as he is of submitting to any amount of discomfort and privation, objects to his cabin being turned into a raft, and to himself and children being compelled to live like water-rats. Up in the Kankakee country, to which I allude, the visitor may succeed in obtaining an extensive view, uninterrupted in any direction by the works of man. I have spent weeks in this isolated region, alone with a companion, who knew not either to lie or cheat, whose eyes spoke what his heart felt, and whose pleasure was to do my will. It was during this stay, at the breaking up of winter, on a day so inclement that the most unfeeling man would scarcely have turned his neighbour's dog out of doors, at least not in the presence of a witness, if he had any desire for the respect of his fellow-citizen, that I went to a marsh-margined stream, to observe the effects of sleet, snow, and wind, upon the migrating host of aquatic birds. My retriever accompanied me, not in obedience to my order, but from choice. The howling of the tempest was only broken by the disagreeable sound,— slush, slush, slush,—made during the process of extracting my feet after each stride from the heavy, wet, saturated soil. Even in the midst of such disadvantageous circumstances, numerous little incidents were constantly coming under my observation indicative of the habits of animal life, amply compensating me for the inconvenience suffered from the severity of the weather.

At length I reached the desired stand, in the centre of a stunted persimmon-bush, the brown withered leaves of which, even at so far advanced a period of the season, clung with tenacity to their branches. In this spot I enjoyed comparative shelter, and it was an excellent place for observation. Numerous flights of aquatic birds, scudding before the blast, rushed past my hiding-place, unconscious of my proximity, or disdaining my presence--sprig-tailed duck preponderating in numbers over all the

N

other species. Even when darkness descended upon the dismal landscape, there was no diminution in the number of these birds, as they fled swiftly past me, betraying their presence only by the noise caused by the rapid movement of their wings.

This bird is about thirty-four inches across the wings, and two feet long. It is more graceful and slender than the majority of ducks; while the neck is markedly longer in proportion to the size of the body. The bill is of a lead colour; the head and upper portion of the neck of a cinnamon hue; while a band of purple, bordered with white, lies above the junction of the neck with the body. The sides of the breast, and the upper part of the shoulders, are white, beautifully pencilled with fine waving lines. The belly is of the lightest fawn colour; the under tail-coverts black, the wing-coverts dull brown—the greater ones being tipped with lines of a golden yellow. The upper tail-coverts on the rump are pale brown, the centre of each feather being dark. The two centre feathers of the tail run to a fine point, and are elongated upwards of six inches over the others. The irides are dark hazel.

But to return to my present position. In the sand beside me I observed the track of a bear, so large that the animal which produced it must have been of gigantic proportions. It was evidently old, however, and Bruin might now be many miles away. There is no mistaking this spoor, it is so much larger than those of any animals which it resembles.

The forenoon passed without any other occurrence worthy of notice. The incessant attacks of mosquitoes, the first that have punished me this season, were the only source of excitement, too irritating to be agreeable. In the afternoon, I long watched an otter pursuing his avocation. Without leaving the pool on which he was engaged, he must have captured, in the course of an hour, half-a-dozen fish. Fastidious in taste, and lavish of the good things which were so abundant around him, he selected a piece out of the shoulder of his prey; the remainder of the carcass being permitted to float down the current, or become corrupt on the surface of the rock where it was landed. I appropriated for my own use a beautiful specimen of the silver cat-fish, not being too proud to sup upon the leavings of the dainty marauder. Being anxious for an early start, we both soon turned in, and were compensated for our discomforts of the previous evening by a sound, refreshing sleep.

While preparing our morning repast, my companion went to look at some snares he had set the previous day, and in one of them found a fine specimen of the variegated hare. This animal is most abundant throughout this region, and from its frequenting open ground would afford capital sport for greyhounds. Although preyed upon by numerous birds and quadrupeds, they so rapidly reproduce, that with no more serious drawbacks to their existence, they never can become scarce.

When we started next morning, horses and riders appeared to be imbued with fresh energy. By mid-day we had crossed the Missouri,—frequently known by the name of 'the great muddy,' on account of the quantity of decayed vegetable matter and soil contained in its water, which in colour resembles weak coffee. The quantity of sediment carried along in it may be imagined from the fact, that if a tumbler of water were drawn from it, and permitted to stand for a quarter-of-an-hour without shaking, the bottom of the vessel would be found filled for one-third its depth with *débris*. However, whatever people may think to the contrary, my belief, as well as that of the inhabitants who dwell upon its margin, is, that no better water can be obtained to drink. The entire appearance of the country here promises that it will some day be the residence of a densely-settled agricultural population. From the depth of the soil, and its rich, black appearance, I could well imagine that at no very distant date it will rival Illinois in its claim to the appellation of the 'garden of the West.'

Although the current was strong, and the width of the river equal to that of the Thames at Richmond, we forded it with ease,—the horses never losing their footing. We remarked numerous buffalo-trails leading in every direction, some of them so broad and tramped, particularly where they led to and from fording-places, that they reminded me of the entrance to a farmyard pond, where domestic horned cattle quenched their thirst. No buffalo, however, were in sight, although their footprints were so fresh that they could not be formed over twenty-four hours. This 'the old man' assured me was an indication that Indians had lately been hunting in the vicinity. As the stream at the part where we struck it ran with a sharp turn towards the west, my companion, who had been here before, stated that we were still some way from the camp of the people we sought,—which was on a small tributary of one of the feeders of the Missouri flowing in from the north. Their exact position, 'the old man' remarked, was easily recognised by a high clay bluff opposite where it debouched into the parent stream, as well as by the proximity of a ridge of high ground, the summit of which was fringed with pines. In his belief, we had not over twenty miles more to traverse before reaching our destination. If his supposition was correct, there was no advantage to be gained by hurrying, as such a distance was more than our cattle in their exhausted condition could accomplish that day, without being goaded on in a manner that would be absolutely cruel. In fact, for the last day or two, to save my mare as much as possible, I had ridden the mule, a service he appeared most unwilling to submit to. While the sun was yet about two hours high, we found a suitable camping-ground, which had apparently been used for that purpose before, as portions of charred wood, and numerous bleached bones lay around. The afternoon, which had been a little hazy, cleared up at sunset; and, to my great delight, a hill, such as my guide had described, was distinctly visible two or more miles to the north. Twice during the night I was awakened by the uneasiness of our cattle; but, after listening intently, I could hear nothing but the distant baying of some wolves, interrupted by the still more distant howl of what I believed to be a wolverine.

In the morning at daybreak we found ourselves positively surrounded by wapiti-deer, whose perfect tameness allowed us frequently to approach within fifty yards of them, before they evinced any inclination to move off. 'The old man,' as usual, moralised on this fact as bearing on our own prospects.

With rather a crest-fallen countenance, he asserted that these animals never would be so familiar if there were a lot of white men within a few miles of them; and, therefore, the persons he sought were gone. The Indians, perhaps, had turned upon them, and taken their scalp-locks.

Our nervous systems being worked up to the greatest amount of tension through the constant alternations of hope, doubt, and fear, caused by these surmises, our minds derived some relief from the appearance of smoke—which, at first, was regarded as a favourable indication; but, on second consideration, was taken as a providential hint that we should exercise more than our habitual caution, — a fire being just as probably the work of Indians as of white men. At length we halted, to consider what course we had better adopt, when two reports of a rifle reverberated through the woods. As Indians will not, as a rule, waste upon game, if procurable in other ways, that precious commodity, gunpowder—their supply of which is uncertain, and very expensive—we began to feel that fortune was more favourably disposed towards us than we had previously supposed. Again pursuing our course, the veteran leading, his tongue was suddenly let loose by the exclamation :—'Darn me, if there ain't one of the boys!' True enough, there was somebody evidently intent on a trap or snare over which he was leaning, but whether it was white or red man I was unable to distinguish. My companion, however, with his keen practised eyes, knew too well the characteristic differences between the two races to entertain such a doubt.

Urging on his Rosinante with a war-whoop, the noise of our approach caused the unknown to raise his head, and at the same time grasp his rifle, which rested against a bush. Although the colour of the stranger's skin was scarcely distinguishable from that of one of the aborigines, his manner and bearing dissipated in a moment all doubt, and we recognized in him a countryman, with whom we immediately made acquaintance.

We continued our route in his company,—

favouring him with a volley of questions; and, half-an-hour after our meeting, we entered the long-sought camp, where we were surrounded by a crew of a dozen as hardy-looking cut-throats, —without disrespect be it said,—as ever trod a pirate's deck.

With the appearance of this community I was not favourably impressed. Their camp was disorderly and dirty; their own personal appearance absolutely filthy. Many of them were half-breeds,— a race to which I had long been the reverse of partial, for I had always found them dishonest, treacherous, and cowardly. All were under the leadership of a chief of their own selection, a powerful, brawny-shouldered Hercules, a man who evidently brooked neither insubordination nor skulking. He gave his orders with that intonation which clearly said,—Do it, or I will make you. A man of any other character could not have managed such a motley crew. He had the reputation of knowing the Indian country from end to end; and had been in more fights with the natives than any of the free trappers of his time. He was also said to be their best rifleshot, and none of his comrades could show so many wounds. A Missourian by birth, he had passed his childhood on the frontier, and his more mature years between that state and the Rocky Mountains. It can scarcely be deemed surprising, therefore, that he hated the Indian as thoroughly as it was possible for him to do. When spoken of by his comrades, he was designated 'the Cap. ;'—his proper appellation, I was informed, was Ned Soulé.

The reception accorded to me was far from being marked by that warmth which I had anticipated. Blunt and gruff, however, as he was with all—why should he make an exception in my favour, more particularly when it was evident that no money was to be squeezed out of me?

I determined, however, only to remain in his camp as long as circumstances compelled me, submitting patiently and without murmur to my share of work. Soulé's society, also, I should take care to avoid as much as possible; feeling convinced that if I pursued another course, there might be some danger of a collision which it would be more prudent to avert by a cautious course of conduct.

In this camp there were fourteen hunters, a few of whom had squaws. Although, in true Indian fashion, all the hard work devolved on these unfortunate women, they did not appear to murmur, but even looked happy, notwithstanding their excessive drudgery. When this camp was formed, each member had possessed a horse; several also had mules; but a disease,—caused, doubtless, by neglect and filth,—had broken out among their cattle, of which only four survivors were left. These were in capital condition, as a stock of forage had been gathered the previous autumn, to supply the wants of the larger number, so that there was now an overplus, which was distributed with no niggardly hand. Of course, my horses came in for their share; and it was astonishing how soon, with rest and abundance, they improved in appearance.

'The old man,' my companion, did not like Soulé a bit more than I did; and as among the assembly he found only a few acquaintances, and no intimates, he remained on the best of terms with me. Although he said very little, I felt convinced that if I should get into any scrape with this rough crowd, I had a friend who would stand by me.

The camp, standing upon a slight elevation above the surrounding country, was conveniently situated for a supply of water. It was well sheltered from the north and west, from which quarters the prevailing winds in winter blow; and was surrounded by a rough fencing of logs and boughs. In the centre of this inclosure was a citadel, composed of logs drawn together, resembling a half-built barn of immense size, loop-holed on every face for musketry. Within shelter of this building, many of the garrison slept. Those who were possessors of dusky wives had shanties, or huts, or whatever they chose to call them, leaning against its outer walls.

This fortress was admirably suited for the purpose for which it was intended. A garrison of a few determined men with an abundant supply of ammunition, might have kept ten times their number at bay, unless attacked on all sides at the same moment, and overpowered before they had time to use their arms. Even after such a *contretemps*, a small number of defenders, if able to secure their retreat into the citadel, could have cleared the inclosure surrounding it.

This day it was bitterly cold, the wind blowing in fitful squalls from the north. Occasionally fragments of snow floated before it, probably the precursors of a heavy fall; but our encampment being possessed of plenty of firewood, no inconvenience was anticipated. A stranger taking a peep into the interior of our citadel, would be struck with the industry, and amused with the diversity of the occupations on which its inmates were engaged. A few days ago it would have been different, for then three-fourths of our numbers would have been trapping, or endeavouring to kill time at eucre or old sledge, the favourite card-games of the western man. As the season, however, was now advanced, and their future course of action had been settled, every spare moment was passed by the trappers in getting ready their rude outfit, so that they might be prepared for all emergencies. Mocassins, leggings, and hunting-shirts, had to be patched; knives sharpened; gun-locks dismembered, washed, and oiled; packs of ammunition and necessaries put together in the most portable shape. It was really surprising to witness with what skill these large, rough, powerful, weather-beaten men handled their needles; many of the alterations and patches made by them being so neatly executed that none but eyewitnesses could have believed that the work did not proceed from the dainty, skilled fingers of women. Many men are unaware of the abilities they possess, until they are forced to utilise them; but, when thrown on their own resources, with no one to perform for them the minor details of life, it is wonderful how soon they become perfect masters of such an art as that of sewing. This explains, I suppose, why sailors are always so handy,—their protracted absence from home forcing them to acquire those useful accomplishments which in general are only possessed by women. No sort of knowledge is a burthen, and, therefore, I always make it a rule to get an insight into all that falls under my observation; and I should advise others to do the same. He that can put a sole upon his boot, or a shoe upon his horse, is a far more desirable travelling-companion than he who must limp along for want of the former, or lame his horse and impede the journey because he has not the skill to do the latter.

If the severe weather continued much longer, we should soon have begun to believe that summer was never coming. Cold does not signify much, if the atmosphere is still, for exercise and clothing will then keep a man warm; but when the icy blast is sufficiently strong to be felt through the thickest covering, the animal heat of the body is soon overpowered. Wind and cold, which are comparatively harmless when separate, do all the mischief when combined.

I listened with curiosity one day to these men

discussing their future proceedings. Some of them appeared as simple, frivolous, and changeable as children. One moment, the fascinations of city life were remembered by them with regret, and a determination to return to town was expressed. The great drawback was, that they were without the means of living, once they got there ; and they had no idea of going back poor. One of the party had a visionary idea of some distant country where the Indians were friendly, and as yet untainted by contact with the white man. Game, he said, was there plentiful, and prospecting for gold certain to lead to the discovery of rich lodes. The physiognomies of one or two of the listeners expressed doubts whether such things were not too good to be true ; but these were convinced by the narrative of some adventurer's experience in this favoured land. Some portions of this story might be true ; but assuredly the greater part of it was imaginary. There were great discrepancies in the narrative ; but the yarn had been spun dozens of times before,—and stories, like snowballs, gather additions in their progress.

Jem Green, a powerful man, with a far from attractive cast of countenance, had all the talk to himself for more than half-an-hour, during which he kept the floor, only occasionally interrupted by such an interjection as, 'That's so !' or a request for further information. As some appeared doubtful of his tale, he turned to a man well known on the plains, who knew them like a book, old Tom Kemble by name, and, looking him in the face, addressed him thus: 'Now, old man, you knew Joe Brown?'

'I did so,' was the response.

'Well, you may bet he was one of the right sort,' continued Jem.

'True for you, he was a bully boy,' pronounced Tom.

'That he was, a whole team of himself; well, he told me on Yellow-stone, just below the Crow-fork, when he was on his way for St. Louis, to raise a company to go back with him, not a week before the Red-skins raised his hair, all about this place; and there ain't a bit of doubt that it's a tip-top diggin'. And if you'll only go along with me, this day twelve months you'll all have more yellow boys in your pockets than will buy a good farm down east. You have all got the proper grit in you, and we would make a big team together. If the venture turned out a good spec, we'd share and share alike. I ain't asking any odds of any man, only all that's fair and square.'

So the matter appeared settled. With no more cogent reasons than those above stated this hardy party of men were willing to start off hundreds of miles on what might well be considered a wild goose chase.

The storm at length blew itself out, the fitful gusts gradually becoming less frequent. The fire was made up for the night, the size of the back-log promising endurance, the quantity of fuel abundant heat. After the evening meal all had a smoke by its flickering light, and ultimately lay down to sleep.

Our bundles served as pillows, and we had no change of raiment. Yet we slept soundly, and rose more refreshed probably than many who have reposed on beds of down under a canopy of damask. Awaking a few hours after midnight, the calmness of night was most impressive. The moon peeped out from behind flitting clouds, and the silence was only broken by the wild yell of a Lucifee exercising his vocal powers half a mile away. We required a few sticks of fresh wood to lay on the fire, and, as I was at the portal of our primitive house, I crossed over to what was known as the wood-pile, stacked ready for consumption. In the act of stooping to obtain a load, a most demoniac yell burst upon my ear, so close at hand that it completely startled me. It was so sudden, so unearthly, and unexpected, that for an instant I was unnerved. The cause of my alarm, however, was only a wolverine, which I distinguished hurrying off (possibly the mate of the first I had heard), who had been induced to visit our camp by the want of food.

CHAPTER X.

LOOKING FOR GAME — ON THE TRACK OF WAPITI DEER — ENCOUNTER WITH A PUMA — AN 'OLD HOSS'S' STORY — SOULÉ AND HIS MEN — SHAMEFUL TREATMENT OF INDIANS — RATTLESNAKES — DEPARTURE FROM THE CAMP — WILD STRAWBERRIES — SHOT AT A BLACK-TAILED DEER — BEAR AND WOLVES — EXCITING ADVENTURE.

THE morning after, I started as soon as day broke, to look for game. There had not been sufficient snow to fill up the old footprints and make tracking good. After traversing lengthwise the piece of timber in which our shanty stood, I determined, as the day was still young, to branch off to the north-west, to a part that I believed was rarely or never disturbed. The wind was bitterly cold across the open country; but I struggled against the blast at a three and a-half mile to the hour pace, though, when I accomplished the distance, I was very cold and very blown. A few minutes communion with my pipe, within the shelter of the trees, afforded me relief from these inconveniences.

On a close examination of the vicinity I saw every reason to congratulate myself on the course I had taken, for the tracks of wapiti deer were most abundant. In one place in particular, where there was a slight depression in the soil, which was entirely free from shrubs, and had a slimy appearance, the surface was as much broken up as if it had been the floor of a well-stocked hog-pen. For this I accounted by concluding that the spot was a salt-lick, always a place of the greatest attraction for tame as well as wild ruminants. I felt convinced if such was the case that I had better keep my weather eye open, for some of the carnivora were certain to be in the vicinity, it being well known that wherever deer assemble in numbers their enemies are not slow to discover their retreat. The trees I remarked were unusually large, and, although they grew sufficiently apart to induce a growth of underbrush, it was not so thick and tangled as to prevent a view of over a hundred yards ahead from my position.

Whether it was the result of animal magnetism or not, I cannot say; but I felt convinced that I was not far distant from animals of some sort. Acting under this impression, I moved cautiously and slowly, making the most careful scrutiny of every object within vision, and employing my ears to the utmost of their abilities. But although I could not observe anything that warranted this precaution, I did not discontinue, but rather redoubled it.

Peering into the labyrinth of limbs, and looking well before me, I saw something move. The smallest glimpse of a portion of the sky, which I had noted, was for a moment obscured; but although I was aware this could not be without a cause, for some time I could not discover what it was. After turning my eyes frequently in

o

the same direction, however, I perceived on a limb twenty feet from the ground, and which traversed exactly the course I was taking, a panther (*puma*), his head over his left leg, his eye fixed on me, the whole body, save a few inches of the tail, perfectly still. The brute's colour was so thoroughly assimilated to that of the surrounding trees, that it no longer appeared to me a matter of wonder that I had not distinguished it when fifty yards further off. Now that I was aware of the vicinity of this agile animal I had nothing to fear; but, from its attitude and expression, I have little doubt that if I had passed under its perch it would have sprung upon me, when its impetus, combined with its weight, would have in an instant prostrated me, and perhaps have rendered me insensible. The moment the puma became aware that it was detected its whole manner changed, and it exhibited signs of nervous timidity, the occasional furtive glances that it cast around plainly expressing a desire to remove from its present position, though it had the instinct not to make too hasty a movement.

Detecting in the brute a skulking coward, I at once took the offensive, being eager to obtain possession of his beautiful soft coat, which, transformed into a rug, would be useful.

Without further delay, therefore, I aimed for behind the shoulder. The bark splintered from the limb on which the creature was stretched, and, at the same time, the puma sprang headlong, but without purpose, into the air, falling a moment afterwards on the earth, where it lay struggling, mortally wounded.

By the time the carcase was skinned it was time to retrace my steps. That night I narrated to an attentive body of listeners the circumstances of the panther's death; and I was heartily congratulated that, in consequence of the correctness of my aim, I had not got into a 'darn'd ugly muss.' But Jem Green, who had generally something to say on every subject, cleared his throat, as if about to speak; and the respect in which he was held induced all to look towards him, temporarily suspending their remarks. When silence was obtained, he prefaced the story he was about to tell by informing the company, in a half-diffident manner, that he was only thinking of a scrape with a painter (*Anglice*, panther) he and his old dad had in Pensilvany. The bait took, and three or four voices requested him to narrate the circumstance.

'Spit it out, old hoss!' said they, in the elegant language of these dwellers in the wilds. And the old hoss proceeded to comply with their request. The yarn I will give as closely as I remember.

'It was when I was about old enough to do some of the "*chores*" around the homestead, that one cold stormy night in winter, when we were going to turn in to roost, both the old man and myself heard a muss among the calves. Now, we had a good dozen of these yearlings in a pound enclosed with rails close to the stock-yard. As wolves and bears were plenty in these parts at that time, we had to shut up the young critters in this way to prevent them being turned into beef before their time. If we had had a barn we would have shut them in it; but we were only squatters, and fresh fixed upon a new location.

'On passing the wood-pile to seê what was the bother, father picked up a club, and, as the axe lay handy, I fetched it along with me. The night was neither terrible dark, nor was it very light, still a fellow could see six or eight rods forenenst him. As we passed the hay-rick we heard the calves crying piteously, as if they were getting terribly roughly handled. At first we could see nothing; but, as our eyes got used to the light, the old man spotted a painter on the top of the fence. Soon I see'd him too, and, as I'm sitting here, the pesky cuss was chasing the heffers round and round the pen, which was not more than two rod square, and, every time he could get a chance from the top of the fence,— for, you see, he never left it—he gave one of the calves a dab with his paw that made it sing out for bare life.

'"Well," says the old man to me, "Jem, give us the axe, and you make tracks to the house for the rifle."

'I did my best to perform his bidding, and run both ways back and forward, still was gone near ten minutes, for the tube (nipple) of the rifle wanted a fresh cap, and, although I have them most of the time in every pocket, so as to be handy, it was some minutes before I could find one.

'When I got back the gun was not wanted: the old man had killed the painter with the axe, although it was a terrible risky thing to do. You see, he got kind of riled at seeing his calves abused; so he jist stepped up to the thief, and, as he was about to spring on the old man, dad let him have the blade fair in the face. The old fellow was one of the smartest choppers that lived in them parts. He could put up four cords of wood in a day, so you may guess he knew how to handle an axe.'

Many of the pipes having gone out before this yarn was finished, perhaps if several of the supposed listeners had been invited to express their satisfaction with it, they would have been found asleep; but, as in more fashionable circles, they did not wish their inattention to be known.

The next day there was a great improvement in the weather. It was a day to break the back-bone of the late trying storms. From feeling indolent, in consequence of an evident disposition to an attack of fever and ague, I remained in camp, and drenched myself with tea made from the bark of the wild plum, which, in the absence of quinine, is the best substitute for that useful article these wilds produce. That evening Soulé came over when I was having supper. Although his manner was slightly improved, I cannot say he had advanced in my estimation. The cause of his visit was a desire to buy, or obtain by barter, either one or both of my animals. Not caring about handing my pets over to one whom I considered likely to be the reverse of a humane master, I declined politely but firmly. No way rebuffed, he told me that, as he would pay a good price for them, I had better reconsider my decision, and, as an inducement to do so, gave me a large cake of cavendish tobacco.

We had been now several days in this camp, and every hour made me dislike my company more. For the sake of my animals I should have preferred to be able to stand it a week longer; but I almost feared the possibility of my doing so, for some wretched half-starved Indians, who arrived to-day, received such treatment as made my face burn with shame that possibly they might regard me as one of the same crew. In order to avoid witnessing again such scenes—for I had not the least power to prevent them—I shouldered my gun, and took a stroll to the north. The country was well wooded along the margin of the streams, and, if I mistake not, trout were abundant in their waters; for several fish broke the surface after the manner of these beauties when feeding on flies.

Deer-trails led in every direction, and, although I only saw a couple of these animals, they certainly frequented this locality in immense numbers. The impressions in the soil produced by some of their feet appeared quite as large as those of two-year-old heifers.

While wandering about I killed a rattlesnake nearly six feet long—a size very seldom reached by these reptiles. Its poison-teeth were as large as the claws of a full-grown domestic cat. These serpents are of all shades of colour, from a very dark greenish-black to yellow. This description refers to the timber variety, not to the massasauga or prairie-rattlesnake, which very rarely exceeds twenty-four inches in length, and is generally of a dirty-brown hue.

I was attracted by a flower resembling the wood anemone when I came across this villain ; but, from the energy with which he sprang his rattle, I had ample warning to keep out of the way of danger.

Pugilistically inclined he evidently was, for while I retired a few paces to cut a stick with which to administer the *coup de grace*, he never moved from his place, but kept his tail vibrating like a telegraph-wire in a gale of wind. Knowing as well as I do the nature and powers of snakes, I experienced no difficulty in depriving him of life by a couple of sharp cuts with my rod.

To the uninitiated I may mention that a rattlesnake cannot jump at you, but simply strikes from an elevation of one-third its length—a height which is obtained by coiling the body up. This reptile, therefore, can only inoculate with poison an object two feet from it. The traveller or sportsman who wears long boots—say up to his knee—experiences little danger from their attacks, as they cannot pierce through strong leather. In fact, so little are these vermin regarded by the settler, that I have frequently seen them kick or tread them to death under foot. Accidents have frequently occurred through them, but I have yet to learn of one proving fatal.

On returning to camp about sunset, 'the old man' communicated to me the best news which had reached my ears for a long time. He informed me that to the north of this place—beyond the very topmost waters of this tributary of the Missouri—were encamped half-a-dozen hunters, an offshoot from the establishment of which we were at that moment inmates. As the intention of Soulé was to break up camp here, and proceed to the south to join the traders, as soon as the Indians brought him in a promised supply of horses to carry their packs of furs, he made arrangements with my old friend to be bearer of his intentions to this still more northern encampment.

From my having ridden my mule a portion of our last journey, and thus saved my mare, my friend's horse was in a less capable state than either of my animals for further work, and we therefore deferred our start for a few days.

With every indication of pleasure he listened to my decision to join him. That night we sat late discussing our plan, retiring only to rest when exhausted nature proclaimed that we were trespassing upon her patience. During the three succeeding days nothing worthy of note occurred. The captain of the camp again broached the subject of purchasing my nags; but, on being informed that I still required them,* he left me in a fit of bad temper, which he took no trouble to disguise, carrying it so far as to refuse to sell me a few pounds of ammunition. However, I succeeded through my companion in obtaining all that was requisite, which enabled me to take the road in better spirits, and with more courage, than if it had been otherwise. The last time I saw Soulé he was swearing loudly at an unfortunate Indian, who had returned from an unsuccessful hunt, and, consequently, was unable to pay off some trifling debt. From his camp I departed with pleasure, hoping if ever I met him again it would be on more equal terms.

Our first morning's ride was by far the pleasantest travelling we had yet enjoyed. The ground was firm and suitable for horses. The scenery was pretty, the atmosphere bright, and the temperature such that more favourable could not have been selected.

The better to husband the strength of the mare I rode the mule; rest had made the long-eared scoundrel so obstreperous that it became necessary to visit his flanks with flagellation. For this purpose I cut a sharp birch-rod, the application of which nearly caused me a spill, for the blackguard made a rear and plunge conjointly, that sent me over his diminutive mis-shapen withers. Through dint of good luck, however, I clambered back into my seat without visiting mother earth.

After progressing for several hours we came out on prairie land, here and there broken by clumps of trees. A variety of pinnated grouse (*Tetrao cupido*) was most abundant, and exhibited so little fear of our presence that many of them remained on the ground within a few yards of our path. One which we forced to take wing was captured by a large hawk, much resembling a falcon, after a chase of a few hundred yards.

Well on in the afternoon we again came to the margin of the stream which we had previously left, on account of its bending off nearly due west. For some miles our course was destitute of trees. Shortly before we reached our usual halting-hour we entered a dense growth of timber, in which many of the trees were pines of considerable size. Every indication from which we could form an opinion convincing us that we were far from man's vicinity, we built a large fire, and with considerable comfort enjoyed a good meal, for the air and exercise had sharpened our appetites. Feeling drowsy, I soon went to roost, and my friend was in dreamland before he had finished his first pipe. I was not long in following suit, but was awakened from my welcome slumbers by a most diabolical noise, which I immediately recognised as that produced by a wolverine. Next day, when we had advanced about twenty miles, we came upon an old and admirable camping-ground, where we determined to halt. After doing so fair a journey from last night's resting-place to this day's camp, I still felt so desirous of more exercise, that I took a cast to the eastward of our intended course on the morrow, to see what game was on the move. I never felt the air more invigorating, every breath bringing renewed energy and a desire for further work. In fact I possessed that sensation which is so graphically expressed by the American when he says, 'I feel all here.' I knew full well that I was in splendid shooting fettle, and that no deer which offered me anything like a fair shot would go off scatheless. I felt assured, indeed, that I could not only hit it, but almost place my lead in what part of the carcase I desired.

The walking was particularly good, the soil firm but springy, and the landscape presented a varied picture. The small timber was broken up into numerous detached clumps. Where the ground was open and grassy wild strawberry-plants were coming up in the utmost profusion, and in some places they were packed so closely that I frequently wished it had been later in the season that I might have enjoyed an abundant feed of them. We all know what a favourite the cultivated berry is; but these little wild ones are infinitely superior in delicacy of flavour.

When ascending the gradual slope of a dip in the land, I was induced to look to the left by hearing such a noise as might be occasioned by an animal hurriedly passing through brush. In a moment after a fine specimen of the black-tailed deer came in view, going at speed, and crossed me at something like eighty yards' range. I pitched my gun well in front, pulled the trigger, and a welcome thud proclaimed the result. The gallant buck struggled hard to retain his feet, but, with all his efforts, he was able only to go about a dozen more paces, when, down the incline, he pitched on his shoulder, and almost turned a summersault from the impulse with which he ran. Satisfied that the game was dead, as soon as I loaded again I turned up to the clump of brush from whence it had come, fully believing that some unknown intruder, and not myself, had started it. I could see nothing, however, except a hare which jumped out of its form—a pretty good proof that no dangerous creature was in the vicinity.

On returning I bled my quarry, and then left it, intending to take as much of the venison as could be carried conveniently when I retraced my steps to camp. Topping the next swell of land I found that a charming mountain-stream babbled down the hollow at my feet. As water-courses are always attractive, whether they be giant rivers or diminutive rills, I directed my steps to it. Although in places not more than a couple of yards wide, it swarmed with fish. From every shoal, and from under each bank, the bright silvery beauties rushed, alarmed by my approach. For half-an-hour I sat perched upon a rock watching a most enticing little pool, which, from the colour of the water at the upper end, had the appearance of great depth, but gradually became more and more shallow towards its exit, till not more than a few inches covered the clear pebbly channel it flowed over in pursuing its downward course. This spot was just of that size that the fly-fisherman could, with ordinary length of line, cover its every corner ; and fortunate would have been the disciple of the gentle art who got such a chance, for every second the dark tortoise-shell-coloured back, or the many brilliant-hued flanks of a trout, would break the surface-water by the precipitous splash it made to secure its insect prey. Canny Scotland, with its purple moors and mountains, its babbling brooks and rocky crags, rose in my memory, and asked not to be remembered less because the rival country in which I was then travelling was quite as lovely to gaze on. But I have neglected to mention an addition to the attraction of the scene—a large white-headed eagle (*H. leucocephalus*)—fitting emblem of the great republic—which hovered aloft as if guarding this demesne from all intruders. When a lazy half-hour had rapidly passed, I turned to the right-about to pick up my load of venison before proceeding to camp. On gaining the ridge that overlooked the spot where the game lay, I was surprised to see a bear, evidently intent in burying the slain deer. Bruin's manner was exactly that of a domestic cat. He did his work gingerly and superficially, occasionally leaving it, but immediately returning to inspect it again, and scratch a few more twigs and grass over his treasure. At length, when he had accomplished his task, he started, but as if unwilling to abandon so precious a prize, he halted again when he had gone about twenty-five yards, and then hurried off at a rapid pace. As I expected, however, that his absence would not be long, I remained in my concealment, waiting for his reappearance. Ten minutes had scarcely passed when two wolves rose from behind a rock, and with the impetuosity of a brace of greyhounds rushed upon the buck. They had been between me and the bear, and as I was to the leeward of all, they had the advantage of Bruin by being to windward of him. The bear's conduct was on the whole rather unaccountable. From his manner I now feel certain that he imagined he was being watched; but if so, what induced him to go off, except, possibly, to communicate to his mate or cubs intelligence of the windfall he had discovered. I am surprised that he did not take the buck with him, for if he had not far to carry it, a bear's strength would not be much taxed by the weight. These wolves, although hunting together, did not appear to be united by any tie of friendship, for they snarled and snapped at each other with the most vindictive animosity while standing over their prey.

After a protracted scene of wrangling, the larger wolf commenced operations on the deer's stomach,—the lesser on the neck; and although there was sufficient and to spare for both, at intervals they would cease eating and have a defiant growl at each other, after which, as if their appetites had been increased by this exertion, they set to again with increased vigour. But if they had known how short a time was allotted for their feast, they, doubtless, would have given more uninterrupted attention to the business of satisfying their appetites, for Bruin again appeared upon the scene in a state of great excitement. For a moment the wolves looked inclined to dispute possession, but their courage failed them, and they reluctantly gave way, but only to take up a position as spectators a few yards off.

It is currently reported that, when a bear buries his prey, all the other wild animals show their respect to the sexton by passing it by without attempting to appropriate it. The spectacle which I saw seemed to be rather an exception to the rule. When at length I made my appearance, going towards the carcase, the wolves moved off to a safer distance, but Bruin did not show me so much respect, but plainly indicated that if I wished to obtain possession of the deer I must fight for it. Not being very short of food, however, and having no desire to shed blood unnecessarily, I left him in possession.

That night the temperature fell suddenly. At dark it felt almost sultry; by nine o'clock it was bitterly cold, with every indication of heavy rain. During my absence my companion had killed a yearling buck, so close to our halting-place that he had shouldered the carcase bodily and brought it into camp, where it was hung from a sapling within ten yards of our sleeping-place. Before turning in for the night I remarked to him on the probability of its attracting carnivorous marauders of the vicinity to our neighbourhood. 'Who cares?' was his reply. 'Well, if you don't, neither do I,' was my response; and in a few minutes more we were both asleep.

It might have been three o'clock—it was certainly more than an hour before daylight—when I was suddenly recalled from dreamland by the report of a rifle, followed by a yell, long, fierce, and vindictive. In a moment I was on my feet, gun in hand. From the flicker of the uncertain blaze of our nearly exhausted fire, I was able at once to comprehend the situation. Our deer had been almost dragged to the ground, and the lower portion of it was in the grasp of a puma, which was tearing at the carcase with teeth and claws. While the old man was reloading I took aim, and a messenger from each of my barrels cut the thread of life of the would-be thief.

My companion explained that the restlessness of the horses had awoke him, when on peering from his blanket to discover the cause of their uneasiness, he was a witness of the misappropriation of his property, and taking the law into his own hands had fired unsuccessfully. The puma, as he had only wounded him, unable to account for his suffering, was venting his rage on the dead deer when he received the *coup de grace*.

This animal was not higher, though it was longer, than a good-sized foxhound, and evidently was only two-thirds grown. The excitement of this adventure had so effectually banished sleep, that neither of us felt inclined again to court the drowsy god. So sitting up we rebuilt our fire, and listened to the howling of a second puma, who could not screw his courage up to the point of bringing himself within range of our arms.

Next morning there was ice on the stagnant pools, and cakes of it were floating in the stream. Wild fowl were also abundant; among which I noticed many specimens of wood-duck (*Anas oscura*), the first of that family I had observed this season. As they are well known at home on all our ornamental waters a description of them is unnecessary.

The appearance of the country, as we continued to progress northward, became far more picturesque. The scenery had a great resemblance to some portions of Montgomeryshire in Wales, only that the timber grew almost to the summit of the high grounds. Pines and other evergreen trees now predominating over every other variety of the vegetable kingdom, threw a sombre hue over the landscape, which required a bright sun to show it to the greatest advantage, a privilege not vouchsafed to us. Our course led us up a constant ascent, in parts very steep and tedious for the horse, forcing us both to march on foot the greater part of the day. Mosquitoes, to my great grief, were becoming very abundant. Oh, that this charming land could be delivered from such frightful plagues! Several wood-grouse, or Canadian partridge (*Tetrao Canadensis*), came under my observation, some of the young of which were almost half-grown.

CHAPTER XI.

BEAUTIFUL SCENERY — THE CHAIN-MOUSE — PLEASANT SHOWER-BATH — UNSUCCESSFUL ATTEMPT TO BRING DOWN A BUFFALO COW — SOLITARY REGION — ENDURING FATIGUE — BEAUTIFUL LAKE — COMMUNION WITH NATURE — WILD DUCK.

WE encamped at night near a small lake, with a long extent of elevated prairie-land at its north-east end, stretching off to a distant horizon. The bosom of this solitary sheet of water was literally covered with wild ducks, while beaver-houses and musk-rat dwellings were most abundant along its margin. While we were preparing the evening meal, both of these animals were seen in numbers, busily pursuing their respective avocations. At the hour of sunset, old Sol vouchsafed to show us his face at the moment when he was going to rest, attended by a host of bright-coloured clouds. The varied scenery, at once warmed and softened by the rich yet subdued light, was a fit subject for the brush of any artist.

The only sound that broke the silence of our contemplations was the voice of a wolf with a sore throat, or some other affection of the bronchial tubes, which every few minutes kept up a most dismal howling as if to solicit sympathy of his friends.

About three hours after dark I was lying in that semi-conscious state that precedes sleep, my jaws having several times relaxed their hold of my pipe-stem—a pretty good indication that I was approaching dreamland. The fragrant birch and hemlock-boughs on which I lay were so yielding that they invited me to repose, an invitation which I was on the point of accepting, when I was recalled to the realities of my position by the sound, in close proximity to me, of breaking limbs. I at once assumed that it was game feeding, and as the full moon was shining brightly, I picked up my double-barrel and stole towards the point from where the noise proceeded. Without even the mishap of breaking a rotten stick, I made a capital stalk towards the invisible quarry, but reached an opening on the edge of the wood without seeing the object of my search.

Listening, however, I detected a noise some way in front of me, the cause of which could not be far distant. I advanced towards it, therefore, but although everything favoured my progress, the only reward I received for all my trouble was that of seeing looming before me the figure of a large bull moose, as it hurried off in a direction that would soon give the brute my wind.

When in the woods at night, the ear is often struck by a short metallic note, which on this evening I heard with frequency and distinctness. For many a day I was ignorant of the cause of this peculiar sound, but I afterwards learned that it emanated from the little chain-mouse.

It being useless to remain abroad longer, I returned to camp, and listening for a time to the strange but attractive notes of the Whip-poor-will, unconsciously glided into repose, and slept a most delightful and refreshing sleep.

I rose with the sun in the morning, and enjoyed a pleasant shower-bath among the spray that fell from a neighbouring miniature cascade. The stream was alive with fish, whose rapid and eccentric movements were apparently so reckless and purposeless, that I began to imagine the scaly gentry, when in undisturbed retreats, were a very harebrained lot. Possibly on this brook there might be few foes—no formidable pikes, with ogre-like eyes, lying in ambush, ready to pounce out upon the unwary; no cruel fish-hawks, with massive talons, quick to swoop down upon the venturous, that floated too near the surface of their liquid home.

The Cockney angler, who travels all the way from his musty-looking town residence to Teddington or Reading, or even finds courage to visit the Lakes or Wales, where he may hook a few half-pound trout, if dropped on Bull-Moose Lake or tributaries, would find the realisation of his brightest dream relating to the capture of the finny tribe. He would not have to ·sit for hours watching an incorrigible float that would not go under water, although the unfortunate worm on the hook wriggled ever so indefatigably, and then return home with a stickle-back and three bites as the result of his day's sport.

Soon after starting, a buffalo cow in excellent condition came out of the bush in the vicinity of our path, and at a good pace went off to the eastward. As the ground was sound I thought to procure some beef for change in our diet. At first the pursued fairly ran away from me, but getting into very heavy ground, which I avoided by making a detour, she soon found me close alongside her flanks, which, in consequence of the violence of her struggle through the morass, were heaving from fatigue. Depressing the muzzle of my gun, I was just about to pull the trigger, when my horse put his foot into a hole and sent me, sky-rocket fashion, over his head, the concussion causing the hammer of each barrel to fall and explode their respective charges. Fortunately I was not hurt, and, more lucky still, did not break the stock of my faithful Dougal gun. On gathering myself together, I found my nag quietly feeding as if nothing had happened, and the buffalo cow still going at her best, and so far off that I was compelled to give up pursuit.

From the margin of this elevated piece of table-land, we struck off into woods which became more dense and sombre the further we advanced. The ground was now so rough that it was deemed more prudent to walk than ride. From this period; indeed, our quadrupeds were comparatively useless.

If a suitable purchaser could be found at our destination, I had resolved to dispose of them, and afterwards, if practicable, make my way on foot or by water to the Red River settlement.

For the two succeeding days, nothing broke the monotony of our course, for very little game was seen. From the roughness of the ground, our progress was slow. From the frequent tracks, however, I judged that the neighbourhood was not always so scantily supplied with animal life. In our route we had to traverse several diminutive streams that were crowded with fish, of which we were seldom able to obtain a supply for the support of the inward man. The trout which we caught were generally small, the size of the brooks operating as it does elsewhere against the growth of their inhabitants. Judging from past experience, I should consider this a splendid country for trapping the more valuable varieties of fur-covered animals; and am much surprised that none of the natives came under our notice, nor did we perceive any indication of their being in the habit of visiting this quarter, which is a dense solitude undisturbed by the presence of man.

No one can more appreciate the pleasure of change of scene than the traveller who has for days tramped through heavily-timbered land without getting a glimpse of objects separated from him by more than a hundred yards. In this instance, the weight of my pack, for the animals had not strength to carry much up such an ascent, added in no small degree to the disgust I felt with the monotony of a scene in which I was surrounded in all directions by pine-stems, all straight, all of the same colour, and all apparently exactly the counterpart of their neighbours.

When scenery is varied, more particularly if it be attractive, pleasure and admiration are excited; and thus, while the mind is actively employed, bodily ailments or fatigue are forgotten; but when there is nothing to distract the attention, the pressure of the pack-straps upon your shoulder, or the chaffing of the string of the mocassins, keep the wearied traveller in a constant state of irritation.

There are very few persons that I have met whom fortune has more favoured with the power of enduring fatigue than myself, but if there is one thing I abominate more than another, it is turning myself into a beast of burthen. On the occasion in question my load was not a heavy one, but the strap that attached it to me was most galling to my shoulder, which it deprived of a portion of the cuticle. Moreover, the journey had been tedious, and we had to traverse hemlock swamps, which were more than usually dense, while the soil beneath was so spongy that the indentation caused by the foot filled immediately after a step was made with water. Is it then to be wondered at, that I hailed with pleasure a gradual decrease in the closeness of the large timber, and a more varied growth of underbrush, both indications that we were about to make our exit from this region of densely-packed forest?

It was near sunset when my surmises that we were approaching an open space no longer remained doubtful. This conviction imparted to me additional vigour, and I unconsciously so sharpened my speed that my companion asked me in a querulous tone, 'where the deuce I was running to.' In a minute afterwards, a view broke upon us so charming, so tranquil, that I was forced to halt and contemplate it at leisure. We had before us a lake, the surface of which, smooth as that of a mirror, was studded with islands covered with the richest foliage. The water was as blue as that of the Mediterranean in the calmest day of summer, as transparent as crystal, and the banks were fringed with the darkest green leaves, while the hue of the distant hills resembled the softest shades of amber and purple; reminding me of those little lakes that have attracted so many delighted visitors to Cumberland.

Beneath a giant birch, hoary with lichen, venerable from the quantity of ragged bark that in dishevelled locks hung around its sides, we disencumbered ourselves of our loads. Although it was my turn to light the camp-fire and take charge of the culinary arrangements, my companion volunteered to perform these duties. I gladly accepted his offer, and wandered off to a distance, wishing to commune alone with the great and beautiful works that on every hand surrounded me. Man and his society

I like at times, but there is an irresistible fascination in solitary communion with Nature; for the sake of which I would abandon the most brilliant scenes of life and civilised society.

On a point of rock that jutted far into the clear, pellucid water I took my stand, and gazed on a scene of surpassing beauty. The sun, resembling an immense orb of fire, just touched the horizon, gilding the clouds with his own regal hues. While I was admiring this unequalled spectacle, my attention was distracted by a family of wild ducks, led by their mother, which came from some neighbouring sedge, and commenced feeding at my feet, not thirty yards intervening between me and the happy little coterie. As they were unaware of my presence, all their actions were natural; they were quite untrammelled by fear, and I watched their proceedings with the greatest pleasure.

Wild-duck, also, unencumbered by domestic ties, winged their way to favourite feeding-grounds, while white-headed eagles and heavy-flighted cranes pursued their course to their roosting-places. With these bidding the landscape good-night, I bowed my adieu ere the drop-curtain of darkness descended to shut out the scene.

Our frugal repast was soon discussed, the soothing pipe was smoked, and I enjoyed a sound sleep, disturbed neither by the owls' complaints to the moon, nor by the howls of the wolf serenading her garish majesty.

Next morning we started soon after sunrise, but ere we had proceeded a quarter of a mile I learned with the greatest regret that the noble birch, under which we had slept, had been set on fire. My friend, untroubled by sentimental considerations, had scraped the embers remaining from our fire against the trunk of the tree that had afforded us temporary shelter, and which gave permanent beauty to the landscape. The consequence was that its pendulous and highly inflammable bark was now in a blaze. If the tree was not killed, it must have been injured for years, and its charred body and limbs would ever afterwards remain a silent witness of the treatment it had received. Knowing remonstrance to be useless, I chewed the cud of bitterness and said nothing.

Around the southern margin of the lake, which we selected for our route as offering the more suitable course for continuing our journey, we passed through great quantities of aquatic weeds. Wild-duck flushed on every side, the old familiar mallard (*Anas boschas*) being by far the most numerous. From our constant association with these fowl, they being the progenitors of our common domestic duck, they usually attract little attention from any but the sportsman. This is scarcely fair, for the drake is as handsome as his race have proved useful. The Eastern and Western hemispheres are alike this noble bird's home, for it is found from the paddy-fields of China to the prairie-margined sloughs of the Far West. While the stamp of serfdom is on the domestic race, the wild beauty is proud and haughty, carries his head aloft, and through his bearing imparts to his variegated plumage an attraction that the farmyard waddler never possesses.

In their wild state migratory, the mallard and the pintails are almost the first to proclaim to the observer the advent of spring and the approach of winter. In America they breed on the margins of the numerous northern lakes that are beyond the route of traders or sportsmen, where they are free from all intrusion, the drake leaving to his mate all the responsibility and onus entailed by the rearing of a family. In their nests, which are rough and slovenly, the number of eggs sometimes amounts to twelve or fourteen. Immediately the young break the shell they are are able to paddle about, but do not obtain the powers of flight till almost of mature growth. It is unnecessary to describe their appearance, for what schoolboy cannot remember in some familiar barn-yard a green-headed drake, and a sombre-plumaged duck, which are in colour the counterparts of their wild relatives? The sportsman also is familiar with these birds, few other species having so often swelled the capacious maw of his game-bag; for, although wary, they are numerous, and not difficult to decoy or stalk if, not forgetting the importance of silence, due attention be paid to wind and cover. The mallards during the day, unless in stormy weather, remain at rest, either floating upon the surface of the water, or on the margin of a stream or lake. Towards sunset or sunrise they visit their feeding-grounds, the time of their appearance being much governed by the temperature and the wind. In tempestuous weather they throw off their shyness, and are less loth to approach the haunts of men. As the mallards feed almost entirely on grain when it can be procured, they are seldom indifferent human food : but should severe frosts drive them to the open sea for their sustenance, they become fishy and consequently disagreeable, even when served from the hands of the most skilful cook. Wild rice, which I believe grows only in American western waters, has immense attractions for the mallard. The sportsman who desires to accomplish their destruction has but to learn where this aquatic vegetable flourishes in abundance, and the season at which its seed is ripe, and in that locality he will find unlimited opportunities for sport.

After another day of hard travelling we found ourselves, almost for the first time, short of food. Although so far in the season, the day following was just such a one as we frequently experience in London in the month of February, when the poor man shivers over his scanty fire, or the little crossing-sweeper trembles with cold before the glowing windows of some luxurious club. This day I had a very severe attack of that commonplace complaint the 'blues.' Although my present position was of my own choosing, there were moments at which I could almost envy these poor vagrants in the streets of

London to whom one occasionally throws an odd copper, for I was perfectly drenched with rain which poured down in incessant showers. Who has not noticed the numerous little streams of water that flow from a thickly-coated water-spaniel immediately after he makes his exit from a river or pond? Although I did not possess the same facilities for collecting the descending streams, I feel assured that the volume of water which came out over my feet was quite equal in the aggregate. In fact, my clothes were a reservoir filled to overflowing, and only requiring to be squeezed or shaken to make their contents run out abundantly. The hemlock-trees and the white pine had drunk more than their fill of rain, and the excess that could not be absorbed by them was glistening from every branch. Each sough of the wind threw a heavy shower of the drops over the surrounding ground. Unwelcome, however, as was the task in such weather, food had to be obtained, and that could be done only by searching for it. So, with the locks of my gun as well protected with wrapping as could be, and carrying that valuable companion at the secure, I started eastward, being particular to note the 'lie' of the country and the principal landmarks, the better to prevent my losing my way.

To the backwoodsman and hunter nothing is of greater importance than a natural talent for acquiring a knowledge of locality, for in the wild lands over which they roam it is a most serious matter to lose one's way, that misfortune not unfrequently entailing death by starvation or fatigue. I suppose it must be the constant exercise of the bump of locality through successive generations that has rendered the North American Indian so sure a guide through pathless forests and over boundless prairies, an instinct, if I may so term it, in which the red man has infinitely the advantage over his white brother.

CHAPTER XII.

BLACK SPRUCE—MINIATURE LAKE—THE MINK—NATURAL ARBOUR—UNSUCCESSFUL STALK AFTER A COW MOOSE—THE CANADA PORCUPINE—SNIPE—WATER-SNAKES—CURLEWS—ROASTED OWL—ENCAMPED ON THE MARGIN OF A LAKE—INGRATITUDE OF A GREY WOLF.

AFTER traversing a considerable space of thickly-wooded, low-laying ground, I came out on rolling prairie sparsely covered with trees. Its surface was extremely irregular, making the walking unusually laborious, for boulders of every size and shape, covered over with a thick and many-coloured clothing of moss, lay around on all sides. To the left, standing alone, bursting from a fissure in the rock, grew a large black spruce, towards which, as it was the most prominent feature in the foreground of the landscape, I directed my steps. The regular growth of this tree always renders it attractive; its cones make it a favourite with young folks; and the favourite summer-beer being procured from it, the good housewife is not without a feeling of tenderness towards it. In the northern New England States, and in the provinces, it is abundant, and consequently has always been associated in my mind with civilisation. The one before me was the first representative of its race I had seen so far to the westward, and, as might be expected, it recalled the past, transferring memory back to a time when I enjoyed the society of kind friends and valued companions, illuminated by the light of merry laughing eyes. Its constant drip, however, soon drove me off; the wanderer in a strange land could find no shelter under its rain-charged branches.

From the vicinity of this tree, however, I obtained a view that caused me to alter my direction. About half a mile further to the left I perceived a miniature lake, the waters of which, under the scourging influence of the fitful blast, fretted and wasted their strength against their rocky boundary. Several mergansers, doubtless tired with the bobbing about they had received from the diminutive waves that disturbed the surface of their favourite element, stood upon the beach beyond the influence of the tiny breakers. Although these birds are generally wild, on this occasion my presence was disregarded by them; and while I stood within fifty yards, those whom the noise of my approach had awakened again replaced their heads under their wings, and in perfect confidence resigned themselves to repose. Meanwhile, remaining perfectly motionless, I scanned carefully the limited horizon. Not a sound proclaimed the vicinity of other animal life, when the ducks, giving utterance to their shrill call of alarm, suddenly took flight. One of the retreating birds exhibited a broken pen-feather in the wing, and

Q

a few fleecy fragments from its breast or coverts floated on the breeze—evidence that I was not the only creature seeking wherewith to satisfy my appetite.

The unknown disturber of the repose of these wild fowls was a mink (*Putorius vison*), a fur-bearing animal widely scattered throughout those parts of North America where lakes and rivers are abundant. The little marauder, which was evidently ignorant of my presence, appeared for a few seconds upon a stone that was some inches above the water, and several yards from its margin. In its weasel-like face and round sharp eye, curiosity was strongly marked, but on noticing me it slipped off its perch and disappeared.

This little animal, which is peculiar to America, has a beautiful pelt, much valued on account of its fineness and rich brown colour. Partially web-footed it is very aquatic in habits, and lives indifferently on all descriptions of small game and fish. Generally easily trapped, and its skin commanding a large price, it is eagerly sought after by the Indian and backwoodsman.

Turning off still further to the left, the ground, as it diminished in elevation, was clothed with more cover. Beneath an overhanging rock I discovered an admirable natural arbour, which might have been rendered perfectly rain-proof by the exercise of a little ingenuity, and the outlay of a small portion of time. Here I made a halt, and treated myself to a pipe. No wonder the weed is popular. It is a better companion than a quarrelsome member of our own race, for it soothes the wearied traveller, while such a companion irritates him.

I had just rested long enough to feel so stiff that I was rather disinclined to leave my seat, when a sound which I well knew told me that game, fit food for any mortal, was close at hand. It was a cow moose talking to her progeny, in a voice soft, low, and melodious, full of solicitude and affection.

Stiffened with the damp and cold, I made slow and awkward efforts to rise, getting on my feet with some difficulty. Utter silence and the greatest stealth were necessary to give me the slightest promise of success, for there is not an animal that roams the forest gifted with greater powers of scent and hearing, or which more unremittingly exercises these qualities. Listening, again, the fretful warning voice once more reached my ear, certainly not more than a hundred yards off. I crept from brush to stone, from stone to brush, having the wind all right, and came at last so near that I could hear the rustling of their movements, still I saw nothing, though once more I heard the baby whispering, so near, that I was surprised I could not see the game. On hands and knees, dragging my stomach on the ground, I attempted to stalk a little further. My sight and hearing were both strained to the greatest tension, and directed to that spot where I believed my quarry lay. Inch after inch I got over the ground. By Jove, I said to myself, if this goes on much longer I shall be stirring up the old cow with the muzzle of my double-barrel; but this was a rather rashly formed conclusion. Taking no observation of what was in my immediate vicinity, I placed my hand upon a hare, which had been asleep till thus ruthlessly disturbed. Which was the more surprised and disconcerted it would be impossible for an impartial judge to decide. I was recalled to the purpose of my present position by hearing the crushing and snapping of brushwood, which clearly told me that my game were off, with a speed that rapidly placed between me and them a wide range of country.

Deeply mortified, out of sorts, hungry, and uncomfortable from the continued state of moisture in which I had remained, I got back to camp, but not without losing my way. It was so late when I reached it, that the little Acadian owls (*Ulula Acadia*) had been for more than an hour singing forth their mysterious bell-like note.

My companion was a better trapper than myself, but he was not so good a hunter. If small game or 'varmint' graced our board, their presence was owing to his skill, when larger and more substantial diet was provided it was usually due to my prowess; and this day the tables were not turned. A savoury stew was in the pot, and several pieces of meat were poised on pointed stakes, sputtering out their fat. My friend complacently nodded when he saw me, accompanying that sign of recognition by a gr[...] way of welcome, at the same time winking and po[...] ing with his knife to some pounds of flesh which lay close by.

Noway wishing to interfere in the cooking arrangements, I eyed the scene with complacency, and inhaled the odours streaming forth to leeward with greater satisfaction than those small boys who muster round a cook-shop, for I knew I was about to become intimate with the fragrant viands, whereas they, poor fellows! rarely, if ever, get on such intimate terms with the steaming joints on which their hungry eyes are so eagerly fixed. At length the moment for assault arrived, and for minutes nothing was heard but the smacking of the cook's lips and the satisfactory grunts that issued from his mouth as he partook of the rich feast which he had provided. And what does the reader suppose we were discussing with so much gusto?—a large portion of a well-fed porcupine which had been so unfortunate as to fall into our hands.

Although assured by a celebrated naturalist that the porcupine of the Atlantic sea-board states is not found in the Far West, my experience has led me to form a different opinion, as this specimen and numerous others I had seen in this part of the world exactly corresponded in appearance with the animal I had known so well in New England.

The Canada porcupine (*Erethizon dorsatus*) is harmless to everything but trees. Although more frequently seeking its food by night, it is not strictly speaking nocturnal. Partial to all varieties of wild fruit, it more especially evinces a liking for straw and blueberries. When attacked by dogs it endeavours to get its head into a hole, and while thus protected in front keeps its assailants at defiance by violently striking its tail, armed with innumerable quills, to the right and left. The prey of many wild animals, its assailants do not always come off scathless, for even the puma has been known to die from wounds caused by some detached spines of this animal sticking in its mouth. In size it much resembles the common porcupine (*Hystrix cristatus*), but is longer and stands less high upon the legs. As food for man it is excellent. When made into a stew, with an abundance of vegetables, the peculiar rich flavour of its flesh justly entitles it to be considered even a delicacy. The quills, which are easily stained any colour, are used by the Indians for their decorative work. The skill with which they are blended, and the beauty of pattern made with them by the Aborigines, have long been subjects of admiration.

As they produce a very strong trail and are slow of foot, they are soon driven into a tree or easily overtaken by dogs. A very small blow on the head instantly deprives them of life.

Although this porcupine weighed over twenty pounds, it is almost with shame I acknowledge that nearly half of it was consumed at that meal. Next morning when we awoke the remainder had been carried off; the foot-tracks of a wolf plainly showing who had been the thief.

There is a wonderful difference between hunting *pour passer le temps* and being compelled to hunt that you may obtain the wherewith to satisfy the cravings of appetite.

To-day I started on an empty stomach, with that sinking feeling I have often experienced when kept waiting longer than usual for breakfast, in fact that very sensation that often induces the dissipated to satisfy their craving by a soda-and-brandy. We are only mortal at best, and I believe myself extremely so, for I have a decided tendency to like this beverage. The popping of the cork of a soda-water bottle would then have been to my ears the very sweetest strain of music imagination could conceive.

I can joke now about it, but my position at the time was far from agreeable, for I had slept badly, was wet through, rather stiff from indications of rheumatism, and decidedly down in spirits. As I was determined, however, if possible, not to go any longer without grub, I settled down to my task and trudged on manfully. The scenery was rather gloomy, quite in harmony with the state of my feelings, while the heavy leaden clouds hung close to the surface, completely keeping out the rays of the sun. Snipe (*Scolopax Wilsonii*) at every step continued flushing before me, while large flocks of plovers (*Charadrius apricarius*) rushed here and there over the surface of such places as were bare; or, uttering their little piping notes, took wing, frightened by my proximity, and sought retreats which they regarded as more secure.

For several days past my ear had been greeted by a new sound. Several times I halted, with the hope of finding out what produced it, but I was for a time unsuccessful; I expected that it emanated from a bird, and this supposition, I think, led me astray. Imagine, therefore, my surprise when I at length obtained convincing proof that it proceeded from a large description of water-snake. The manner in which I made this discovery was rather strange. As I was moving onwards, I was surprised to see a large flat stone turned over, twenty yards in front of me, without any apparent cause to account for the phenomenon. In the indentation which its weight had made in the soil, I observed a dozen or more of these reptiles forming a perfect Gordian knot; and, on stirring them up with my stick, they expressed their objection to such cavalier treatment by uttering the short, unknown sound, the origin of which had so much puzzled me.

On the high grounds, some way removed from the bed of the river, I saw several pairs of curlews (*Scolopax borealis*), which were evidently there for the purpose of nesting. As I had ever found it the case with all this family, they were extremely wild, not permitting me to approach them nearer than one hundred yards. They are a much more showy bird in plumage than our English species, and strike me as much stronger on the wing. I have killed them frequently near Cape May, and on several occasions on the prairies. As they are well worthy of the sportsman's notice, I will describe them. The head is dark-brown, with a longitudinal mark over each eye, and one up the forehead, of buff. The iris is of a dirty-brown colour. The breast is very pale cinnamon-brown; the back of the neck, dark and light-brown in alternate lines; back, cinnamon-coloured, with dark-brown bars, and edged with spots of white towards the tail-coverts; the belly and vent, white; the latter in portions showing a tendency to brown; tarsi, greenish lead colour. From end of bill to termination of tail, this bird is twenty-one inches long, and thirty-two across the wings.

In pursuing the curlew, great skill and patience are generally necessary in order to bring the sportsman within gunshot. They also require very hard hitting, being capable of carrying off as much shot as a wood-pigeon. If one is disabled and left struggling on the ground, it will attract to the spot all its companions within sight. Is it not too bad to take advantage of these creatures and deprive them of life when they are exhibiting so noble a trait in their character; while they are illustrating the parable of the good Samaritan, for, doubtless, they collect on such occasions to condole or help their wounded fellows?

In Labrador I have frequently found the nest of

this species of curlew. The name commonly applied to them in the United States, that of Esquimaux-curlew, has doubtless been suggested by the fact that they frequent that northern region in summer. Their eggs are very large, and not unlike those of the lapwing in colour.

They feed upon shell-fish and aquatic insects, become very fat soon after they have terminated their migration, and are a great delicacy when well cooked, except when they exclusively confine their diet to hermit-crabs, which has the effect of giving their flesh a rank taste.

Some readers might not unjustly inquire, why, in the presence of so much animal life, I remained hungry? My explanation is that I possessed no shot sufficiently small to kill plover and snipe, while the larger curlews would not permit me to come within range of them.

Where all the deer had gone was beyond conception. That they had once roamed over this neighbourhood in great numbers was very apparent, for on every hand their old tracks could be discerned; yet not one could I now see. What could be the cause of this? The only reason I could imagine was that there must have been a pack of wolves in the neighbourhood, which had very lately been making this their hunting-ground. A jolly life these marauders must lead, when they select for their retreat a locality as free from human intrusion as this. With comfortable dens, plenty of food, abundance of sport, jolly companions, and no anxiety about dress, their time must pass very pleasantly. Enjoy it while you can, your hunting-ground, like the Indians', will soon be wrested from you.

Indefatigable as I was in my tramp after game,—for I was urged on by hunger,—the only live animal I came across was a Canadian owl. On a previous occasion, when similarly hard-up for food, I had once attempted to eat one of these gentry, an experiment which I think I can safely promise never to repeat or forget. I had been out in search of sport on the northern shores of Lake Huron, one of the most desolate regions, and possessed of less game than any other locality I wot of. I was going home with an empty game-bag, and a stomach almost as empty, the shades of night falling around me, and no prospect of anything wherewith to break my fast; when, about a quarter of a mile from the encampment, one of the companions of Minerva, from the summit of a lofty pine, thought fit to disturb the solitude by exercising his vocal powers. A single note betrayed his retreat; and, ere he had time to emit a second, a ball from my rifle brought him struggling to the ground. In the prospect of being able at last to appease my hunger, I gloated over my prize, smacking my lips when I thought of the feast in store for me. As I hurried home, I stole a march on time by plucking the snow-white plumage of my victim, that there might be no delay in the preparation of my anticipated banquet. When ready for the spit, the appearance of my *bonne bouche* was far from tempting, notwithstanding the ingenuity I displayed in trussing it. The fact is, it appeared to me to have more resemblance to the body of a baby than to that of any fowl I had ever seen.

A London poulterer, I had no doubt, with that happy ingenuity which they possess, would, by breaking the breast-bone, and performing sundry other operations, have rendered my prize not only plump in appearance, but enticing to the eye. Although frizzled meat of almost every description smells about the same, I had no sooner commenced roasting this owl than I remarked that it did not smell like anything with which I was acquainted, except, possibly, a cage in which white mice or guinea-pigs had been kept.

At length it was done to a turn; and the better to enjoy my anticipated feast I selected the softest part of a log for my seat. Drawing my hunting knife, I then tried to amputate a limb; but I could not dissolve the partnership. At mess I always enjoyed the credit of being a respectable carver, and was therefore surprised at my lack of skill on the present occasion; but, remembering how fresh was the game, how blunt my knife, and how awkward my position, I renewed my efforts, and at length a leg was sawn off, in a mangled state. By the drumstick end I picked it up, and inserted it between my teeth; but when they closed on the anticipated delicacy, they found they lacked the strength to penetrate a substance as firm as glue and as stringy as cat-gut. The flavour was—well, the least said soonest mended. I threw the repulsive carcase away, carefully wiped my knife, in case any of the fragments of the unsavoury morsel should remain attached to it, and give it a taste and odour which would not leave it for days. As I put it into my pocket I could not help moralising—a capital thing to do when hungry—to the effect that, smart as I imagined myself, yet I, like others, was sometimes sold. My pointer, who, like others of the same species, was of a very hungry type,—a fellow that could crack into splinters a shank mutton-bone, or pick out tit-bits from a squatter's ash-pit in a nearly thoroughly decomposed state and apparently enjoy them, actually, on being offered owl, turned his nose up, and steadfastly refused to touch it. I need not say that after such experience as this, hungry as I was, I spared the emblem of wisdom. Happily my forbearance was rewarded, for when I joined the old man, who had pushed forward with the horses, I found that he had captured another porcupine, of which we made our evening meal.

Our camp was this night on the margin of a lake several miles long, which, from the transparency and colour of its waters, I judged to be very deep. The scenery that surrounded its north-west shore was grand in the extreme, perpendicular rocks rising in some places from the water's edge to an elevation of over a hundred feet, while from every crack and fissure hung luxuriant evergreen shrubs, inducing in the mind of the spectator a feeling of astonishment that they could retain their position in situations apparently so ill adapted for their growth.

While engaged in cooking, a very large grey wolf came out of the bush, and, coolly seating himself in the open, viewed with envious eyes our provisions. As he was probably hungry, like ourselves, I conquered for the moment my feelings of hostility, and left him unmolested to enjoy a feast in imagination.

When we had finished supper, I was generous enough to leave the refuse for his use. Having collected the fragments, I placed them on a rock about fifty yards from our camp, and the moment after I retired the powerful jaws of the beggar were hard at work, performing their labours so satisfactorily that in a few minutes not a particle remained. Like all his race, however, he was incapable of any feeling but that of the basest ingratitude, for not half-an-hour after my act of charity, the skulking scoundrel was seen in such close proximity to one of the horses and with such an unmistakable look of guilty intentions in his countenance, that I had not the slightest doubt he was only waiting for an opportunity to convert the quadruped into carrion.

So disreputable a scoundrel was not fit to live, and his death-warrant was signed, the sentence being carried out by means of a pill warranted to cure all earthly ills.

Although unable to capture any fish, I saw that this lake swarmed with them. Several immense trout, perfect leviathans of their race, continued rising within stone-throw of the margin. White fish also were constantly passing by in shoals, floating so close to the surface that their dorsal fins were frequently out of the water. With such an abundance of wholesome food within sight, it was rather tantalising not to be able to obtain some of it.

It was with regret I saw most clearly that unless we reached our destination soon our poor animals would be utterly knocked up from fatigue and want of food. They were, without exaggeration, regular bags of bones, possessed neither of energy nor of strength. I would willingly have left them here, in the hope that the return party might find them; but if such a course had been adopted, they would not have survived twenty-four hours, as the wolves would have been certain to take advantage of their unprotected condition, and harass them to death.

My companion informed me this evening that he was beginning to fear that he was out of his reckoning, for, to the best of his calculation, we had travelled all the necessary distance to transfer us from the camp we had left to the one we sought. A pleasant prospect truly! Still there was no use murmuring; the old fellow had done his best, and 'the best can do no more.' 'A stout heart to a stiff brae,' is a good old Scotch saying. Remembering it, I determined to prove to the satisfaction of my old friend—for often he had expressed opinions to the contrary—that there were other nationalities as well as his own possessed of what he was pleased to denominate 'true grit.'

About noon, as we were slowly traversing some wet, open ground, which was almost sticky enough to be designated a swamp, and which was trying most severely the strength of the nags, I almost succeeded in obtaining a shot at an immense bull-moose. When first I saw him he was straddling down a sapling to get at the leaves, but the distance was too great to hope for a killing shot. I endeavoured, therefore, to shorten the range, and, while doing so, the noise produced by the horses caused him such alarm that he suddenly decamped. However, we were not destined to go supperless to roost. Shortly before halting I obtained a chance to rake a flock of wild-ducks (*Anas boschas*). Although the missiles in my gun were buck-shot, so closely did the birds float together, that I killed six at one discharge. If possessed of an abundance of small shot, the sportsman here need never be in dread of short commons, for both Canadian and ruffed grouse, as well as ducks, and other varieties of feathered game, are plentiful. Buck-shot is not suited for rapid shooting at small objects, more particularly when many of the discharges must be snap-shots. My having nothing smaller in size than the missiles mentioned was the cause that our provision of food was often reduced to the lowest ebb.

CHAPTER XIII.

GOOD CAMPING-GROUND — NIGHT FISHING ON THE LAKE — TRAPPERS' STOCK-HOUSE — SALE OF MY QUADRUPEDS — IMMENSE SWAMP — THE AMERICAN RAIL — BEAUTIFUL SCENERY — MY DEBUT IN RAIL-SHOOTING — MY 'PUSHER' SOLD.

AT night we found a good camping-ground, with many indications scattered around to show that it had been employed previously for a similar purpose. The horses, also, were not so badly off, for among the sedge on the margin of the lake they appeared to obtain an abundance of aquatic vegetation suited to their palates. In front of us was a beautiful little island, covered with trees to the water's edge. Swamp-maple, birch, and elm, were interspersed with pine, hemlock, and cedar, thus removing much of the sombre hue so common in the northern portion of the American landscape.

About half-an-hour after dark to our surprise a light upon the water was distinctly visible, moving slowly along towards the north. My companion saw it at the same moment as I did; but possibly doubting the veracity of his eyes, made no remark. The more I gazed, the more certain I became of the correctness of a supposition I had formed that it was the torch-light of fishermen.

At once I piled more fuel on the embers that

remained from our fire, and a flame soon blazed joyfully aloft. The unknown tried to outstrip us by heaping fuel on their fire, for it sent forth a loftier flame than previously. They had evidently recognised our signal, for their course was now directly towards us. In twenty minutes afterwards, the welcome sound of voices speaking our own tongue hailed us. The strangers were the persons we sought.

Never in the whole course of my life was I more agreeably surprised than with the three men who landed from the canoe. I had expected them to be similar to the crowd from whom they were an offshoot, but the case was quite the reverse, thus accounting for their dissolution of partnership. All were dressed in rough attire, but their manner was kind, and denoted education. The principal, who was about five-and-thirty, and did not stand over five feet six, looked and spoke like a gentleman, and he, with the others, extended to us a most hearty welcome, offering us a share of their camp, and food as long as we thought proper to accept their hospitality. In a trice a number of their best fish were cooking on our fire, and every office that demanded exertion was executed by them in spite of all we could say to the contrary. Our poor horses, even, received their attentions, and many a word of condolence was vouchsafed them, many a caress was bestowed upon them, intermingled with expressions of commiseration for their shattered condition.

Before retiring it was arranged that my companion and myself should accompany the chief in their canoe to camp, while the two others drove our horses round the top of the lake—an indifferent route of some distance, on which walking was a very tedious affair.

A little after sunrise we embarked, and before three hours our voyage terminated. We landed in a sheltered cove, where birch and hemlock kissed the water. Soon after we entered a rough stock-house, admirably suited for the purpose for which it was intended, clean as a barrack-room, but unfortunately smelling strongly of the numerous furs with which its upper floor was packed. After suffering from short commons and protracted fatigue, the first few days devoted to rest, if provided with plenty of the necessaries of life, are truly delightful, more particularly if associated with persons agreeable to your taste. Thus a week passed, each day being spent as its predecessor, till again I commenced to long for change and excitement, a desire which was soon to be gratified, for the party of trappers whose guests we were had arranged to start in a few days for the south, in order to engage in their annual summer trade, viz., dispose of their stock of peltries, and lay in ammunition, traps, and groceries for the coming winter.

As my beasts of burthen were of no further use to me, I disposed of them to the chief man, with feelings of great regret, but satisfied at least in one respect, viz., that they had obtained a kind and feeling master. Several times I had the idea of knocking them on the head, to prevent their having to endure a repetition of the trials which they had suffered when with me, but having a desire for cash, I argued successfully against my thoughts, and was thus induced to spare them. After all, were they not playing the part destined for them?—and if they could still be useful to my fellow-men, how selfish would it have been in me to have wantonly sacrificed their lives.

The fourth day after our arrival here, when wandering to the westward of our camp I discovered an immense stretch of swamp. Wild fowls of many varieties were most abundant, also that noble bird, the sand-hill crane, whose whooping notes I could incessantly hear, although hovering so far aloft as to be beyond the reach of vision. Another most interesting feathered beauty abounding here was the American rail (*Rallus Carolinus*), which is frequently called by those persons who reside in the vicinity of its haunts, the 'sorra,' and which resembles in many respects our familiar land-rail or corn-crake. It is migratory, arriving in, and disappearing from, the localities which it frequents with wonderful precision of date. As this bird is so much prized as a table delicacy, and affords a favourite pastime to the lovers of sport, a description of its appearance and habits, as well as of the method employed in its pursuit, may not be uninteresting.

Among the writings of an observant naturalist I find the following short and precise sketch of its distinguishing peculiarities :—' The American rail is nine inches long and fourteen across the wings ; bill, yellow, and blackish towards the point, with black stripe down the throat ; sides of the crown, neck, and upper parts generally olive brown, streaked with black on a brown olive ground, and edged with white; wings, plain olive brown; tertials marked with black and long lines of white ; tail, pointed and dusky olive brown, lined with black ; lower part of the breast marked with semi-circular lines of white on a light ash ground ; belly, white ; vent, brownish buff; legs, feet, and naked parts of the thighs, yellowish green, eyes, reddish hazel. The female has little or no black on the head, the throat white, and the plumage generally of a lighter colour, and more inclined to olive than in the male.'

From this description it will be seen that these birds are more than usually attractive in colours, but they blend so admirably, and harmonise so beautifully, that it is almost impossible to distinguish them at a short distance, when among the water-loving plants that luxuriate in their chief haunts. This peculiarity, combined with their extraordinary speed of foot, enables them, with comparative safety, to frequent places that, but for these wise provisions of nature, would be fatal to their existence, for, like nearly all creatures provided with the means of fleeing from danger, they are harmless and timid, becoming an easy prey whenever opportunity offers, to hawks, snakes, and numerous other vermin.

When on the wing the rail appears too heavy to accomplish more than the shortest flight, while the limbs hang down as if they were dragging their proprietor to the ground by their weight.

It may be imagined how easy a shot the rail then presents for the sportsman; but this tardiness of locomotion only exists for a few seconds after taking wing and when near the surface of the ground, for when a certain elevation is obtained, such for instance as is required for distant flights, its progress through the air is both sustained and rapid.

Migratory in the strict acceptation of the term, rails accomplish journeys of great length, which are always performed in the night, from which circumstance have doubtless arisen many of the marvellous stories of their mysterious performances told by the ignorant. Being peculiarly sensitive to cold weather, they do not come north until a return of frost for the season has ceased to be probable, while the journey to the southward is undertaken at such a time in autumn as will enable them to avoid all possibility of similar mishaps. Thus they do not remain over three months on their northern feeding-grounds, the remainder of the year being spent in the mangrove-swamps of Central America and reed-margined lagoons of southern Mexico.

On their influx into their summer retreats, they are very low in flesh, and impart to the observer an impression of suffering from extreme weakness. Only a few days, however, are required for their restoration, when they become fat and throw off all indication of lassitude. In this condition they are a great table delicacy, and can be oftener and more freely partaken of than any description of fowl with which I am acquainted. Their sensitiveness to a depression of temperature, on the advent of cold weather, is one of their peculiar characteristics. The marsh which absolutely swarmed with them to-day, to-morrow will be deserted, though the thermometer has only fallen a few degrees. When such an exodus has taken place, the observer may feel assured that cold weather is not far distant.

The fluvial portion of the majority of North American streams that enter the sea south of the Hudson, overflows an immense extent of low-lying meadow-land, covered with great varieties of aquatic weeds, but principally with the *Zizania aquatica*, or wild reed, whose seed seems to be the favourite food of this rail, for when it is ripe these birds are always more abundant, stronger on the wing, and more delicate of flavour. In fact, I believe it plays as important a part in reference to the sorra as the *Valisinera* does to the canvas-back duck. Although the stems of this reed are very tall, their intermediate parts are laced together by broken-down and decaying vegetation, forming a kind of platform over the less entwined roots. Under this screen, hid from the eyes of their numerous winged foes, the rails find their food. It is but seldom that a human being can obtain a look into these obscure haunts. On one occasion I was able to command a view of several yards through a natural vista, probably opened by a current. Such an opportunity of acquiring an insight into the habits of these timid birds I could not let pass. After remaining nearly a quarter of an hour in a state of perfect quiescence, the feathered strangers seemed to gain confidence. Coming to the conclusion apparently that my boat was tenantless, several mild but suspicious eyes were seen taking observations, first from one and then from another tuft of vegetable *débris*. Satisfied with the inspection, the birds came successively into or crossed the line of my sight. Previous to this I was disposed to believe the diet of rails almost entirely vegetable, but I now learned that animal food was not objected to. The rapidity of this bird when on the ground is surprising, its feet moving so rapidly that they can scarcely be distinguished as they run. On such occasions the body is reached forward and depressed very low in front, while their tails nervously and incessantly twitch every few moments.

All seasons and places have their peculiar attractions, and the beauty of some of these immense marshes, covered with a wild crop of the richest and ripest hues, is very remarkable. The dense growth of water-plants, gently waving before the last breath of the breeze as it dies out with the declining day, the whole mellowed with the soft, subdued, hazy light of such a sunset as follows a warm summer day, forms a scene that can always be remembered with pleasure. Sometimes the extent of these tidal overflowed lands is so great, that the navigator of the numerous water-courses that traverse them, or the rail-shooter who poles his way over their bosom at high tide, can see nothing but a wide expanse of plumed reeds, transferring to the mind similar impressions of boundlessness to those that strike you on first viewing the great prairies of the Far West. There are, I suppose, some people who care not for such scenes; who, if alone in such a spot, with nought but God's untutored children for companions, would sigh for the busy haunts of man and the dissipations of city life. Well, every one to his taste! but the note of the little reed-warbler, the sight of the ever-changing, yet always mathematical figures formed by a flight of duck, the sound caused by the croaking of the bull-frog, or the melancholy but sweet and appealing call of the curlew, are as elevating, as purifying to my mind as a stroll through a graveyard, or an hour spent under the lofty roof, in the subdued light of Westminster Abbey. Thoughts and impressions such as these can be obtained by all whose temperament is similar to my own, nowhere better than in the haunts of the sorra-rail.

Delaware, Pennsylvania, and New Jersey in all probability are the most celebrated places for rail-shooting; but it must not be imagined that these birds are confined to these localities alone. The wet prairies of Western Indiana, the sloughs of

Illinois, the gigantic marsh that margins the Detroit river to the northward and eastward, are also their homes; but the latter localities, not being subject to the influences of tides, such quantities cannot be obtained by the sportsman as in the former states. Nevertheless, I believe from observation that they more frequently select them as their breeding-grounds.

When residing in the vicinity of the grand prairie during those months that constitute the close season, when game was sacred even to me, a keen sportsman living, as many believe, only to wantonly shed blood, I have frequently in the cool of the summer evening, when giving my setters a run, found the young of this rail, little, soft, shapeless, awkward, timid creatures, clothed in a dark suit of burnt cork-coloured plumage, capable of making good use of their legs, but most amusingly awkward in their movements when forced to take flight. A noble old setter, who was a perfect retriever, and often took liberties with me on account of the length and strength of our affection for each other, has frequently brought me one of these tiny balls of down in his mouth, which was so capacious that scarcely the smallest part of the young birds could be observed, while they were held within his powerful jaws. When ordered he would release the trembling captive, or deposit it in my hand, specially satisfied, as was indicated by the intelligent twinkle of his eyes, and the speaking gestures of his body, when the latter was the case.

In the State of Delaware I made my *debût* in rail-shooting. Everything favoured me, for the wind was blowing and had been for some days from seaward, and the moon was full, two circumstances that predicted a very high tide, of all things the greatest guarantee of sport. About noon I joined my 'pusher,' who had promised me his services for this occasion in return for the consideration of five dollars. This description of shooting cannot be enjoyed without such an attendant, and his qualities require to be so varied and extensive, that the apprenticeship of a lifetime is not too long to produce a perfect pusher, who must have skill in poling a boat, eyes keen as a cat's to mark the killed game, a knowledge of the locality, and familiarity with the resorts and habits of the quarry.

I was far from favourably impressed with my temporary companion. His first remark on meeting, previous to our start, was so offensive as almost to produce an instantaneous dissolution of partnership. He told me in the coolest and most off-handed way, that he guessed I had better stick to store business, and leave gunning to my betters. It must be acknowledged this was a fearful rub to me, an ex-military man, rather conservative in my opinions and sentiments, thus to be taken for a counter-hopper, a measurer of ribbon, an expounder of the various qualities of cottons and stay-laces; but not believing in the expediency of 'cutting off my nose to spite my face,' I submitted without protest to my fate, congratulating myself that the period of our intercourse was limited.

At length we got under way. The sun was warm and I was impatient, so without making allowance for the heat, and believing that as more than a mile or so had been traversed, I might retaliate on my insulter, I hinted that he was taking his work easy; but, as has often happened in such cases, I found myself in the wrong box. My pusher abruptly sat down, gently hinting that he had no objection to my trying my hand at poling if I was so inclined, adding that he was darn'd certain that such a change of work as would allow him to do the gunning would be certain to result in a heavier bag.

Obstinate, pig-headed, low-bred, good-for-nothing brute, were among the invectives that hovered on the tip of my tongue, but there was one of those indescribable but easily imagined twinkles in his eye that warned me how much better it would be not to express my feelings. A suspension of verbal hostilities, therefore, ensued for ten minutes, during which time the tide was rapidly carrying us homeward, and until we disembarked I had determined to say nothing, but to open the vials of my wrath when safe on *terra firma*. However, a blue-winged teal coming up the watercourse, which, when it saw us, deviated to the left, and passed ahead out of range, suddenly wheeled to the right-about, and came down wind within long range. The temptation was too great. I pitched my gun to my shoulder, held well in front, and really made a clever and difficult shot. 'Guess you do know how to handle a shooting-iron,' my boatman remarked. 'Come, let us have a tod of that old rye,' alluding to a flask of whisky I had with me, 'and we'll hitch teams and travel the same road.' Feeling like one who has in the shafts a nag that wants coaxing more than coercion, I produced my pocket pistol; and while I drunk to the Queen, he toasted General Jackson. However, the *entente cordiale* was established, and I learned a lesson that was not without its benefit in after life.

Though poling under a vertical sun is not light labour, my democratic friend stuck to it, and forced me through and over almost insuperable obstacles. The rails, as usual, were lumbering and slow on the wing when just flushed, and the majority getting up under the bow of the boat, I take small credit to myself for missing very few, although I fired away as rapidly as I could load. Moreover, I was so wonderfully successful in finding the dead and dying that the list of slain began to assume a formidable appearance. The tide, however, commencing to run out, first slowly, but, by degrees, more rapidly, the game again had mother earth to traverse, a warning, that was not disregarded, for us to discontinue further labour.

With a bag numbering many dozens, I landed, well satisfied with the sport; and, as our bargain was now concluded, and no more was to be gained by holding my tongue, I determined to fire into the enemy a parting broadside that would there and then floor him.

'I say, Ike, you took me for a Yorker.'

'Jist so.'

'Well, I'm not.'

'Guess you are not far short of it.'

'Yes, I am; for I am a Britisher.'

'Well, darn me, if that's not the second time I've been sold the same fashion;'—adding (and here spoke the true Republican), 'but one that can handle a shooting-iron the same fashion you did this day, gi'n he Yankee or Britisher, must be some punkins.'

The number of these rails killed at a tide is sometimes enormous. Suffice it to say, that I have known a rather indifferent shot bring ten dozen to bag. In no description of sport are the advantages of the breech-loader over the old form of gun so apparent as when shooting sorra-rails in the immense marshes that margin the embouchures of many of the American rivers.

CHAPTER XIV.

JOURNEY TO THE BARRENS—ROCK CREVICES—MINERAL WEALTH—UNUSUAL CONFIDENCE OF THE WILD ANIMALS—ECONOMY IN THE USE OF AMMUNITION—LAST NIGHT IN CAMP—AGAIN EN ROUTE—TIMBER—A BEE-TREE—MY COMPANION—BEE-HUNTERS—PTARMIGAN—ADVENTURE WITH A GLUTTON.

WHILE here, I was induced to visit a locality which some of the trappers spoke of under the name of the Barrens, situated a journey of two days off, and which I performed alone.

The appearance of the country in that neighbourhood is remarkable, differing from all the localities I had previously seen. Here rocks crop up in abrupt piles, and in the most unaccountable manner, through the surface of the soil, while the crevices between them are filled with pebbles of various dimensions and shapes. The apparent disorder impresses the traveller so forcibly with the idea of mismanagement, that he cannot help imagining that this part of the earth must be of later construction than other portions, and that the necessary materials having become scarce, all the rubbish that could be collected was thrown together in one common jumble. Many of these rocks are furrowed with deep seams, produced, one would imagine, by the blows of some giant mechanic who had used his mallet and chisel upon their surface. These crevices have been attributed by some to the action of water, and by others to that of drift ice, at a time when the world was far younger than it is at present. I lean to the latter surmise; for not only here, but also further south, there are remarkable and convincing proofs that bergs once were frequent in this region. The process by which these appearances must have been produced, is easily imaginable. An immense iceberg, acres in extent, and over a hundred feet in height, floating at the mercy of the winds and waves, its immense mass having barely depth enough to float, and its submerged portion having numerous large boulders firmly imbedded in it, would, when it grounded and scraped against the bottom, tear it up with an herculean force that would produce exactly such crevices as those described. Where watercourses abound, these piles of rock are more numerous; the current of the existing stream probably washing away the *débris* which otherwise would hide them from observation.

That this district is rich in mineral wealth I have no doubt, from its similarity to the copper-producing districts on the shores of Lake Superior. It is not improbable that when, between emigration and the reproduction of the human family, the arable grounds of the more favoured neighbouring climates are all settled by a race devoted to agricultural purposes, this wild country will become the centre from which the engineers and contractors of the future will obtain the material for their iron roads and complicated machinery. Coal is also abundant. In many places it can be observed cropping out through the surface; while shale, a long acknowledged indicator of the presence of petroleum, is observable where the under strata are exposed.

A country rich in coal and metal, particularly when they lie close to the surface, would, but for the value which man attaches to these mineral treasures, prove so unattractive that it would remain a desert; for in such districts the landscape possesses an air of inhospitality, the timber is stunted and gnarled, the brushwood scarce, the grass patchy and of irregular growth, in fact, all is destitute of the verdant colouring which is so fascinating to the sight.

The silence is here so oppressive that the report of a gun, or the sound of a human voice, seems to be heard with such joy that it is again and again repeated by the echoes; the little hills and rocks rejoice over it; and even the mighty mountains seem to laugh and nod at a music which is new to them.

From the rocks and decayed timber beautiful mosses hung in considerable variety, waving playfully in the breeze; but as I generally associate these with dank caverns, and climates adverse to the growth of more substantial vegetation, I gaze with greater pleasure upon the feathery graceful birch, the stately elm, or the lordly oak.

It must not be supposed, however, from what I have said, that animal life is wanting in this part of the continent; but the most numerous species are of a diminutive size. Man being a rare intruder on their solitudes, they exhibit the most remarkable confidence in his good intentions. Though this unusual characteristic of the wild animals might be attributed partly to ignorance, it was evident, from the manner in which they noted my presence, that it was blended with curiosity. Thus the ptarmigans (*Lagopi*), of which there are here several varieties, and the mountain hares, instead of hurrying to place such a distance between me and them as would render them safe, would stop and gaze earnestly at me, following all my movements with eager looks, and frequently permitting me to approach so close to them that I might almost have captured them with the hand.

As ammunition is always a valuable commodity in these distant regions, it behoves the sportsman or traveller not to be lavish in his expenditure of it. On this account, when it was possible to make half a charge suffice, I invariably did so. Indeed, in shooting small game here, I never used more, for the distance that intervened between me and the object of my pursuit would seldom be more than ten or fifteen yards. Although it was necessary to shoot for my support, I am not ashamed to confess that I often felt grieved at taking the lives of the harmless, beautiful inhabitants of this region, whose trustfulness and confidence placed them so completely in my power.

All the streams and lakes swarm with fish. The gravelly-bottomed, rock-margined rivers are admirably suited for the residence and reproduction of Salmonidæ; and the temperature, from the elevation of the region, can scarcely ever be so high as to heat the waters, and thus force the residents of these mountain brooks from their favourite river-haunts to the frigid springs feeding the lakes, as it does in the less elevated country further to the east.

My stay here was not long, a few days sufficing to gratify my curiosity; and as I was desirous of starting for civilisation as soon as possible, at daybreak, on a dismal, threatening morning, I directed my steps to the south, the weather improving and becoming brighter as I advanced. This I welcomed as ominous of a favourable journey, raising my spirits, and giving such additional vigour to my limbs that in three days I was again among my temporary companions.

Camp was now all bustle and confusion, the order and regularity that had hitherto prevailed, being completely disregarded, for arms, accoutrements, and packs lay scattered around on every hand.

One of the hunters, on this the last day of our stay in camp, informed the old man that two years since he, with several companions, came from the east by the very course we propose taking; and that when they left Moose River, a branch of the Saskatchewan, they hid their two canoes in case they might be required on a future occasion. A description of their exact position was given us, and we had permission to appropriate them if we should succeed in finding them. This we hoped to do, as they would prove of the greatest utility, and save us much time, fatigue, and exposure.

Our last night at this ever-to-be-remembered agreeable camp was pleasantly passed, and all appeared to look with regret to the coming day which was to break up a little coterie that in all probability should never again be reunited. The camp-fire was supplied with additional fuel, and the blazes leaped aloft in savage glee, causing the giant trunks of the trees to appear in their recesses like sombre-robed mourners grieving at the prospect of our approaching departure.

But the night waned; one after another, each fell asleep where he had sat, the earth his bed, and the fretted sky his canopy; oblivion both of the present and of the past embraced all.

Next morning I caressed the soft muzzles of my mule and mare, mentally wishing them God speed, while I told their new owner that my friend or foe he should be in the future according to how he treated them.

Anxious to get on as rapidly as possible, we were *en route* before the sun came forth. The weather was so changeable that it baffled all my calculations; as often as I came to the conclusion that it would either clear up or commence raining, so often I found myself wrong. The fatigue of walking over soft ground, rendered still softer by occasional showers, and the heavy drip from the surrounding foliage, more penetrating by far than rain, did not conduce to render the journey agreeable. After a fatiguing day we reached a bad halting-place; but, overcome with fatigue, we were satisfied with it. A blister over the right shoulder, produced by the pressure of my pack, did not tend to add to my comfort. By degrees, however, my pack had become considerably diminished. Experience taught me that I could do without this and that article of my equipment; and these discarded portions were stuck up in some conspicuous place, that the wayfarer, whether red-skin or white man, coming across them, might have his brains puzzled by the question how they came there, or by speculations as to their use. A knife, fork, and spoon, a hairbrush, an empty powder canister, a roll of bandage, and what once had been a pair of woollen socks, now almost footless, would be prizes to an Indian family. With what curiosity would they be inspected! and who can tell the uses to which they might be turned?

As we progressed to the northward there was a marked change in the quantity and variety of the timber. The quivering-leafed poplar was particularly abundant, fir and spruce-trees were also numerous, while an occasional white pine and birch, by their silver-coated bark, added a pleasing variety among the surrounding dark tree-stems. About two o'clock I proposed a halt. The old man was not loth to accede, for although the distance traversed was far from equal to our usual day's march, still it had been most fatiguing. While we were making the necessary arrangements the sun shone out for the first time that day, as if in approval of our conduct, and soon after our blankets were stretched before his friendly rays, to divest them of some of the wet with which they were saturated.

While cleaning my gun, which had suffered sadly from the wet, my companion went off, evidently with the intention of looking for game. After an absence of more than an hour, he returned with the information that he had discovered a bee-tree. Neither of us being possessed of an axe, I could not see how we were to be benefited by what he considered a great piece of luck. However, at his request I accompanied him to the tree. In an opening, that looked as if it had once been cleared by man, stood an unusually large girdling, perfectly denuded of branches, while the upper portion leaned almost at an angle of forty-five degrees towards the south. Near the top he pointed out an orifice, which he stated was the entrance to the hive. In answer to my inquiry as to how he intended getting at it, he informed me that by sounding he had discovered that the tree was hollow, and if we chose it could soon be burnt down. Not having a particularly sweet tooth, I vetoed the trouble. Though my associate concurred in my opinion, in fact, I believe, approved of it, he did it with so bad a grace that an observer would have thought I was making a victim of him.

With all his eccentricities and his frequently disagreeable ways, my companion—I would say friend, but for the fear that he might some day peruse these lines, and deny that I had the right to use the epithet—was a sterling old fellow, though he had a peculiar way of showing it. Although for days little more than monosyllables in answer to my inquiries could be obtained from him, and these more resembling the grunts of an angry bear than civil responses to necessary questions, I knew that at any moment he would have risked his life for my protection.

Curious as it may seem, we never hunted together, never communicated to each other how we intended passing our spare time, seldom ever spoke of our plans for the morrow. When the hour for starting arrived, we mounted our packs together, the movement of the one to do so being the cue for the other to follow suit. In the early portion of the day the old man invariably led the way, voluntarily dropping in rear when half the distance we intended to traverse was accomplished.

To discover a hive of wild bees requires a good deal of experience and keen sight. In America there are persons in the unsettled districts who devote their time almost entirely to this occupation, and are consequently known as bee-hunters. Their *modus operandi* is as follows :—On observing a loaded bee they follow it as long as possible, then wait till they see others going in the same direction. These, as they successively pass, they keep in sight, and by this course are brought nearer and nearer to the hive. After the tree in which the industrious insects have their stores laid up is reached, it often requires time and trouble to discover the entrance to the hive, and much experience to know whether there will be a sufficiency to recompense the hunter for the trouble of cutting it down, for a bee-tree is generally one of the largest proportions. Wet and damp weather is best suited for this description of hunting, for then the insects fly more slowly, and closer to the ground.

In strolling around the camp within a circumference of a mile or two, I saw several deer, and could have killed without difficulty a couple of them, for even after they were aware of my presence, they remained staring at me, scarcely evincing any feelings of alarm. It was evident from their manner that they were as yet unacquainted with the destructive powers of fire-arms. As we had plenty of food, the old man having struck on the head a porcupine, which, fortunately for us, ran across his track in the vicinity of the bee-tree, I did not molest these beauties, it affording me much gratification to be able to leave them alone.

For three days nothing of importance occurred. The country became more and more swampy, and densely timbered. At length we commenced to ascend what evidently was the base of an extensive table-land, and in a short time camped beside a splendid stream, in every way fitted for fly-fishing.

To-night I could not sleep; although tired and anxious for rest, Somnus refused to come to my assistance. In whatever position I placed myself, my arms and ribs appeared to be in the way, and got chafed or bruised in consequence. In fact, I was in one of my blue fits, which was not alleviated by the sight of my friend enjoying his rest. Not even the wolverines, repeating their unearthly call, nor the owls freely practising their objectionable music, could disturb the placidity of his slumbers.

As the blaze of the camp-fire gradually subsided, I took my bed upon my shoulders—for it consisted only of a blanket—and went forth to collect an armful of fuel, no easy matter in the opaque darkness of a close and densely-foliaged wood. Moccasins, not being possessed of a hard sole, do not afford much protection for the toes, as I found to my cost. I soon procured, however, sufficient fuel to replenish the fire, and when it once more gave forth its ruddy flame, which leaped aloft in fantastic figures, as I lay down to rest beside it; but although I courted sleep with all the assiduity of a lover courting his lady-love, the fickle jade would not smile on me. To pass the time I lit my pipe, but the tobacco-fumes tasted nauseous, and I tossed about till it was almost morning, when I became unconscious to the outer world. The sun was quite an hour high when my companion awoke me, so far from refreshed that, when I shouldered my load and started, I regretted much that cruel fate forced upon me a long tramp, to which I felt far from equal.

During our march we flushed several couples of ptarmigan as we crossed a high ridge of land that was covered with stunted birch. These birds were so excessively tame that their flights seldom exceeded a hundred yards. Perched on a point of rock that stood several feet over the level of the surrounding neighbourhood, we came upon an old cock-bird, who, although I hurled at him several stones, one of which ricochetted within a few inches of his head, refused to take wing till I had approached within half-a-dozen yards.

From the elevated ground which we traversed to-day, the view was very extensive, for the vision was not restricted by timber, which only here grows luxuriantly where shelter from the biting wintry blasts of the prevailing winds can be obtained. To the northward lay a high range of hills, on whose sides snow still was plentiful. Their outline was jagged and irregular,—indication of the stoniness of their surface. Towards noon we descended again among timber, the edges of which were cut up in every direction by American reindeer, or cariboo tracks. Never on a Scotch mountain had I seen sheep-paths more abundant, but the producers of these runs were doubtless far off to the north, where they would remain till the forerunning voice of winter ordered them to return to these pastures.

The hour for halting had almost arrived—in fact, ere this, if a desirable situation for camp had been found, we would have ceased our march for the day—when I espied a large animal on the ground, much resembling in size and shape an otter, save that the head was more pointed, and the tail almost rudimentary. From its manner I felt sure that it was aware of our proximity, so speaking *sotto voce*, I told my friend not to look to the left, but continue following in my tracks, for that a wolverine was in that direction, watching our proceedings.

Gradually altering our course, and deviating in the direction of this animal, I stopped when we got within forty yards of it. The creature noted my movement, and at once sprang into a tree; but there he was not safe from the contents of my gun. Firing a snap-shot I knocked him off his perch. Falling on the ground with a heavy thud, I thought the brute dead. While loading, not a movement of the game indicated the existence of life. Convinced, therefore, that the animal was dead, I approached it sufficiently close to administer to it a dig in the ribs with the point of my toe; but the glutton was only playing 'possum, and turned upon me with the rapidity and vindictiveness of a wild cat. The first blow of its paw ripped open the covering of my right leg, and as I stepped back to obtain space to administer a *coup de grace* my heel caught in a bush, and over I went full length on my back. So thoroughly was I disconcerted at this awkward turn of affairs, that I entirely neglected firing, though in an instant more I knew the wounded savage would be on me, and in such close proximity that nothing but my knife could be useful to me in such an emergency. Scarcely had I time to realise the awkwardness of my position, when I heard the sharp report of a small-bore rifle that seldom spoke in vain, and in an instant my enemy was incapable of further mischief.

My companion who had thus promptly, and not a moment too soon, come to my aid, pronounced it 'a tarnation big crittur,' and heavier than ever he had seen before. Of one thing I was certain, that if the length of its claws were to be taken as an index of its powers of doing mischief, then I would sooner fight something else with my knife than a wolverine.

The habitat of this animal is much restricted, and even there it is scarce. With little speed of foot it has to resort to stratagem to procure the food it most preys upon. Cariboo are doubtless its principal victims, to capture which it lies out on a branch of a tree which projects over their most frequented runs. When the reindeer passes beneath the destroyer drops upon it, seizing the back of the victim's neck with its teeth, and clutching to the flanks with its immense talons. In vain the deer seeks safety in flight, rushing through the woods or bounding over the rocky soil; it is doomed, and nothing but the distant chance of man's intervention can save it.

An Indian hunter told me that he had once witnessed the following scene. He was shooting cariboo, and had approached within easy range of four or five full-grown animals. As he pitched his rifle to his shoulder to kill one of them, the stag of the party gave a bound, for a previously unseen animal had sprung upon its back. For a quarter of an hour the buck struggled, and made the most violent efforts to rid itself of its assailant, but all was fruitless, and the antlered monarch of the forest at length succumbed under the terrible teeth and giant claws of its foe, which, it almost is unnecessary to add, was a glutton.

CHAPTER XV.

THE RED-MEN — AN INDIAN 'FLITTING'— INTERVIEW WITH AN INDIAN FAMILY—HORSE-INDIANS — TIMBER-INDIANS — FISH-INDIANS — THE MUSTANG — PICTURESQUE CAMP — AMERICAN CHAR — RECKLESSNESS OF MY FELLOW-TRAVELLER — VIOLENT GALE — EMIGRATION.

THIS night we encamped upon a rather exposed stony ridge, but the weather was favourable, and after a good night's rest we were again *en route* by sunrise.

'Indians are poison' is a common expression throughout the United States, very indicative of the feelings with which the red-man is regarded by our trans-Atlantic cousins. My sentiments towards these aborigines are very different, and I think I have good grounds for entertaining a more favourable opinion of them. When the hunting-ground of a tribe lies so far to the north as to be out of the track of the white man, the adventurer may safely trust himself among them, for they are brave, honest, and proud. But if the white man with his fire-water has had long and constant intercourse with these children of the forest, they are to be avoided. Apt scholars, they soon learn the vices of civilisation, viz., to lie, cheat, and steal.

In England people are very prone to blame the American's Indian policy, but are there no black spots on our own escutcheon? Are we quite free from blame in our treatment of the aborigines of newly-discovered lands? Let those that live in glass houses beware of throwing stones, for abroad there are ugly tales afloat, in reference to England as well as America.

Descending the brow of a hill, I observed a family party of Indians, winding their way in single file along the margin of the stream. It was evident from the load with which each was encumbered, that they were making, what is called in Scotland, 'a flitting.' By using as shelter such intervening obstacles as brush and boulders, I got within a quarter of a mile of them ere my presence became known, and believe I could have even come nearer, but that the sharp ears, or possibly sharper noses, of their curs, warned them that an intruder was close, information they were not slow to impart to their owners. On approaching, I discovered that the party consisted of a family on the tramp. Though my advent was not regarded without suspicion, an old man at their head stood his ground, while his squaw and two half-grown children by retiring showed every evidence of a desire to seek safety in flight. However, after a close inspection, during which the throats of their vociferous pack had become so dry from excessive exercise as to produce a temporary lull in their vocal practice, I felt satisfied that the impression I had made was not unfavourable.

Seating myself on the ground I induced my new

acquaintance to do the same. With pantomimic gestures I endeavoured to convince him how wonderfully partial I was to all his race, and to himself in particular. After the manner of his breed he grunted an apparent approval of my pretty speeches. To cap all by a favourable climax, with the greatest gravity and formality I produced my pipe, which, from its proportions, would have been called a 'dutheen' in Ireland. With the point of my knife the charred embers were removed, not thrown away, but saved for a top-dressing to the new charge of tobacco, and the better to assist the lighting. My plug of cavendish was brought forth; the shavings that I sliced off were carefully rubbed between my palms and placed in the bowl. A few strokes of my flint and steel produced a light; half-a-dozen long, steady puffs kindled a fine glowing coal, when, removing it from my own lips, I transferred it to those of my associate.

Cluck, cluck, went his mouth in evident enjoyment. Again and again the pipe changed hands, and the ceremony performed its work, for we were now friends.

It is usually regarded as a mark of friendship for two persons to drink out of the same cup, and smoking out of the same pipe, particularly if it be an old and short one, must be considered expressive of even stronger feelings of regard. Thus the noble savage and the white wanderer hobnobbed over the fragrant fumes arising from a thimbleful of honey-dew.

In the meantime the old squaw had drawn near, with her two hopefuls clinging to her. When the pipe was produced she squatted, but as the pou-wow was not one in which her sex is allowed to share, she amused herself in searching the black elfin locks of her youngest child for certain unnecessary parasites. The skill with which the monkeys at Regent's Park Gardens perform this office for each other, and the celerity with which the captives are secured and dealt with, was on this occasion quite equalled by the loving and anxious mother. Assuming an additional air of pompousness I drew the eyes of all towards myself, while with great gravity I produced a small package of scarlet cloth, which, while the eyes of all glittered with curiosity, I unfolded with the greatest care, taking from it two brightly-tinned fish-hooks. These I gave to the youngest son, who accepted them with diffident eagerness, while the orbits of his parents and brother glowed with covetousness. Two more hooks were handed to the elder boy, who smiled with pleasure as he received them. Three were then handed to the old woman, and four to her lord and master, all evincing the most indisputable evidences of satisfaction.

As it was now late in the afternoon I took leave of this happy family, with many protestations of friendship, and joined my friend about sunset. My protracted absence had caused him some alarm, for in his route he had passed trails that indicated the presence of Indians; and, like a true American, their vicinity was regarded by him as dangerous. But experience had taught me that the tribes of the north are much less to be feared than those of the southern plains.

Horse-Indians, Timber-Indians, and Fish-Indians are designations which will explain the various leading characteristics of the aborigines of North America. The first are the most treacherous, the second the most skilful hunters, and the third the most improvident, squalid, and filthy, although all are dirty enough. The Horse-Indians reside on the great plains extending for over a thousand miles of latitude to the north of Mexico and Texas. The Timber-Indians, who have suffered more than any others by the advent of the white man into the western continent, inhabited at one time all the forest-lands from the Atlantic to the verge of the great plains. The Fish-Indians, who even at the present day are sparsely supplied with fire-arms, reside principally in the vicinity of those rivers that flow into the Pacific or Arctic Ocean and produce salmon. The first-mentioned are indifferent walkers, from passing their lives on horseback; are small in stature and badly formed, are invariably treacherous and bloodthirsty. The Timber-Indian is well made, straight as a lath, noble in carriage, capable of performing long and rapid journeys on foot. They have often handsome features, and are honourable and brave, but revengeful. The Fish-Indians are unprepossessing, debased, and cowardly; inferior to the others in intelligence, capable of bearing fatigue, and possessed of great powers of enduring the fluctuations from heat to cold peculiar to their habitat. The Timber-Indian may be regarded as the highest type of the red man, the Horse-Indian next, and lowest those whose principal support is fish.

The mustang, a pony in size, which is the horse of the Western wilds, is descended from European progenitors introduced into America at the period of the Spanish invasion. They are occasionally used by the Timber-Indians, possessed in herds by Horse-Indians, and are almost unknown to the Fish-Indians. But even among those possessed of steeds, that type of the noble savage which schoolboys and the uninitiated delight to gaze on, decked out with gorgeous plumes and handsome ornaments, so frequently represented on tobacco-boxes, or in mammoth figures outside the doors of dealers in the Nicotian leaf, has never yet come under my observation.

This night we had a more picturesque camp than can possibly be imagined. It was on the summit of an acclivity, with a beautiful stream flowing around three sides of it. At sunset I seated myself on a rock, perpendicular on all sides except where it joined the bank, and from this perch overlooked a long, placid pool, the surface of which was incessantly disturbed by trout rising at the ephemera that floated upon the surface of the water.

One fish that broke water several times almost

immediately below my perch, would doubtless have turned the scales at ten pounds. I had only momentary views of him, still they sufficed to show the brilliant robing of the American char, by far the most gorgeously coloured of the Salmonidæ that I know of. A fly-rod and light tackle would afford its happy possessor in this part of the world pleasure never to be forgotten.

With the decay of light an otter put in his appearance, and with his advent the scaly inhabitants of the placid stream disappeared.

If my companion was not the most provokingly obstinate old man living, he was the next to it; and the more I think, the more I am puzzled that his utter recklessness had not deprived him of life long before he reached so respectable an old age. By reason of the up-country rains the stream was much swollen and discoloured this morning; and although my venerable friend had not the most remote idea of swimming, he attempted, in spite of all I could say or do, to wade across to the other side, although quite ignorant whether the river was thirty or three feet deep. Moreover, the current, at the part where he entered, was sufficiently swift to have borne a raft or boat at the pace of four or five miles an hour.

Having long learned how useless it was to argue with my companion, I sat upon the margin, and put my trust in Providence, at the same time unfastening some of my outer garments, that I might be the more rapidly prepared to render him assistance, if necessary.

In a few steps the object of my solicitude was up to the knees, and in a few more up to the waist, his stalwart figure staunchly resisting the powerful current. Not once did he cast back his eyes; the goal was in front, and he was determined to reach it. When, on advancing a few paces, his body became further submerged, I exclaimed, 'Come back; you are attempting an impossibility,' narey a come back in response floated to my ears. 'Go on and be —— well drowned,' I was about to utter, when Mr. Obstinacy placed his foot either on a slippery stone or tripped, and in a moment afterwards was struggling in deep water. In an instant I comprehended the danger of his position. There was no time for hesitation. My clothes that were outermost were kicked off, and in a twinkling I was up to my neck. Half-a-dozen strokes brought me alongside the victim of his stupidity. Having on several occasions rescued indiscreet individuals in similarly precarious predicaments, I was not unaware of the danger to be braved under such circumstances, so had armed myself with the branch of a tree to give the drowning man to lay hold of, and thus keep him at arm's length, while I towed him to the shore.

Success rewarded my efforts, and the old reprobate has now to thank me that he still is in the land of the living, yet with the utmost pertinacity he insisted that he should have sooner or later drifted into shoal water. To this I remarked that it should have been so much later that he would have been in an excellent state to furnish food for the craw-fish and eels, or to be employed as bait for wolves. This little adventure curtailed our day's journey, so we passed the evening at the camp of last night.

During the day we had a specimen of how it could blow in this neighbourhood; and if the gentleman who had charge of this section of the country for Boreas did not do his work in a thorough manner, then I must be acknowledged no judge of the power of the winds. The gusts were fiercer than any I had ever felt at sea, and of much longer continuance. It is generally supposed that the gales of the temperate regions are much more moderate in comparison with those of tropical climates, but such is not the case. The latter, coming on more suddenly, and often being preceded by little or no prophetic indications, are more destructive. The gales of lower latitudes are moreover marked by more frequent lulls, some of these enduring even minutes, whereas here, and generally in similar latitudes, the blow may increase or diminish in violence, but seldom entirely breaks off even for a moment. Although we had got ample warning of what might be expected by the lowering, overcast look of the heavens, and the excessive rarefaction of the atmosphere, distant objects looking close and looming up double their proper size, still, when the storm burst upon us, we were out in a most unprotected position, and so great was the clap with which it assailed us, that we were almost thrown down. If this had happened where our footing was precarious, or the surface steep, without brush to cling to, we should literally have been blown away.

Much of the neighbourhood that we are now in is admirably suited for the emigrant. Wood and water are abundant, and the surface is sufficiently level and free from stones to promise easy cultivation. But I am adverse to emigration from our country. The reasons may be selfish, but they are patriotic; and on a subject of so much interest to the nation, I may take the opportunity of making a few remarks. So much has lately been written on emigration—more particularly to Canada—that for the benefit of those about to leave their homes to found new ones in this distant land, I will give some of my experiences, with the hope that the remarks I have to make may be instrumental in mitigating or preventing many of the discomforts that are certain to attend the stranger, especially when accompanied by a family, on his advent in his adopted country.

There are two classes who should never think of emigrating to Canada—viz., the educated without means, and those who deem good society essential to their happiness, for the former in nine cases out of ten, unless professional men, will starve, while the latter, from being unable to find congenial acquaintances, will become morose and dissatisfied, constantly pining after the land of their birth, and ultimately relapsing into morbid and often dissipated habits, producing unhappiness and discomfort among all those with whom they are thrown in contact. Retired military and naval men, professional persons advanced in years, all whose habits of life have become formed, had better be satisfied to reside at home, however parsimoniously they are compelled to live, to risking the chance of being successful across the ocean. Many such people, having large families, believe it a duty they owe their children thus to expatriate themselves. They know by experience that education is expensive in England, and they are well aware that it is difficult to obtain suitable employment for their progeny. This I grant, but the same objection is applicable to Canada; and worse still, there are very few young gentlemen brought up in the bush who do not relapse into the condition of boors, or worse still become even utter blackguards. Nor is this to be wondered at, when too frequently they have no other society but that of teamsters, woodchoppers, Indian traders, and half-breeds. Life in a frontier cabin, though it may be free and independent, with a certain amount of romance, is unfortunately idle. A youngster, after living it for some years is as unqualified for settled mercantile or professional pursuits as the retired veteran soldier to become a laborious artisan. I know Canada from east to west, from the shores of the great lakes and St. Lawrence to the barriers that form the northern boundary; have visited and re-visited it time after time, lived for months in succession in different parts of it, and therefore do not make statements without having had sufficient experience to justify me.

Between thirty and forty years ago, our government, desirous of introducing fresh and loyal blood into a disaffected colony (through grants of land and flowery descriptions of the productiveness of the soil, and statements of the facility with which all could soon become possessed of beautiful and productive farms, handsome dwellings, and immense herds of cattle), encouraged a great number of veterans who had served under the 'Duke' in France and Spain, and who had been placed on half-pay through the reduction of the army, to emigrate to the lands lying to the north of Toronto. Those who had private means were able to subsist, but those who had none relapsed into a state of destitution and drunkenness, cursing the deceivers who had been instrumental in causing them to leave their own country; and hoping against hope that some unknown combination of circumstances might bring them the means once more to visit the resting-place of their fathers. Nearly all these were married men. What then has become of their sons and daughters? They will be found, with few exceptions, in the lowest grades of society, broken-spirited, unhappy, useless members of the community, who never fail to tell who they are, and from whom you cannot help recoiling, cruel and uncharitable as such conduct may appear.

With the mechanic and farm-labourer it is different; they go prepared to work, and capable of doing so. Any change that takes place in their circumstances must be for the better. The associates they are thrown in contact with are as well educated as themselves, possibly better; while in tastes, pleasures, and habits of life, they entirely sympathise.

If the educated man does not succeed in England, it is very improbable he will in Canada. The mechanic and labourer who has never known but short commons at home, will most likely be able there to enjoy abundance. Prosperity or the reverse has this effect: the country in which the former is enjoyed is loved, where the latter is suffered, hated. The better class hate the new land and crave for home; the lower class love the new land, and soon learn to hate the old. The former become broken-hearted, useless members of the community; the latter disaffected, and too frequently rebellious subjects to the parent country. Thus Government, instead of fostering and encouraging those who would remain faithful to the end of time, entirely neglects them, and sends out gratuitously those who will ultimately cut her throat.

Those who emigrate make a great mistake if they suppose that Canada will long remain under the

British flag. A few years—very few, I think—will see it attached to the United States. This is a result which we may predict with as much certainty as we can foretell anything in human affairs. No one knows better than I do the grasping spirit of the Great Republic; few are more satisfied of its immense power, and this they can wield at any moment desired, to appropriate this land. Canada, with a partially disaffected and tainted population, with about fifteen hundred miles of frontier, a great portion of which adjoins the most densely populated part of the country of the future aggressor, would but be a sop to Cerberus, obtainable without an effort:—but so few will agree with me on this point, that possibly the less said the better.

CHAPTER XVI.

PRAIRIE-FIRES — TERROR AND FLIGHT OF WILD ANIMALS — CARIBOO-TRACKS — SPONGY SOIL — UNSUCCESSFUL STALK — LARGE GREY WOLF — WILD DUCKS — SIGNS OF A CHANGE OF WEATHER — WILD GEESE — MOOSE RIVER — CONSTRUCTION OF A RAFT — VOYAGE OF DISCOVERY — BIRCH-BARK CANOES.

THE sky last night was brilliantly illuminated, so much so that I could not help surmising that the scrub,—for such is the nature of the vegetation we are now come to,—was on fire. This morning confirmed my surmises. Heavy clouds hung on the horizon, rolling over each other, and swallowing up their predecessors like the fresh waves of ocean. Up to windward a lurid glare, deepening in intensity, as unnatural and forbidding as one might imagine if the earth were being destroyed by fire, advanced towards us. The smell of burning soon became sickening, and the sound made by the conflagration in effecting its work of destruction was heard like the hum of traffic in a large city.

It is an uncommon occurrence for such fires to take place so early in the season. Spring had made vegetation unusually damp, while no protracted dry summer had followed to parch it. In my lengthened experience, I do not remember an instance of such conflagrations taking place till the end of autumn, when they are generally caused by the carelessness of travellers, or by the deliberate act of Indians, who often take this means of driving off the game from the country of a hostile tribe.

Although we were some distance from water, no danger was apprehended, as it required but little experience to avoid accidents. The means we adopted, and which is invariably employed, was to set fire to the grass to leeward of our position. The flames we had lighted soon increased, the blaze spread right and left, licking up every particle of vegetable matter on which it could feed, acre after acre becoming denuded of all substances that burn, thus presenting an impassable barrier to the advance of the portion of the devouring element. Here on the ground cleared by your fire, the traveller can take his stand with feelings of perfect safety, and if he remain as close up to the line of debarkation— that is, between the burnt and the burning grass— as the stifling smoke will allow, he will see animal life under a phase never witnessed by the constant dwellers in towns and cities.

It is most curious to watch the conduct of horses under such an ordeal,—what different traits of character and education each will exhibit. Thus one will evince perfect indifference, apparently relying entirely in its owner's judgment; another will testify such fear as almost to be helpless and incapable; while a third, intoxicated with excitement, with starting eyeballs and wide expanded nostrils, may be seen struggling with herculean efforts to break loose and obtain safety by flight.

An extract from a former journal will give some explanation of such scenes :—' My companion's mount, which was a ragged-looking, weather-beaten veteran, lopped his ears, and appeared to doze, possibly suffering from disinclination to exercise, augmented by the oppression of the smoke-charged atmosphere. The baggage-nag sweat profusely, yet it made no effort to be released, while my Bucephalus struggled and tore around, lashed, reared, and threw itself about, perfectly regardless of consequences. But that its moorings,—as a sailor would call them,—were strong, it must have broken away, when I should, as far as its services were concerned, have to resort to the ever popular shanks's mare. With no small effort, we secured the struggling brute, but not until it was thrown, when I took my outer hunting-shirt off, placed the animal's head in it—a capital illustration of the saying "put your head in a bag."

'Hours before the line of flame had neared us, a visible movement was apparent among both birds and beasts. The former flitted past on rapid wings, while the latter exhibited all the evidences of the greatest alarm, as if the emergency had deprived them of sense, many of them hurrying on with uncertain steps, at a loss to determine which route to select.

'As the flame approached the atmosphere became

more and more oppressive. Fragments of burnt vegetation floated by or rested upon us, fouling all with which it came in contact. As the flames advanced, I had an opportunity of witnessing the sight for which I had remained, still in a very lessened form from what I had anticipated—a circumstance I much regretted. Urged on by the devouring element there passed, close to us, first, a splendid buffalo bull, evidently in prime condition and age. His coat was soiled from sweat and earth, his eyes were expanded to their utmost, and his tail was raised aloft, while his gait denoted that notwithstanding his strength he was exhausted by fatigue. Scarcely deigning to look at us, he inclined neither to the right nor to the left, but, intent on self-preservation, held forward on an undeviating course, in the direction which his instinct told him led to safety. Fortunate for him that we were not short of food, or else his blind fear would have caused his destruction. It is marvellous with what celerity these ponderous animals move, and for what a length of time they can remain on foot, fleeing before the pursuing flames. Nevertheless, hundreds must perish every year in these conflagrations. Next came an interesting coterie, composed of two grey and three prairie wolves, a coalition of five thorough blackguards. I call them interesting because it is often fashionable to make an unmitigated scoundrel the lion of the hour, and all admirers of sensational heroes seek him out, and take the liveliest interest in his welfare, appreciating him the more for the fiendish character of his crimes.

Now, wolves are a sort of four-footed banditti of the forests and the prairies, and possibly, therefore, in accordance with the diseased sentimentalism of the time, I, according to my humour, lavish my sympathy and admiration upon them. The wolves were followed by bands of deer, and the more closely they were pursued by the flames, the less did these refugees seem to regard our presence or that of the other animals, their enemies, the common danger having for the moment extirpated their mutual fears and jealousies.

However, to return to my present position, the next and succeeding days we found the fire had done us much injury, for quadrupeds of all kinds had disappeared, and we were reduced to short commons.

Nothing is more trying to the temper than an unsuccessful hunt. It is annoying to suffer from fatigue and exposure without obtaining adequate remuneration, but more so if the chase has been prolonged, and the game so wild as to have kept constantly at a safe distance from your missiles. The pangs of hunger, added to our other sufferings, I am sorry to say, have frequently proved adverse to both our courtesy and our forbearance.

The scenery to-day reminded me much of what is to be found in Dumfries-shire,—rugged stretches of undulating hills, covered by stunted vegetation, with streams tumbling down their sloping sides, and hurrying on to pour their crystal waters into some of the innumerable little lakes that appeared on every side. In all directions, where the ground was sufficiently sound, I could see cariboo-tracks crossing and recrossing each other, telling plainly how numerous these animals must be in this remote range at certain seasons of the year. The surface, however, in occasional places was so spongy that such traces had disappeared, and care had to be taken not to trespass upon them too recklessly. Experience and observation had taught me that those parts where the vegetation on the surface was greenest were the most impassable. At the same time, I know that in Ireland, where this brilliancy of herbage is regarded as a warning to trespassers, there are many sober, brown-looking pieces of bog where, without suspecting danger, the unwary may find themselves caught in a toil as firm in its grip as the grasp of the usurer upon the unfledged subaltern.

I feel convinced that if we had reached here months sooner we should have witnessed an exodus of reindeer to the north, equal in numbers to those herds of buffalo that have never failed to strike with astonishment the traversers of the Western plains. However, in all probability they would have been low in flesh, for if this were their winter quarters,—and I strongly surmise such to be the case,—the depth of the snow which lies on the soil of such high latitudes in uncultivated regions, even late on in spring, could scarcely fail to cause these hardy ruminants great difficulty in obtaining a sufficiency of food.

Although I started soon after daylight, and was on my feet till night, I only saw three head of cariboo, and these were all so wary that I could not come within anything approaching justifiable shooting distance. All of these were males, and their new horns were only sufficiently developed to be ornamental. One male, taller by over an inch than its fellows, I spent an hour trying to stalk; but all was useless, the brute marked my every movement, noted each dodge I put in execution, and satisfied itself by keeping just sufficiently from me to laugh at my futile efforts. At length, in a fit of desperation, probably temper, I fired at him a long shot. Although I made allowance for the distance by giving plenty of elevation, my bullet lobbed close to his feet. A frightened start, a movement of a few hurried paces, a halt and toss of the head, and the splendid animal walked away at no faster pace than that common to a Blackheath donkey. But that my supply of ammunition was limited, I should have persevered. The first essay was encouraging, and its shortcomings might have been corrected.

I saw this day the largest grey wolf that has yet come under my observation. The scoundrel looked most ragged and gaunt, but carried himself very jauntily. Perfectly aware of my presence, there was no attempt to escape observation, for, though all his movements were hurried, they were perfectly natural. I would have given much for a brace of good greyhounds trained to wolf-coursing, to enable me to have the pleasure of taking the conceit out of the braggart, for I owed him a grudge, as I have no doubt it was he who, like certain dissipated 'fast persons' at home, kept me awake all night by a series of howls which reminded me of a ditty, doleful when sung by half-intoxicated Bacchanals, but regarded with great favour by those who delight in drunken orgies, 'We won't go home till morning.' If I could have succeeded in tying a kettle to Mr. Lupus's tail, although thereby I should have made myself amenable to that excellent Institution for the Prevention of Cruelty to Animals, I certainly would have done so.

The last sight I had of my grizzly friend he was scratching himself after the manner of a dog; at the same time, with his weather-eye open, looking over his shoulder in my direction. Possibly after my back was turned he shook his lugs, after the manner of Burns's 'dougs,' and rejoiced that he was not a man.

To-day the country improved, and wild ducks were numerous wherever there was a deposit of water. Many families of young birds, already half grown, I disturbed, their anxious mothers exercising all their ingenuity, by assuming lameness and incapacity of flight, to draw me away from their defenceless brood.

What a beautiful example of maternal affection these birds display! Could some of those gin-drinking mothers who are ever to be found in our gigantic Babylon loafing about the numerous tinsel-decked public-houses, baby in hand, not learn from them a lesson worthy of being studied? And yet the lately-hatched young duck is not half so helpless as the newly-born babe; for the former the parent would give its life, while for the latter, the mother would not temporarily forego the gratification of a debasing passion.

Next day was successful with hook and line, so we had plenty of fish in our larder, and in consequence supped on them; but, although fish are a great delicacy, particularly char from these mountain retreats, the feast, without other concomitants, is rather unsatisfactory. Cold lamb and salad are excellent when combined, but all salad and no lamb forms but a sorry meal. Brook-trout may be admirable as an *entrée*, when fried with cream, or served with drawn butter, accompanied by new potatoes and bread; but brook-trout and nothing else for days together, are enough to give one a distaste to fly-fishing, however skilled and devoted he be to the gentle art.

This night was clear and calm, the stars stood out in bold relief from the azure space in which they are set; and we had but to peer steadfastly into the canopy above, to discover innumerable luminaries whose radiance was only dimmed by distance. Though these were all indications of fine weather, I felt certain that a change was not distant; for the little wood-frog (*Rana sylvatica*) was piping his song unceasingly. The loon was uttering its prolonged weird note, and the large white owl (*Surnia nictea*), possibly regretting the termination of such splendid weather for its nocturnal rambles, vented its disappointment in dolorous notes of grief. But all these heralds of coming storm failed to keep me awake when I wrapped myself in my dirty blanket, for I immediately glided unconsciously into dreamland, from which I was not recalled until the sun had shown his face over the eastern horizon.

Being again short of food, I paid a visit to the neighbouring stream, on the margin of which I cut a wand for a rod. For some time I hunted in vain for bait, but at length in turning over a large stone ousted out a small lizard. Hoping that this would prove an attractive lure, I impaled the unfortunate on my hook, and soon had several sparkling, many-hued beauties struggling at my feet. My bait first lost its tail, and soon afterwards its hind-quarters, but even thus disfigured it proved so attractive that I believe I could have continued to take with it, so long as a fragment remained upon the hook.

While eating our morning meal, a full-grown wolf showed itself, evidently attracted by the odour that arose from our cooking operations, and, with an amount of assurance with which I should have credited only the man about town living on his wits, sat down within easy shooting distance, and surveyed our preparations. The cool impudence of his conduct, arising of course from his ignorance of the danger of his position, amused me so much that I did not molest him, but in charitable frame of mind left him a portion of our spoils.

Wild geese (*Anas Canadensis*) were passing all the afternoon in large flocks from the north. These birds, according to the season, are to be found from about 30 degrees north latitude to the Arctic circle,— some authorities say even farther north. Very few persons—certainly none possessed of ordinary powers of observation—who have travelled in the sparsely-populated portions of Canada or the United States, can fail to recall occasions on which they have heard the often-repeated notes of 'honk! honk! honk!' emanating from flocks of wild geese making their aerial passage to unknown parts. Not so large as our domestic bird, wild geese are much handsomer in form, and more attractive in plumage. When walking they bear themselves as if conscious of the value of liberty, and appear to take good care not to place themselves within reach of those who may deprive them of it. Nevertheless they do not always escape. When from prolonged severe weather, the poor birds are deprived of food, they become so reckless of consequences that, in their longing to gratify their craving appetites, they stoop to decoys, or alter their course in answer to the skilfully-uttered call of the sportsman. So abundant are they said to be in parts of North America, that if the writer were to repeat the stories he has heard of the slaughters made of them, he would be accused of drawing the long bow.

We at last reached Moose River. Here deer were abundant. I already felt rewarded for my labours; doubly so if we found the canoes.

After passing a thoroughly refreshing night, undisturbed by mosquitoes or by wild beasts, we rose early to inspect the locality.

Both of us had come to the conclusion that we were too far to the south, or, in other words, not sufficiently down the course of Moose River to find the birch-barks. To avoid the fatigue of walking along the rocky margin of the streams, or penetrating through the hemlock and cedar-swamps that in places abut upon the water, we decided to build a raft out of drift-wood, and upon it proceed provided cataracts or other obstacles did not occur.

If we had been furnished with axes, forming a raft would have been an easy matter, but as that was not the case, nearly a day was lost in labouring to accomplish our purpose. However at length we succeeded, and on the most primitive of crafts, bound together with the stems of the wild grape-vine, we started upon our voyage of discovery. For two days our troubles were unceasing. First we got into a rapid that threatened to dismember our boat; next we stuck on a rock; and, lastly, we were in imminent danger of going over a waterfall; but being destined for some other fate than drowning, we safely came through all perils.

Game was unusually abundant, particularly deer, so much so that on occasions the demesnes of many of our English noblemen were recalled to mind. A buck (*Cervus Canadensis*) which I saw was as large and heavy as an ordinary two-year-old steer, while its imperfectly-developed horns promised that at some not remote day this lord of the manor would carry a splendid head.

The stag of Canada, more familiarly known as the wapiti, is as noble and graceful an animal as the eye can rest on. Larger than the red deer of Scotland, and in the season possessed of ponderous but handsome-shaped horns, the lover of nature gazes with delight on his massive proportions. The species is fast disappearing however, and the day is not far distant when it will become exceedingly rare — possibly extinct.

In our progress down the river we passed an island, which the old man proclaimed as marking the vicinity of the canoes, a surmise which was perfectly correct, for we soon afterwards discovered them. After much carpentering and caulking the smaller of the two was considered seaworthy. Although a birch-bark canoe is a fragile conveyance, and far from easy to handle, yet with time and practice a white man can succeed in becoming tolerably skilled in its management. Among the Canadian voyageurs, and even lumbermen, I have met with persons who could almost rival their redskin neighbours in the pilotage of these vessels; but they are exceptions to the rule. In the western Indian country I received my first lessons with the paddle, and being a good boatman was an apt pupil. In after years I enjoyed much practice in this style of navigation in the lumber districts of Maine.

My readers, therefore, must not be incredulous if I go so far as to state that I believe myself almost master of the art. At all events, I can shoot a rapid with the rocks projecting in many parts of the channel, and can jump a fall of a foot or two, although the moment after the leap is taken, my buoyant craft must be shot off at right angles to its original course to avoid a rut. The old man soon found this out, and saddled me with a great proportion of the duties of Palinurus; respecting age, and being aware of its infirmities, I permitted myself to be imposed upon.

Our patching was a success in one respect, and not in another; for although the canoe was made watertight and capable of bearing us on our way, from having a big side where a new rib had been put in, it took an enormous amount of exertion to bring it round to starboard, and when it commenced to come, it did so all of a rush, making the strongest amount of port-paddle necessary to prevent the head of the cockle-shell from turning to where its tail should be. I did not find this out before an unenlightened eye-witness would several times have imagined that our course was against stream, not with it.

However difficult it may be to navigate a birch-bark canoe, it is more difficult to build one. I never knew a white man succeed in accomplishing this task so well as the veriest lout of a red-skin. It is *par excellence* their craft, and although we may hourly witness their construction, the secret of their success still remains hidden.

We now enjoyed the relief afforded our hard-worked legs, to an extent that could not be over-rated. With unalloyed pleasure we could gaze upon the changes of the landscape, and take note of the numerous islands as we passed them, and all without any exertion on our part, and, better still, every mile we traversed brought us nearer our destination.

At the same time, travelling upon these far western waters is a dangerous mode of locomotion, for out on the broad expanse of a river you are an object of attraction to all eyes, and if a war party of young braves belonging to a tribe of hostile Indians discover you, your predicament will be far from enviable, for you will be incapable of defence, and at the same time present a most enticing target, the ribs and bark of such slender crafts not being so adapted for defence and shelter as the sides of an ironclad. By turns replacing each other in the stern, in spite of a small inward monitor which kept whispering words of caution, homeward we progressed. While the smoke from our pipes circled aloft, and we knelt or reclined upon our blankets, we lived in anticipation of a happy ending to our journey, and reckless of the consequences our present rashness might entail. 'A short life and a merry one' was the motto which my old companion continually quoted. I thoroughly agreed in his choice of this adage, but pointed out as a strange contradiction to it his grey hairs and numerous years.

As we proceeded wild ducks became more numerous, as well as many of the smaller species of aquatic fowls. Wherever the water-lilies and reeds were abundant, these little beauties sported in multitudes. Surrounded by such interesting objects no one could feel lonely, nature, in her infinite wisdom, affording constant food for contemplation.

Audubon, the ornithologist, was a fortunate man in having such a comparatively new field open for his researches. He certainly did his work well, but still there is room for others, for there are yet birds to be found here whose existence is far from universally known. One of these is a species of jacana, not so large as the bird of South America, but possessed of very similar characteristics. Another is a diminutive teal, fawn-coloured, with a tinge of pink throughout the plumage, excessively swift upon the wing and difficult of approach. For some time I had known of its existence, as a year previously I killed one on a slough in a favourite shooting ground, at which time I was disposed to believe it a *lusus naturæ*. This day I saw over a dozen, all members of the same flock.

I am inclined to believe that many different

breeds of wild fowl, under such compulsory circumstances as being unable to obtain a mate of their own species, will breed with another race, and thus produce hybrids which are apt to be mistaken for new specimens. On several occasions I have shot most peculiarly marked and oddly-formed ducks with the characteristic of the mallard and dusky-duck strongly defined, and from observation and inquiry I am inclined to believe that these were crosses between the two species.

CHAPTER XVII.

DELICATE LUXURY — A HURRICANE — CONTRETEMPS TO THE CANOE — DISTURBED IN A DAY-DREAM — NARROW ESCAPE FROM A BEAR — TICKS — GREY WOLVES — MUSIC OF THE WINDS — THE CANOE IN A RAPID — HUMBUG — AN AUTHORITY ON NATURAL HISTORY.

THE majority of English readers will scarcely agree with me when I assert—for the antipathies of the bulk of my countrymen are strong against using such food—that there is not a more delicate luxury than frogs. Day and night these creatures were croaking round us in great numbers, so I determined to have a dish of them when opportunity offered. This afternoon such an occasion happened, and, with great satisfaction, I availed myself of it. As snags were abundant, and a collision with one would probably have scuttled our flimsy craft, we landed among the reeds about an hour previous to sunset. Procuring a long rod, I fastened on the end of it, attached to six inches of thin string, a hook, with a small piece of my red woollen shirt lashed to its shank, and hanging over the barb. With this novel implement I was most successful, for I had but to dangle the lure in front of a croaker and immediately he jumped at it. Sometimes the first effort was unsuccessful, but the second or third seldom failed to secure the prize.

These frogs are not identical with the edible frog of the south of Europe, but are the common bull-frog of America. As with the former, the hind-legs only are eaten. The limbs should be skinned the moment the victim is captured, a process which is easily accomplished when the *modus operandi* is known. When served, the flesh looks exactly like that of the most delicate spring chicken, while the flavour is superior.

My fellow-traveller was unacquainted with those fastidious qualms on the subject of diet peculiar to the well-fed children of Albion, so enjoyed his feast with such gusto that I was soon aware that to dawdle over my meal would insure an insufficiency of grub to satisfy my inward man. The result was a race, in which either might have claimed the victory. That each had obtained enough was apparent, for soon after the savoury stew had disappeared, not one, but several reefs were let out in our waist-belts.

Soon after dark, ominous clouds commenced rising in the west, rushing across the face of the heavens, with the precipitous headlong haste of a stricken army flying before its discomforters, and the glittering, thread-like crescent of the new moon ceased to struggle for the power to light up the shadow-draped landscape. Such indications told of storm and rain. Man, with his want of perception, at this late hour, when the cyclone was about to burst, knew it was nigh, while the wild, uncivilised, and uneducated children of nature had, twenty-four hours ago, expressed their warning,—told it, in truth,—to the self-styled Lords of Creation, too proud to acknowledge the superior foresight; told it to the minor weaker animals, too thankful to receive and profit by the admonition.

About midnight, the advance-guard of the hurricane struck us; its power impressed us with the belief that the main body would accomplish our destruction. The canoe we had placed edgewise on its beam to windward, firmly braced with withes and poles, to afford some protection. At the first squall it was spun round like a cockle-shell, and dropped upon us like a gigantic extinguisher. More braces and props being attached to it, again it was deemed strong enough to cope with the warring elements; but we were wrong, for we had just deemed our work complete, when the canoe was torn from its situation, and hurled against a log with sufficient violence to demolish it to atoms. Here is an end to our aquatic progression, thought I, and, what's more, expressed it, but my comrade neither thought nor spoke, but rushed after the object of our solicitude. In a moment he had seized it by the stern; an instant after a fresh gust struck it; the strength of one human being was not enough to resist, so the old fellow was thrown down in a most unceremonious manner, minus our treasure, but which, before rolling many paces, was, fortunately, checked by coming broadside on to a thick clump of hazel-bushes.

Apparently little injured the canoe was brought

back to its former perch, and care, patience, and skill finally made it a fixture. In this little *contre-temps* I regret to say my fellow-traveller received several severe contusions, as well as incurring the loss of considerable cuticle from his nose, forehead, and shins.

As is frequent with summer gales, this one was of short duration, and day broke so still and balmy that the experiences of the previous evening appeared impossibilities.

The inspection of our canoe, however, tells us that the storm of last night is not a mental delusion, for its gunwale is bent and strained, while several rifts in its bottom foretell that hours of labour will be necessary before it can again dance safely and buoyantly upon the sparkling, laughing waters.

Circumstances and places frequently alter our ideas of subjects; thus I account for abusing an animal at one time, or praising it at another, or attributing to a brute motives which I afterwards have had reason to doubt it possessed. Politicians are blamed for turning their coats. If they do so from seeing the errors of their past ways, commendation should be awarded to them, for the policy that promises the most good at one period may not do so at an after.

As the senator gets blamed so may I, unless what is unpardonable in the whale is unworthy of notice in the sprat.

Off to the North, distant about five miles from our present position, is a hill, portions of which are destitute of timber. On those slopes, devoted to grass and bush-wood, the sun has shone so brightly that I cannot resist the attraction, so determine to pay it a visit, for the canoe can be caulked without my aid, and the old man does not object to my shirking my part of the work.

The day was wonderfully warm and oppressive, the flies were more than usually troublesome, and I felt such fatigue as made exertion almost painful; thus I was far from being on the *qui vive*, as I traversed the intermediate ground, so doubtless would have walked by a deer, or possibly a buffalo, if they had been distant fifty yards from my course, without being cognisant of their presence. A dip occurred in the landscape; it was not sufficiently steep to be designated a ravine, yet the shelter it afforded caused the wild raspberry-bushes to grow in unusual abundance. As there were several tracks made by deer which exactly led in the route I was going this brush did not inconvenience my course.

The load which I carried—only my double-gun and side-arms, viz., revolver and bowie-knife—made the distance traversed appear longer, for already I began to look forward to the time for a retrograde movement, the loll about camp, the hour or two's rest before sleeping-time. Moreover, possibly, my thoughts wandered across the Atlantic—to an old-fashioned house covered with ivy and monthly roses; to a wide extent of grazing country spread out before it, or in imagination I heard the bells of the village church toll, as they invited all, rich and poor, happy and afflicted, to the quiet repose, and to listen to the good words to be heard within its walls; but this I do know, I was far away in mind from my position and circumstances. Ruthlessly my dreams were broken and dispelled. An angry grunt, half of alarm and defiance, fell upon my ear; in a moment my gun on my shoulder fell to the port, and instinctively both barrels were cocked, as the eye hastily scanned the immediate vicinity of my position. Not a moment too soon had I taken these precautions, twenty yards to my front and left was a full-grown grizzly-bear, absolutely 'pointing' me.

In the earlier portions of my life I have never done the duty of the breed of dogs that bear this name, but have frequently been their backer; so it is not surprising that I felt nervous at such a novel situation. I profess to have—let the reader decide with what amount of justice—a knowledge of the habits, possibly of the motives, of game, but never till this moment did I realise thoroughly a poor partridge's feelings. Not without an effort I recovered the proud dignity of a descendant of Adam, and prepared myself to do my progenitor credit.

A gun like mine carries a heavy bullet, a regular bone-crusher, but to enable it to do its work in a finished manner the range must be short; so I bridled my impatience, and endeavoured to better the distance between me and Bruin.

If I had selected the loads for the job in hand

it could not have been more admirably suited, for I had a bullet in both barrels with three drachms of powder behind each, and the charging had taken place a few minutes before to-day's start, with the weather dry ever since.

No miss-fire did I apprehend, for the caps were in their places; no passing piece of brush had disengaged them, as I saw, so I may say I sought, certainly did not avoid, the pending contest.

Do not, gentle reader, rush off at rash conclusions, and give me credit for an unusual amount of pluck. I was but doing like the gamester playing at loo, who holds in his hand the queen and knave of trumps; the odds were all in my favour, although it was just possible to lose.

For me to advance on the foe was unnecessary, for the brute had the fortitude to draw to me. Where I stood the ground was firm and comparatively smooth, so I remained upon it. My adversary had a splendid box of grinders; from their colour his tooth-brush had no sinecure, and, as if proud of them, he took more trouble than the veriest dandy to show them; further he curled his nose up like a snarling cur (causing me to draw a comparison not in his favour), making it look heavenward, but at the same time giving him a most disagreeable expression.

I have tickled up 'Sampson,' Barnum's (the celebrated showman of New York) grizzly; but then the unfortunate was in a cage. The physiognomy of his wild relation was a counterpart to his; the expression of either was not highly indicative of brotherly love: the looking aloft certainly did not possess observers with Christian intentions.

Ten, more probably eight yards intervened between us; my gun was pointed for his heart; bang went one barrel, but the foe did not fall; rapid as lightning the left was put in and the huge creature fell. Stepping a few paces back I hastened to load; the right bullet went down smoothly, but the left was obstreperous. The temporarily suspended animation in my antagonist was rapidly becoming restored; the more I hurried the worse I succeeded, and, while making renewed efforts, the bear gained his feet. In an instant he comprehended the situation and sprang at me. The right barrel was fired without my gun being brought to my shoulder; for an instant the assailant staggered, but only for an instant, and I received a blow that knocked me almost out of time, sending my gun from my hands with the rapidity of electricity. However, I avoided for a second the effort that was made to lay hold of me; the next instant my right hand drew my revolver; one—two shots were fired in rapid succession into the creature's mouth and chest, which was almost within touching distance, when he heeled over, quivered for a moment, gave several convulsive struggles, and what had possessed animation became a corpse.

My escape was a close one, and I sat down

beside my trophy, nervous and excited, thankful that I had suffered no mauling, happy so successfully to have got out of what at one time looked an ugly affair, and grateful to that overlooking Providence that takes the unfledged birds and parentless children under its protection.

With a claw and ear of my antagonist I joined my companion a couple of hours afterwards, for well I knew from previous experience of the old man that, although he would not be rude enough to express doubts, yet, unless I had stronger proofs than words to show him, he would be a disbeliever in any one's prowess, more particularly an Englishman's, being equal to his own. All the game I killed I have failed to mention; but such as made an impression on my susceptibility by its gameness and gallant efforts to almost successfully fight its foe, have found their way into these pages.

On my return to camp I found the canoe fit again to trust to the pellucid stream, for, between a portion of the old man's shirt-tail and an abundance of gum and fat judiciously mixed together, the leak that resulted from the rough handling our craft had received in last night's tornado, had been stopped, and all wounds healed.

This night I could not sleep when first I retired to rest; the cause I could not understand, but my skin felt so heated and irritated, that for the moment I supposed I had contracted some complaint like prickly-heat. Flesh and blood could stand the constant itching no longer, so by the light of the watch-fire I made an examination. The result was that I discovered that in my tramp I had picked up several ticks, which were endeavouring to bury themselves in my hide. Half-an-hour's close search relieved me of these vermin, but the caresses of Somnus, so ruthlessly dispelled, could not be recalled although I sought him with the most devoted assiduity.

The kat-I-dids and whip-poor-wills sung out without cessation their soothing and plaintive notes, but my ears would not listen to the voices of those charmers which so often previously had invited me to rest.

Over the hills and far away my spirit ultimately fled, to be recalled to my present situation by the voice of a midnight prowler whose deeds were by choice those of darkness. What incomprehensible beings we are! How seldom are our likes and dislikes the same! Tired, wearied, possibly disgusted with life, I find myself with a maudlin regard for an animal I should hate. When I was a child an unknown sound, particularly heard at night, would cause a cold shiver to pervade my system. A ghost story would so terrify me, that even when provided with a candle I feared to pass through the hall and passages that were necessary to traverse to reach my dormitory; but a story of a bloodthirsty tiger, or a sanguinary wolf that had ravaged a neighbourhood, eaten any quantity of women and children, and intimidated all by making night fearful with his howlings, would actually prevent my going to the orchard,—ay, even at the period when apples were ripe,—for fear a representative of these dreaded races had made his escape from a menagerie, and taken up his residence near our home. Yet here I am a hundred yards from my camp fire, where I have gone, the better to listen to the deep, yet shrill and quivering voice of a wolf, which has either been disappointed of his supper or wishes to express his disgust at the moon shining so brightly, so as to reveal his skulking actions to less bloodthirsty but more harmless denizens of our planet. To-night I am partial to wolves,—for I am out of temper,—especially grey ones, for they are the worst; for they are out-and-out scoundrels without guile, decided characters, brutes possessed of the inclination to do evil, and no repugnance or make-believe qualms of conscience in doing so. In fact they are uncompromising villains, going about with a placard, not on paste-board, but *tout ensemble*, to warn all that their society or neighbourhood is dangerous. If honesty is but policy, and consequently to be followed, the honesty of this animal's character deserves commendation; for it never assumes disguises by which to gain the confidence of the lamb or the fawn, but from earliest days declares itself their foe, and if such a warning does not fore-arm them, why, let them take the consequence of their inattention. Better, far better, is the character of the wolf than that of many men, who under the mask of friendship will ruin the too confiding. To draw comparisons between the lords of the creation and the inferior animals does not generally make the former appear to advantage; there is room here for thought, and such will result in favour of the *feræ naturæ*, which must become increased the more we ponder on the subject.

An hour before break of day I again sought sleep—this time successfully, although a severe gale had commenced to blow; but then there is no music like that of the untrammelled winds singing their requiem through the forest glades. In this instance it was a lullaby to repose which the exhausted mind and body could not resist.

Although the day broke ominous of protracted bad weather, and numerous impetuous squalls gave warning that more than ordinary skill and watchfulness would be required by the steerer, we embarked a couple of hours after sunrise. Our canoe had not been improved by the rough handling it had received the previous evening, therefore much method was required to trim the frail craft, so as to prevent a portion the stem, where existed the largest leak, from becoming submerged. But when our course brought us into a seething rapid, where the miniature waves jumped in very ecstasy of glee at the precipitousness of their course, an occasional pitch by the head could not be avoided,' thus forcing us to ship water. Twice in a few hours we were compelled to land and turn our water-logged boat upside down; but the grounding or the constant motion made matters so much worse, that by two o'clock we were obliged to determine on a disembarcation and devote our talents to the task of endeavouring to cobble up afresh those places that ceased to resist the invasion of water. The country since morning had become more open and park-like, with the surface more rolling and rocky. By sunset I had made the last stitch that completed our repairs, and the sun, as if approving our industry, showed his roseate face to cheer our depressed spirits. Constant wet, more especially when one is insufficiently clothed, is excessively weakening, and with exhaustion invariably come the blues.

During the afternoon the old man had set a fall trap within a short distance of our encampment. A couple of hours after dark he heard it go down, for the gale had died out, and all nature was reposing in most perfect silence, as if to rest from the fatigue resulting from past exertions. In a few minutes my companion returned with the prize. Although professing an intimate knowledge of the animal I felt convinced from a casual remark he made, that he was ignorant of its name, and supposed it to belong to a different race. But as he never would acknowledge ignorance on any subject, possibly with the intention of teasing, I pestered him to tell me its *sobriquet*. All the *finesse* I used was of no avail; my queries were adroitly avoided and the tables turned upon me. So I gave up the attempt, at the same time informing him that the unknown was a half-grown fischer.

'Of course it is,' said he. 'I guess with all your knowledge of natural history it took you some time to find that out; some of you reading men ain't as smart as you make believe. I'd like to buy most of you at my price, and sell you at your own.'

And the old fellow chuckled with satisfaction, as he thought to himself how he had sold me.

 'So ye bees do not make honey for yourselves;
  Se ye sheep do not bear wool for yourselves,'

is possibly not a literal, but a rough translation from a favourite author, but as true now as it was the day it was inscribed. The thought calls me back to home, to a little episode which did more to open my eyes to the humbug of this age and world than aught that ever occurred in my life.

It may be a digression from my narrative, but it may impress upon the youthful reader the good old proverb, 'All that glitters is not gold,' and thus do him a benefit.

I was asked to visit an establishment in the metropolis of the world at which an immense fish was to be viewed. Visitors were numerous; one called it one thing, one another, but these were lesser luminaries of the scientific clique. At length a buzz of welcome and sycophantish worship told that a great gun had arrived to view the unfortunate—now strongly smelling—late denizen of the deep. Like Metamora, both in form and feature, I never met a more amusing creature, yet so simple that he preferred talking in language that much approached the dialect so much in vogue among fond parents. With an air at once childish and strongly tinctured with *bonhomie*, right and left he interchanged jokes, and looked at the mammoth attraction, but never a word did he say as to its name. At length some one with more brass than discretion asked this would-be great naturalist what was the name of the great unknown monster before us. The heretofore suave, courteous, and rubicund features now assumed a look of severe displeasure, the speaker was disconcerted, and if he did not disappear into mother earth, it was the fault of the hardness of her surface, not of his wishes.

Amontillado was produced, a beverage to which more than myself are partial. It acted like applying oil to machinery, for the cog-wheels and checks upon the company's tongues became loosened, and the heretofore most taciturn became voluble. Still, to my surprise, no one pronounced the name of the fish. Although a copy of Couch's admirable work was constantly alluded to, all spectators seemed ashamed to ask the question, 'What is it?' for each believed his neighbour not only conversant with its name, but also with its haunts and habits, and therefore feared to show his own ignorance.

Although not bright, 'I commenced to smell a mice,' as the Dutchman says, so I determined to have some fun; for the fish I knew, very well, I might say, having resided for years in lands where the neighbouring seas were its principal habitat.

The great naturalist had chin-chinned every one.

My turn came next, and although I had remarked the discomfiture of him who had been too curious, I determined to risk the punishment of a snubbing, for what did it matter? I was nobody, as far as reputation for knowledge went, so, being accredited ignorant, I determined to avail myself of liberties which only would be admissible for one labouring under such a stigma.

I have said the great high-priest approached me. He vouchsafed me a smile of approbation and a nod of recognition. With an air of innocence I appealingly asked, 'What is the name of this wonderful creature?' By the button I was taken on one side. When out of ear-shot the query was put to me, 'Now, don't you know? You have been a traveller; I am certain if you would think a moment you would not require to ask that question.'

For some time I pleaded ignorance, and urged to have its cognomen imparted to me.

This was of no avail; the accepted authority on these subjects was equal to the occasion, and my repeated inquiries were only answered by the polite request that I would state what were my surmises.

At length I gave way, and uttered the name.

'You stick to that,' said the great man, as he turned to leave me; when, going to his secretary, on pretence of some brilliant idea that had struck him, he, *sotto voce*, ordered him to hunt up in the infallible Couch the chapter devoted to this species of the finny tribe.

In a few minutes afterwards, with more pompousness than is to be found in a pouter-pigeon, the great professor came forward. A buzz of approbation from the small fry around greeted him. He waited for a cessation of the noise, but evidently would have liked an *encore*. His supporters, although used to the '*claque*,' had not managed the matter properly, so there was none.

There being, therefore, no cause for delay, for the secretary had counted all the minor fins between the dorsal and caudal ones, and reported that they agreed with Jonathan Couch's work in every respect, the great authority on fish, like a second Bacchus, inflated his lungs with an extra addition of breath, and thus spoke,—

'I have observed among the gentlemen here present what I might attribute either to reticence or ignorance. I would be pleased to consider it the former, in reference to the name of the fish now before us. To prevent any further doubt upon the subject, if such exists, permit me to tell you that it is a——'

The crowd dispersed, and soon after might be seen an article in a great periodical, not only giving the name of the previously unknown fish to the public, but pitching into contemporary newspapers for having miscalled it. There is an immense deal of such humbug in this world; appropriation of the emanation of others' brains is worse, it is dishonest; but then the appropriators have a reputation to keep up, or a reputation to gain. Of course those who crave not for notoriety, and do not strive to soar above their fellow-men, will think this very wrong, and inwardly believe nought could induce them to do the same; but then they have never had inducements to make them think otherwise. Let not the man boast of honesty, that ne'er has tempted been. That great poet and deep judge of human nature, Burns, wisely said that many do not fall because they are never tempted; and that, when we are ready to condemn others for backslidings, we should first try to learn how much more temptation the backslider may have resisted. At least this is my prosaic paraphrase of Burns' exquisite Doric lines to this effect, which embody the very essence of Christian charity.

CHAPTER XVIII.

DANGEROUS NAVIGATION — NARROW ESCAPE — MOOSE RIVER — BEAU-
TIFUL CASCADE — AMERICAN RIVERS — BRILLIANTLY-COLOURED FISH
— BEAVERS — TRACES OF AN ENCAMPMENT — MAN AND NATURE —
EFFRONTERY OF A WHITE EAGLE — THE CANOE OVERTURNED BY A
BEAR — DINNER AT THE SOUTHERN HOTEL, ST. LOUIS.

But to return to the Great West. Day broke bright and clear. A gentle, mellow, balmy breeze kissed the landscape with feathery touch, and the country looked so reposed and peaceful that, if it ever continued so, the world we live in would too favourably compare with the spirits' home beyond the clouds. Sleep and dry clothes had done me much benefit, for my head feels clear, my step is elastic, my hand steady; so when the canoe is shot out on the liquid element, deep and strong is the hold I take of the water with my paddle, while, to the disgust of my companion, I cannot restrain expressing my feelings of pleasure by whistling snatches of airs forgotten in my misfortunes, and whose dulcet strains had never before spoken to the surrounding echoes.

The further we progress the more rapid and dangerous becomes the navigation; boulders and rocks, some towering high, as if glorying in their magnitude, others conscious of their insignificance, like sneaking cowards, only occasionally exposing their summits over the broken water, lie in our route; one moment a headlong current drags us towards exposed dangers; next instant an unseen undertow almost wrecks our frail bark upon a dangerous reef. But the pace is fast, the excitement intense, and recklessness of danger results. But a distant ponderous sound by degrees becomes more apparent; louder and louder it breaks upon the ear, as faster and faster we hurry on our downward course; yet our canoe is under control, and well it is so, for soon it breaks upon my brain with the rapidity of a thunder-clap that we are galloping to the margin of a cataract.

Deeper and deeper goes the paddle-blade into the crystal stream, slowly but steadily our stem obeys the pressure; our head is pointed to a sandy cove; in a moment more a strong stroke drives us out of the foaming stream into the eddying back current of the little haven.

After-inspection proved how narrow had been our escape; for a mile or more, right to the edge of the waterfall, no other landing-place could have been found, and the margin was so steep that even a friendly limb to cling by, to arrest our progress, was not visible. Even snags, those generally invariable adjuncts to American river scenery, found no resting-place on which to anchor, so did not here exist.

For the two following days we had laborious work, carrying our canoe to where it could again be launched, for there was no portage, and logs had to be straddled, trees avoided, and brushwood traversed; still we toiled, and in the end reaped our reward.

The cascade which I inspected was neither as perpendicular as Montmorency, nor so protracted as Chaudier, still quite sufficient to have made fragments of our craft and sent us by express to the happy hunting-grounds.

Like the fiery colt which from rest and abundant food rushes with headlong, uncontrolled speed till exhausted, when he settles down to be a well-behaved nag, so Moose river, after coursing so frantically for miles and precipitating itself over an abyss of thirty feet, flowed peacefully on as if incapable of a continuance of such violent exercise, or as if rejoicing in the reaction.

Thankful again to enjoy the ease of travelling by water, for hours we glided slowly along, more disposed for rest than conversation. The country became more level and more wooded, while the river expanded in width. During the day several minx were seen and constant evidences of the vicinity of beavers. With these exceptions and the monotonous tapping of woodpeckers, animal life did not appear to exist.

When the declining sun was nearly touching the tree-tops, we entered the mouth of a tributary about sixty feet wide; a hundred yards above its *embouchure* was a beautiful waterfall, just too high for salmon to pass over. The basin in which the water fell was perfectly thronged with char (*Salmo fontinalis*). As the neighbourhood was suitable we determined to come to a halt for the night.

After lifting our canoe ashore I left my comrade busily arranging camp, to try if the denizens of this Naiad-like retreat were gifted with that sublunary ailment—appetite. Soon I discovered that they were suffering from the vulgar adjunct, a craving stomach. This misfortune was the cause of a dozen or more being ruthlessly dragged from home, and kith, and kin.

It is my opinion that nothing presents greater attractions to the lover of nature than a river. In childhood we regard it with awe, for we know not from whence it comes and whither it goes; in more mature years, when the mind is better developed, it is looked at with astonishment for its erratic course, and reckless career, while the space which it traverses attracts our admiration; in age it softens to the vision the landscape, speaks of peace and plenty, of utility to man, and luxury and abundance to the animal life that dwells upon its margin.

The schoolboy in his half-holiday directs his steps to the nearest river, with deadly intent in his mind against the lovely children of its liquid haunts, or to bathe, splash, or with *abandon* enjoy himself in its gurgling eddies or silent pools; the old man to listen to its voice, and, charmed with the sweet lullaby it sings over its pebbly pavement, unconsciously to glide into dreamland, there for the time forgetting under this soothing influence the troubles of the past and the trials that he believes in store for him.

But in our little island home of England, so curtailed in space by sea as almost to be to its inhabitants as limited in extent as a hive is to a swarm of bees, those ideas of boundlessness, those manifestations of grandeur, are always wanting; to see them in perfection the Atlantic must be crossed, and the traveller stand on the margin of the reckless, headstrong Niagara, navigate the blue rapids of the Mississippi, drift down the muddy, heavily timbered Missouri, or visit other equally attractive but less known streams. To trace a river from birth to death, from where it bubbles from the mountain ravine to where it passes into the all-absorbing ocean, is a pleasure that requires no enhancing. In England a transit of one hundred miles will generally accomplish this end; in America, in some instances, twenty times this distance will not be sufficient, and the greater portion of the space traversed is not unfrequently all latitude, or, in other words, through a country the position of which is most affected by changes of temperature, sufficient reason, all will understand, to make such a journey more than usually attractive to the naturalist, for in his course he will possibly find residents of the Frigid, Temperate, and Torrid Zones. Although it has often in early days been imparted to me by the old and wise that the rolling stone gathers no moss, it has failed to make me less desirous of travelling, or to ease my craving for visiting countries unsubdued by the husbandman, not intruded upon by the settler, or that remain exactly in the same state as they emanated from the Creator's hands. And where is this passion so thoroughly to be gratified as on the boundless steppes, the barren wastes, the flower-clothed prairies, the densely-planted forests, or verdant savannahs of the Western Hemisphere? But it is not always possible to gratify our cravings; so time rolled on, and boyhood glided into maturity, delay in realising my wishes did not damp my ardour, only made me more eager for the arrival of the time when they could be consummated. Now I am obtaining the consummation of my hopes, for I stand on the margin of a stream not larger than a Scotch mountain brook, which, clear and pellucid as liquid crystal, with eager and unrestrained haste tumbles precipitously headlong from rock to rock. At one moment hurrying round a boulder, at another eddying in deep shadowed pools, or lashing itself against the rough margin, it hurries on towards the ocean in whose embrace it loses all identity. Whence it comes I know not; whither it goes I am aware. Before to-day I have been in positions to revel in these thoughts, the *tout ensemble* might have been adverse, or my thoughts wandering on other subjects; this evening they are revived with intensified pleasure.

I do not think I ever saw more brilliantly marked specimens of fish of western waters than those I captured here. Again and again I gazed with rapture on their changing hues, as lovely as the most gorgeous colouring of the shells of ocean. The mariners of old with justice lauded the dolphin; had they seen the resplendent robing of my prizes, the American char, and not the dolphin, would have been the theme of their song and admiration.

At an early hour we got under way, and not without regret did I see the headlands and marginal trees shut out from view as sweet a spot as ever the setting sun illuminated with golden-hued and gently sloping rays.

The part of Moose river traversed to-day is tranquil and pretty. No one could believe it the swash-buckler among streams that we navigated a week since; possibly when the water gets thus far, it has sown its wild oats; if such is the case, I have no objection. Several times during the day we have seen beavers; towards evening we drifted into a regular village of these rodents, a reckless specimen perishing through his own sheer foolhardiness. It is customary for people to go into ecstasies over the beaver, as it is generally supposed to be a model of industry, perseverance, and frugality. Accepting that the habits of this animal justify its receiving such enviable notoriety, why do those that laud its doings to the skies not go and do likewise? I fear it is much like the case of the physician who says, Do as I say, not as I do.

But to come to facts, really the beaver is a very

much overrated animal; for it has neither the sagacity and intelligence of the dog or horse, the forethought of the squirrel, nor the perseverance of the domestic rat ; in reality he is a very lazy fellow, fond of gadding about, and much given to gossiping.

These conclusions I arrive at from having watched them in an undisturbed state of nature, where their life was free from molestation, and where climate and locality were both suited to their requirements.

This evening I lay in a bed of osier watching the castors, as the French Canadians still term them, going through the usual routine of life. Although the stream is abundantly peopled with these interesting beasts, not one put in an appearance till I was nearly exhausted. Obtaining food seemed to be their first object after coming forth. Appetite satisfied, a general pow-wow takes place, terminating with flirtations, in which it appears to be a matter of indifference whose partner becomes the object of each gallant's attention. Possibly they may have degenerated since the advent of Mormonism into the Western wilds.

At our halting-place for this evening, we have discovered unmistakable evidence that human beings —and those white men—have been here lately ; for the ashes of a camp-fire are fresh, the grass around it still broken with the pressure of traffic, chips of wood unsoiled by exposure lie around, and tracks of feet in the sand, with the sharp edges not obliterated by the lapse of time, are numerous. Robinson Crusoe's surprise at the discovery of footprints in the sand of Juan Fernandez could not have been more genuine than ours, to find that once more we were so near to our own flesh and blood. Whether the sensations of my companion on this occasion were those of pleasure or not I cannot say; but, speaking for myself, I can safely state they were the reverse, for I wished to enjoy to the last moment with no other society than that I now possessed, the solitude of these wilds untraversed by human paths.

The scenery that surrounded us was lovely. Moreover, there was a tranquil repose resting upon it that invited the sojourner to halt, and absent himself for ever from contact with the selfish population of the cultivated portions of the world. This neighbourhood will not long remain possessed of these seductive attractions. It requires little foresight to predict that the date is not far distant when man's dwellings will dot its surface; its now graceful trees be laid prostrate from contact with the woodman's axe, and the flowers and herbage lie torn from their roots by the cruel culter of the husbandman's plough. But such is as it should be, many, the majority of my race, will say; the world is made alone for man, and all that's in it must suffer to forward his selfish views.

But let those that know what war is recall to memory its results; ruined dwellings, smouldering farm-yards, charred and dead trees, scattered and broken fences, the atmosphere redolent with noxious stenches, and the earth encumbered with rotting carrion, and he can regret that all habitable portions of this planet will some day be encumbered with population, and subjected to the horror of such scenes. If civilisation did what its advocates claim for it, my regrets for the inroads of my race into new countries might not be, but it only teaches us to restrain ourselves while our safety depends on doing so. The savage son of man is less a savage than his educated brother, for when the fortunes of war have turned in favour of the latter, and he can without fear of punishment gratify his lusts and smothered, but not destroyed, love of bloodshed, he does so to excess. How comes it I possess so low an opinion of my own race? It is formed upon experience, from my association with comrades, my conflict with enemies, and by studying myself.

Our camp this evening was not as cheerful as usual, or as its position and the beauty of the night would be expected to produce. The vicinity of strangers had caused results possibly very different upon myself and companion, but the old man's manner reverted to that of restraint, similar to what had marked it in our earlier associations. Possibly he possessed some extraordinary idea that it would militate against him in the eyes of the world, if supposed to be capable of unbending and becoming the genuine, sincere, natural person which his true self was.

Got afloat at an early hour, the current of the stream again commences to increase in velocity, while the banks became more elevated and densely clothed with timber. Twice were we compelled to leave the river, and make portages to avoid rapids, so turbulent and swift, at the same time pierced by numerous rocks, that an attempt to shoot them would entail certain destruction.

On one fine pool, fanned by a thousand dancing graceful branches, my companion knocked over a mallard. As it lay struggling on the surface, a large white-headed eagle swooped from his perch, the summit of a lofty solitary pine, and appropriated the prize, which, with the coolest effrontery, he carried to his roosting-place, and commenced to feed upon.

'It's easy seeing we are again near white men, such a piece of cheek could only be learned from them,' said the 'old man;' continuing afterwards to mutter to himself, 'We'll soon see plenty of such work, when we get back to the settlements, ay, that we will, that we will——'

Our journey for the day, although scarcely more than ten miles, had been very fatiguing, so we halted early. The place we selected had but a day or two since been used by others for the same purpose; the most prominent among numerous evidences that such was the case being a smouldering stump.

Who knows the Tay at Dunkeld? Remove from

it the traces of man's work, add to the size and density of the timber around its margin, and double the volume of water, and the reader will have a picture so like the landscape we traversed this morning, that this one might be mistaken for the Scotch river. Turning sharply round a point in the bank, which was densely clothed with hemlock, completely hiding objects up stream from those beneath, we came suddenly upon a patriarch bull-moose of the most gigantic proportions, floating with all except his head submerged to avoid the persecution of a swarm of flies that hovered over him. As soon as he observed us, he made a plunge forward for shore like a buck-jumping horse, causing by his bulk and impetuosity the water to fly for yards around in spray; again and again the bounds were repeated, each carrying him further into shoal-water, and exposing more of his massive proportions. My double-barrel in a moment usurps in my hands the place of the paddle, the current, as if favouring my effort, swings the now uncontrolled canoe into an admirable position for shooting, the but comes cleanly to my shoulder, the eye and sight in a moment are aligned upon my object; the finger presses the trigger, and a dull thud rapidly succeeds the report. The bullet is well placed, for the stricken animal's back hollows, the head is thrown up, and the legs move with uncertain action. Every step appears to be the unfortunate's last, but still he struggles gamely forward and gains the shore. At length he enters the brush, and the green screen parted by his force closes behind him. Certain that the animal's career on earth is short, I refrain from putting in the second barrel, but content myself with reloading that which has been discharged. This duty performed, again the lithe paddle dips deep and strong, again our craft is under control, and like an animated creature, speeds upon the desired course. Ere it touches the shore, with a dexterous back stroke, the stern is swung round, and I spring upon the beach. Cautiously the verdant hemlocks are parted, and my eyes, strained to their greatest power, peer into the shady solitude. Half-a-dozen steps forward, and I am gratified with a view of what I seek. The monarch of his genus stands towering in front of me, the only movement in his body denoting animation being that of his long flaccid tongue, apathetically licking in the gloats of his heart's blood, as if he knew that his life depended on retaining them. But no earthly aid can now save him, his doom is sealed, and his glassy eyes shall never again look upon the favourite haunts of his youth. Closer to the victim I approach; at length his lustreless eyes see me; to be revenged on his destroyer, he nerves himself for a final effort, but, brave as is the resolve, it is too lately formed to be carried into effect, for the effort brings him crashing headlong to the ground; the limbs refuse a further call to serve, and express their incapacity so to do by a few spasmodic struggles, gradually ceasing till all is still. No whoop of joy proclaims my victory, for upon my doings I gazed with more of pain than gratification.

When the hot blood of youth coursed through my veins, and the future was looked forward to with such feelings as anticipate pleasure, it was otherwise. Experience teaches; man becomes drunk on carnage, nor does he cease to revel in blood, till satiety comes from excess. The drunkard may crave for the demon that is killing him, but the veteran soldier looks back with horror on the scenes which result from his own handywork. In the same manner does the experienced hunter detest uselessly to sacrifice animal life.

With as great a supply of the carcass as could be kept fresh till we consumed it, we resumed our voyage; but the day was now waning, so when we sighted a deserted but still smoking camping-place, we drew our frail bark on shore, and arranged to pass the night. For the previous twenty-four hours I had felt symptoms of fever and ague; an hour after supper I was suffering from such a severe chill, that my teeth chattered, and my knees knocked together. My fellow-voyager again and again piled fresh fuel on the fire; all was of no avail in making me feel warm, so with every bone in my body expressing its ailments, helplessly I had to bide the period till the shake thought fit to leave. At length to my great relief it did, and I felt so thoroughly prostrated as to be powerless; at length balmy sleep stole over me, and the sun was hours above the horizon before I awoke. But that I had contracted fever and ague previously, I do not believe I should have now suffered from it; where we are is too far to the north, and too pure and clear in atmosphere to engender it. in those who have not previously suffered from this complaint.

'A stern chase is a long chase.' Evidently the persons who leave behind them indications of their presence are pursuing the same route as ourselves, and as the current is our and their motive power, we have not overtaken them. The scenery still continues lovely, more beautiful possibly than heretofore, for the mellowed tints of autumn are commencing to show themselves.

Soon after the sun had ceased to be due south, when near the entrance to a rapid that terminated a long stretch of smooth water, we perceived a bear enter the river, evidently intent on traversing to the opposite shore. As my companion wanted his hide, I applied additional force to my paddle. The distance between pursuer and pursued was not great, so soon we were within shooting distance. Again and again I asked my comrade to fire; closer and closer we approached to Bruin, who only acknowledged consciousness of our vicinity by curling his upper lip.

At length not more than ten feet severed us, the ponderous rifle of the old man came slowly to his shoulder, and he fired, but his aim was faulty or the motion of the canoe disconcerted him, for his ball only grazed the apex of the bear's skull.

But that was sufficient to stir up his wrath. In an instant he turned upon his back, and before I could clear the 'birch-bark' from his vicinity, he was under our counter. A chance to shoot was thus refused me, but my regret was short-lived, an immense paw made its appearance over the bulwark, and in a moment after I was, gun in hand, struggling in the water. The canoe turned upside down, with my companion hanging to it. Bruin appeared as much astonished at the consequence of his handiwork as we were disgusted, for, either frightened or satisfied at the result, with rapid stroke he pursued his former course. My first anxiety was for the old man, but I found that was unnecessary, as there was evidently sufficient buoyancy in our craft to float him. That weight being off my mind, I made for shore. When nearly accomplishing my purpose I got into a rapid, which, with almost crushing strength, dashed me against a rock. My gun I instinctively pushed forward to save me. Doubtless it did to some extent, but the price of the service rendered by it was a heavy one, for my faithful and well-tried 'Dougall,' the gun that had never for a moment failed me, got broken across the small of the stock.

More dead than alive and almost drowned, I at length succeed in clambering on shore, and dripping wet, numbed from the coldness of the northern stream, my arms destroyed, and my ammunition lost, away in the distant forest, I was truly an object worthy of pity.

While feeling bewildered at the magnitude of my misfortunes, I had the satisfaction to see my comrade land a couple of hundred yards beneath me, and fortunately on the same side as myself, with the canoe still in his grasp. Soon after I joined him. Glum he certainly looked, for his poking old single-barrel had dropped from his hand in the excitement of the moment. Well, if its barrel forms a safe lurking place for young *salmonidæ*, it is being put to a use more suited to its appearance and deserts than ever it was before.

Could the most unfeeling man have looked down upon us two poor wayfarers at the moment of our reunion, compassion must have found its way into his heart.

My narrative is finished. Two days afterwards we overtook the party in front of us; in their society in due course of time we reached Pembina, from there St. Joseph's, and afterwards St. Louis, where, at the Southern Hotel, I succeeded in making the 'old man' jolly, but not until he had imbibed several glasses of whisky-punch, after a dinner, the like of which for fixings, he said, he had never seen before.

THE END.

London: STRANGEWAYS and WALDEN, Printers, Castle St. Leicester Sq.